W9-CFN-562

Genre and Second Language Writing

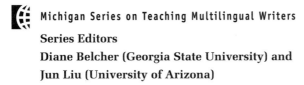 **Michigan Series on Teaching Multilingual Writers**

Series Editors

Diane Belcher (Georgia State University) and

Jun Liu (University of Arizona)

Genre and Second Language Writing

Ken Hyland
University of London

 Michigan Series on Teaching Multilingual Writers

THE UNIVERSITY OF MICHIGAN PRESS
Ann Arbor

Copyright © by the University of Michigan Press 2004
All rights reserved
Published in the United States of America by
The University of Michigan Press
Manufactured in the United States of America
⊗Printed on acid-free paper

2007   2006   2005   2004   4   3   2   1

No part of this publication may be reproduced,
stored in a retrieval system, or transmitted
in any form or by any means, electronic,
mechanical, or otherwise, without the written
permission of the publisher.

*A CIP catalog record for this book is
available from the British Library*

Library of Congress Cataloging-in-Publication Data

Hyland, Ken.
    Genre and second language writing / Ken Hyland.
        p.   cm. — (Michigan series on teaching multilingual writers)
    Includes bibliographical references and index.
    ISBN 0-472-03014-0 (pbk. : alk. paper)
    1. Rhetoric—Study and teaching.   I. Title.   II. Series.
    P53.27H948   2004
    808'.042'071—dc22

                                                    2004053687

Acknowledgments

This book results from a sustained interest in genre that owes a great deal to the many excellent colleagues and friends who have shared their ideas and texts with me over many years. Among these I am particularly indebted to Sue Hood, Bev Derewianka, Susan Feez, and Jim Martin in Australia, to John Swales and Ann Johns in the United States, and to Chris Candlin and Vijay Bhatia in Hong Kong. Their varied influence is obvious on every page of this text, and I hope they find something in it they can all agree with. I am also grateful to Diane Belcher and Jun Liu for coming up with the idea for this series and for asking me to contribute to it and to my research assistant, Polly Tse, for sweet biscuits and sympathy during the ups and downs of writing. Finally, my thanks go to my wife, Fiona, whose love, encouragement, and conversations about writing enormously enrich my life and my work.

Grateful acknowledgment is made to the following authors, publishers, and journals for permission to reprint previously published materials.

Michael Barlow, Athelstan, for a screenshot from "MonoConc Pro."

Butterworth-Heinemann for "Letter to the Editor," from *The Laurie Taylor Guide to Higher Education,* by L. Taylor, copyright © 1994. Reprinted by permission of Butterworth-Heinemann.

Cambridge University Press for adapted Figure 3.2 and Figure 5.2 from *Second Language Writing,* by K. Hyland, copyright © 2003. Reprinted with the permission of Cambridge University Press.

Elsevier for "A Genre-Based Approach to the Teaching of Report Writing," pp. 1–13 (Appendix pp. 11–13) of *English for Specific Purposes,* vol. 10, by S. Marshall, copyright © 1991. Reprinted with permission from Elsevier.

Peter Knapp for figure from p. 152 of *Context—Text—Grammar: Teaching the Genres and Grammar of School Writing in Infants and Primary Classrooms,* by P. Knapp and M. Watkins, copyright © 1994.

John Milton, Copulang, for a screenshot from "WordPilot 2000."

National Centre for English Language Teaching and Research (NCELTR), Macquarie University, Australia, for the following figures:

"Deisigning a Course," p. 79, from *Focus on Speaking,* by A. Burns and H. Joyce, copyright © 1997.

"Description of a Narrative Structure," pp. 225–26, from *Using Functional Grammar: An Explorer's Guide,* 2nd ed., by D. Butt, R. Fahey, S. Feez, S. Spinks, and C. Yallop, copyright © 2000.

"Teacher-Learner Collaboration," p. 27; "Teaching Learning Cycle," p. 28; "Assessment Checklist," p. 131; "Sample Analysis of Learner Descriptive Text," pp. 132–34; and "Objectives," p. 134, from *Text-Based Syllabus Design,* by S. Feez, copyright © 1998.

NSW Adult Migrant English Services, Australia, for excerpts from *CSWE* test materials, copyright © 1987.

Routledge for figures from p. 126, and pp. 128–29 of *Extending Literacy: Children Reading and Writing Non-Fiction,* by D. Wray and M. Lewis, copyright © 1997.

Mike Scott, Liverpool University, for a screenshot from "WordSmith Tools."

The University of Michigan Press for material from *English in Today's Research World: A Writing Guide,* by J. Swales and C. Feak, copyright © 2000.

The University of Michigan Press for a figure from *Genre and the Language Learning Classroom*, by B. Paltridge, copyright © 2001.

Every effort has been made to contact the copyright holders for permission to reprint borrowed material. We regret any oversights that may have occurred and will rectify them in future printings of this book.

Contents

Series Foreword

Since the publication of John Swales's groundbreaking book-length look at genre analysis in 1990, it is safe to say that there has been increasing interest in the pedagogical potential of genre among language educators, whether teachers of first, second, or third language speakers. Recent publications such as Paltridge's (2001) *Genre and the Language Learning Classroom* and Johns's (2002) edited volume *Genre in the Classroom* certainly attest to the ongoing interest in the pedagogical implications of genre research and theory. Growing interest in genre, however, has not brought with it agreement on the immediate value of genre analysis for the classroom, as opposed to other more "authentic" environments such as the workplace. Perceptions of the teachability of genre, in fact, have run the gamut from a conviction that genres are so complex, varied, and unstable as to be virtually unteachable in a classroom setting, to a view of them as fixed and transparent enough to be straightforwardly, even formulaically taught as relatively easy to notice textual conventions.

Ken Hyland aims for more of a happy medium: a text-oriented yet at the same time highly socially situated view of genre. Hyland's approach to genre, derived from his experience with it both as a researcher (see, for example, *Disciplinary Discourses*) and as an EAP teacher for the past 25 years, makes it possible for him to present the potential pedagogical power of genre in persuasively practitioner-centered terms. Through Hyland's window on genre studies, genre appears capable not only of enabling comprehension and generation of a multitude of text types that may be quite new to many multilingual writers (and sometimes to teachers as well) but also of facilitating their entry into seemingly and in effect exclusive discourse communities. It is this nuanced textual and socially sensitive perspective on genre that readers will find throughout *Genre and Second Language Writing*.

Those familiar with many of the publications on genre will easily recognize the novelty of Hyland's latest contribution to the literature. In *Genre and Second Language Writing*, readers are provided with a wealth of practical pedagogical information but also with the theory and research that should serve as the motivation and guiding principles of genre use in the writing classroom. Hyland's book begins with an overview of the major theoretical perspectives on genre and steadily moves toward more concrete classroom-oriented concerns, such as how to determine students' genre-knowledge needs, how to design a genre-consciousness-raising syllabus, how to select sample texts, how to develop genre scaffolding tasks and writing assignments, and how to assess writing with the help of genre awareness. Perhaps most unique is the final chapter, which encourages teacher and student autonomy by guiding teachers and their students toward their own investigations of genre, empowering them as discourse analysts and, as a result, as writing teachers and writers.

Almost 40 years ago, Robert Kaplan (1966) ushered in the new field of second language writing by pointing out the need for teachers of multilingual writers to look and hence teach beyond the bounds of their students' sentences. Accomplishing this pedagogical feat, however, has always been more easily advised than done. Genre analysis, perhaps more than any other pedagogical approach, offers us a research- and theory-based, text- and community-aware means of teaching beyond the sentence, and Ken Hyland, with his extensive and intimate knowledge as a researcher and teacher of the value of genre, has given us a book that will take teachers and their students well beyond the sentence.

References

Hyland, K. (2000). *Disciplinary discourses: Social interactions in academic writing*. London: Longman.

Johns, A. (Ed.). (2002). *Genre in the classroom: Multiple perspectives*. Mahwah, NJ: Lawrence Erlbaum.

Kaplan, R. (1966). "Cultural thought patterns in intercultural education." *Language Learning, 16(1)*, 1–20.

Paltridge, B. (2001). *Genre and the language learning classroom*. Ann Arbor: University of Michigan Press.

Swales, J. (1990). *Genre analysis: English in academic and research settings*. Cambridge: Cambridge University Press.

Diane Belcher,
Georgia State University

Jun Liu,
University of Arizona

Introduction

It is now ten years since Candlin (1993, p. ix) described genre as "a concept that has found its time," and since then, genre has confirmed much of its potential as one of the most lively and influential concepts in second language teaching and research. Essentially, genres are resources for getting things done using language: they represent a repertoire of responses that we can call on to engage in recurring situations. Recognizing their importance, few teachers now neglect text structure or the importance of context in teaching writing, and familiar process methods co-exist with genre techniques in many L2 classrooms. Despite the established significance of genre-based instruction, however, the insights of a growing literature often fail to reach teachers of multilingual writers. This book addresses this problem by providing a synthesis of theory, research, and practice specifically devoted to an understanding of genre theory and its relevance for the second language writing class.

The term *genre,* of course, is not new. It dates back to the study of classical rhetoric and for the last century or more has been associated with literature and literary criticism. Modern conceptions of genre, however, extend its use beyond literary texts, into films, music, and computer games and into professional, academic, and everyday forms of speech and writing. Today, studies of genre also stress a concern with context as well as form and emphasize the importance of description and analysis rather than simple classification. It is also true that genre has become a key concept in modern thought, not only in linguistics and language teaching but in many areas of contemporary social and cultural studies. This is because language is seen as a central way in which we construct our lives. It is through genres that individuals develop relationships, establish communities, and achieve their goals. Without the familiar structure that genres give to social events, we would be unable to conduct the most basic interactions of everyday life.

My own contact with the ideas developed in this book began in the 1980s while I was teaching in Papua New Guinea. At that time, my colleagues and I were beginning to use the insights into written genres filtering through from Australia in our ESP writing classes, and one colleague had developed a genre-based computer program to grade engineering student reports (Marshall, 1991). This activity encouraged me to carry out a move analysis of the argumentative essays stacked in my office, a step that led to one of my first publications (Hyland, 1990) and a continuing interest in the ways written text are constructed and the possibilities this presents for instruction.

This book is part of that continuing interest, focusing on the multilingual writing classroom and taking as its starting point the belief that a better understanding of genre greatly assists what we do as teachers. It sets out to provide an accessible and practical introduction to the theory of genre and to elaborate how teachers can use this theory to extend the ways they teach writing, offering a scholarly foundation for using genre-based practices. In this way, it is intended to serve as a resource not only for students of writing and teachers in training but also for experienced teachers of EFL/ESL writing who are perhaps skeptical of genre approaches or who are looking for ways of introducing such approaches into their classes.

I have to come clean at the outset, however, and admit that this book is informed by a long association with and affection for an approach to genre influenced by English for Specific Purposes and functional linguistics. It emphasizes the central role of language in all social activity and argues that texts are a good starting point for understanding and teaching students to communicate effectively in writing. My understanding of genre is therefore grounded in writing and the sense writers have of who they are and who they are writing for. I am aware of arguments that the genres students need in the real world cannot be adequately taught in the classroom—the view that because teaching and learning occur uniquely in each setting "what is learnt in context *is* the context" (Dias & Pare, 2000, p. 3). But while we can acknowledge that the move from the writing class to the world of work, community, and further study represents an enormous transition for learners, this is no reason why we should not seek to prepare them for the communicative demands that will confront them there.

I agree that genres are more than forms. They function as frames for the ways we act, the thoughts we have, and the interactions we engage in. Nor do I deny that writing is usually only separately attended to in language classes and that learning genres continues into the domains where they are used. Yet, as Bazerman (1997, p. 19) reminds us, when we travel to new domains we see them through the forms we already know; we bring perceptions and ways of communicating with us that we have developed in other situations. This is why it is both *necessary and essential* to provide students with the frames that will help them do this. The whole edifice of education is premised on the idea that the knowledge and skills required for particular tasks can be identified, analyzed, and taught before engaging in those tasks, and although communicative behaviors may be the most important of these skills, I can see no reason why we should make an exception for them. To teach genres, if we teach them in a way that is sensitive to change, diversity, and flexibility, offers the best way we can help our students to be the best they can be.

The book is organized in the following way: The first three chapters provide an **overview of genre,** why it is useful in multilingual writing classes, how it is understood and used in different perspectives, and the key features associated with it. Chapters 4–6 are concerned with the practicalities of **implementing genre-based teaching,** dealing with genre as an organizing principle, teaching and learning practices, and assessment. The final chapter deals with **analyzing written genres** and suggests a number of small-scale research tasks.

Chapter 1

Why Genre?

$Genre$ is a term for grouping texts together, representing how writers typically use language to respond to recurring situations. For many people, it is an intuitively attractive concept that helps to organize the common-sense labels we use to categorize texts and the situations in which they occur. The concept of genre is based on the idea that members of a community usually have little difficulty in recognizing similarities in the texts they use frequently and are able to draw on their repeated experiences with such texts to read, understand, and perhaps write them relatively easily. This is, in part, because writing is a practice based on expectations: *the reader's chances of interpreting the writer's purpose are increased if the writer takes the trouble to anticipate what the reader might be expecting based on previous texts he or she has read of the same kind.*

Hoey (2001) likens readers and writers to dancers following each other's steps, each assembling sense from a text by anticipating what the other is likely to do by making connections to prior texts. While writing, like dancing, allows for creativity and the unexpected, established patterns often form the basis of any variations. We know immediately, for example, whether a text is a recipe, a joke, or a love letter and can respond to it immediately and even construct a similar one if we need to. As teachers, we are able to engage in more specialized genres such as lesson plans, student reports, and class examinations, bringing a degree of expertise to the ways we understand or write familiar texts. In more precise terms, we possess a *schema* of prior knowledge that we share with others and can bring to the situations in which we read and write to express ourselves efficiently and effectively.

Today, *genre* is one of the most important and influential concepts in language education, signifying what Ann Johns (2002, p. 3) has recently referred to as "a major paradigm shift" in literacy studies and teaching. We will return to a more detailed discussion of what genre is in chapter 2, but it might be useful here, at the beginning of a book about genre, to ask why there has been such a shift.

What is it about genre that gives it such a central place in current writing theory and teaching? This chapter sets out to answer this question, raising some of the main advantages and problems with genre and placing it in the context of current L2 writing teaching.

Genre-Based Writing Teaching

Genre-based teaching is concerned with what learners do when they write. An understanding of the concept allows writing teachers to identify the kinds of texts that students will have to write in their target occupational, academic, or social contexts and to organize their courses to meet these needs. Curriculum materials and activities are therefore devised to support learners by drawing on texts and tasks directly related to the skills they need to participate effectively in the world outside the ESL classroom.

For writing teachers, genre pedagogies promise very real benefits. The concept of genre enables teachers to look beyond content, composing processes, and textual forms to see writing as an attempt to communicate with readers—to better understand the ways that language patterns are used to accomplish coherent, purposeful prose. Genre adherents argue that people don't just *write,* they write *something* to achieve some *purpose:* writing is a way of getting things done. To get things done, to tell a story, request an overdraft, craft an essay, describe a technical process, and so on, we follow certain social conventions for organizing messages, and these conventions can be described and taught. For writing teachers, therefore, genre is a useful concept because it pulls together language, content, and contexts, offering teachers a means of presenting students with explicit and systematic explanations of the ways writing works to communicate.

It is important to note that genre approaches to writing instruction do not represent a single set of teaching techniques that can simply be followed in a paint-by-numbers fashion in every classroom. Students have different proficiencies, motivations, goals, and language needs. They study in contexts where English is taught as a second or foreign language,[1] and they learn to write for different purposes and in different genres. But while genre is a term that embraces a variety of classroom practices, at its core it recognizes that the features of a similar group of texts depend on the social contexts in which the texts are created and used and that those features should form part of a writing syllabus.

Why Genre Is Gaining Attention in L2 Writing Instruction

While genre theories have evolved in different circumstances and in response to different problems, they have attracted growing interest because the idea of genre can help us to un-

---

1. EFL/ESL is a distinction based on the language spoken by the community in which English is being studied. Where the local community is largely English speaking (such as Australia, the United States, or the U.K.), this is referred to as an ESL situation, while EFL contexts are those where English is not the host language. Unfortunately, this obscures more complex realities as ESL learners may be as different as migrants or students planning to return home after their courses, while EFL can refer to learners in contexts where an indigenized variety has emerged (Singapore, India) or where English is rarely encountered (Korea, Japan). These differences will have an impact on such factors as students' language needs and motivation, teaching and learning resources, the cultural and linguistic homogeneity of the students, etc. However, there are enough similarities that concern all teachers of writing to non-native English speakers that it is convenient to discuss these groups together. As a result, I shall use the acronym *L2* to refer to all multilingual writers of English and *ESL* as shorthand for all contexts where they are learning English.

derstand the ways individuals use language to engage in particular communicative situations and to employ this knowledge to help student writers create communicatively effective texts. Genre pedagogies have emerged in L2 writing classes as a *response to process pedagogies,* as an *outcome of communicative methods,* and in consequence of our growing *understanding of literacy.*

Genre as a Response to Process Methods

In part, L2 classroom applications of genre represent a corrective reaction to the individualistic, discovery-oriented approaches to writing that characterized learner-centered classrooms until recently. In the 1970s and 1980s, psycholinguistic and cognitive theories dominated language teaching, and writing teachers were encouraged to focus on general principles of thinking and composing. Writing was seen as a skill that was essentially learned, not taught, and the teacher's role was to be non-directive, facilitating writing through an encouraging and cooperative environment with minimal interference. There is little doubt that this approach has served to instill greater respect for individual writers and for the writing process itself, but because it has little to say about the ways meanings are socially negotiated, it failed to consider the forces outside the individual that help guide purposes, establish relationships, and ultimately shape writing.

Essentially, process methods often postpone input on form and expression to the end of the drafting and revising process so that writers can learn to freely express themselves unencumbered by thoughts of "correctness." This is particularly true in the Expressivist orientation, which urges teachers to provide considerable opportunities for writing, encourage creativity, and respond to the ideas that learners produce, rather than dwell on formal errors (e.g., Murray, 1985). In more cognitively influenced versions, there may be some attention given to discourse structure early in the process (e.g., Raimes, 1992). There is, however, still an emphasis on a planning-writing-reviewing framework (Flower and Hayes, 1981), which tends to focus learners on reflecting on the strategies they use to write rather than on the language and patterns they require to do this effectively. Students are generally expected to discover the language they need in the process of writing itself.

Unfortunately, many teachers felt that such a hands-off facilitative approach cast them in the role of well-meaning bystanders with little to say about the ways texts are conventionally structured and used. They found it was unreasonable to presuppose that their students were familiar with key genres as, in fact, L2 writers often have an incomplete control of English and rely on teachers to help them develop the linguistic resources they need to express themselves effectively (Cope & Kalantzis, 1993; Hasan, 1996). Delpit (1988, p. 287), for example, makes the point strongly:

> Adherents to process approaches to writing create situations in which students ultimately find themselves held accountable for knowing a set of rules about which no one has ever directly informed them. Teachers do students no service to suggest, even implicitly, that "product" is not important. In this country [U.S.] students will be judged on their product regardless of the process they utilized to achieve it. And that product, based as it is on the specific codes of a particular culture, is more readily produced when the directives of how to produce it are made explicit.

For genre teachers, it is not enough to equip students with the strategies of good writers and step back to let them get on with it. Providing students with the "freedom" to write may encourage fluency, but it does not liberate them from the constraints of grammar and form in public contexts of writing.

Genre and Communicative Language Teaching

In another sense, genre-based writing instruction is the heir of communicative approaches to language teaching that emerged in the 1970s. Hymes (1972) introduced the idea of *communicative competence* to account for the two kinds of knowledge crucial to successful language use: *the knowledge of language and the knowledge of when to use it appropriately.* The term generated a range of approaches known collectively as Communicative Language Teaching (see Richards & Rogers, 1986) constructed around this core idea of the role language plays in social contexts. Genre-based teaching continues this communicative tradition by guiding students to the ways they can most effectively achieve their purposes by systematically relating language to context.

Genre-based pedagogies rest on the idea that ways of writing are community resources for creating social relationships, rather than solely the property of individual writers struggling with personal expression. Good writers are aware that what a reader finds in a text is always influenced by what he or she has found in previous texts and that what writers want to say is necessarily affected by what readers expect them to say. Because of this, context is not just the background against which writing takes place; it is co-constructed by the writer and reader anticipating each other's responses and needs and co-constructing meaning through discourse. Writers are always influenced by the social activity they are engaged in, by their relationship with readers, and by the development of the progress of the interaction. Their choices of grammar, vocabulary, content, and organization therefore depend on the situations in which they are writing, and these options can form the basis of L2 writing programs.

Genre and New Literacy

Closely linked to their relationship to communicative teaching, genre pedagogies complement research in New Literacy Studies, which regards literacy as social practice (e.g., Barton & Hamilton, 1998). This view of literacy shows that writing (and reading) vary with context and cannot be distilled to a set of abstract cognitive or technical abilities. There are a wide variety of practices relevant to and appropriate for particular times, places, participants, and purposes, and these practices are not something that we simply pick up and put down; they are integral to our individual identity, social relationships, and group memberships.

In New Literacy views, literacies are mainly acquired through exposure to discourses from a variety of social contexts, and through this exposure, individuals gradually develop theories of genre. In educational contexts, reading and writing are therefore curriculum-wide processes rather than simply "English" activities as each curriculum area requires and offers opportunities for different kinds of writing. This means that students can naturally encounter and may need to be taught a wide range of genres. It also suggests that teachers cannot ignore the diverse genres and literacy demands students will face outside the classroom and should provide texts and tasks that mirror the kinds of interactions they will have with these. In practice, this means recognizing that writing is always purposeful, that it demands a range of skills and understandings of various genres, that it relies on knowledge of other texts, and that it has definite outcomes. Writing, in other words, is always situated.

This view also offers writing teachers a radical new perspective on what they do, for the naive assumption that writing and teaching writing are somehow neutral, value-free activities is no longer defensible. This view encourages us to acknowledge not only that writing is used in many ways across many social contexts but also that only some of these have institutional and cultural stature. It is not the case that all genres are created equal, because they are associated with and are used to regulate entry into social communities possessing more or less prestige and influence.

Advantages of Genre-Based Writing Instruction

A number of advantages are often given for the use of genre-based writing instruction. The main advantages can be summarized as follows. Genre teaching is:

Explicit. Makes clear what is to be learned to facilitate the acquisition of writing skills

Systematic. Provides a coherent framework for focusing on both language and contexts

Needs-based. Ensures that course objectives and content are derived from student needs

Supportive. Gives teachers a central role in scaffolding student learning and creativity

Empowering. Provides access to the patterns and possibilities of variation in valued texts

Critical. Provides the resources for students to understand and challenge valued discourses

Consciousness raising. Increases teacher awareness of texts to confidently advise students on their writing

These advantages are set out more fully in the following sections.

Genre-Based Teaching Is Explicit

Perhaps the most important advantage is that genre-based writing instruction seeks to offer writers an explicit understanding of how target texts are structured and why they are written in the ways they are. ESL teachers can rarely rely on their students having the appropriate cultural, social, and linguistic background they need to write effectively in English for Anglophone audiences. They have to assume that students' current literacy abilities may be widely different from those that they need in such contexts. Clear and explicit genre descriptions are required to bridge this gap. Learning to write involves acquiring an ability to exercise appropriate linguistic choices, both within and beyond the sentence, and teachers can assist this by providing students with examples of the language they need to create effective texts. As Christie (1989, p. 45) observes, making clear "the ways in which patterns of language work for the shaping of meanings" empowers both writers and teachers.

This explicitness gives teachers and learners something to shoot for, a "visible pedagogy" that makes clear what is to be learned rather than relying on hit-or-miss inductive methods whereby learners are expected to acquire the genres they need from the growing experience of repetition or the teacher's notes in the margins of their essays (Hyland, 2003). Providing writers with a knowledge of appropriate language forms shifts writing instruction from the implicit and exploratory to a conscious manipulation of language and choice.

Genre-Based Teaching Systematically Addresses Texts and Contexts

A second key advantage is that a genre orientation incorporates both discourse and contextual aspects of language use that may be neglected when attending to only structures or processes. To create a well-formed and effective text, students need to know how such texts are organized and the lexicogrammatical patterns that are typically used to express meanings in the genre. In addition, however, they also need to know the social purposes of the text type; the kinds of situation in which its use is appropriate; who the probable audience is, what readers are likely to know, and the roles and relationships of text users; the types of textual variation that are typical and possible; how the genre is related to others in the target context; and so on.

Linking texts and contexts in this way has two important advantages. First, it means that teaching materials are based on the ways language is actually used in particular writing contexts rather than on our general impressions of what happens. Teaching, in other words, is *data-driven* rather than *intuition-driven*. Second, while genre teachers focus on texts, this is not simple training in reproducing discourse forms, nor is it a narrow focus of disembodied grammar. Instead, linguistic patterns are seen as pointing to contexts beyond the page, implying a range of social constraints and choices, so that students are offered a way of seeing how different texts are created in distinct and recognizable ways in terms of their purpose, audience, and message.

Genre-Based Teaching Is Based on Writer Needs

Genres also offer a principled way of determining the content and organization of a writing course by basing instruction on the typical patterns and choices available to students in the texts they will need to write. These needs may not always be obvious, and it is often necessary to conduct a survey of target writing contexts to determine the kinds of writing practices that the student will be faced with. However, if writing is embedded in familiar, real-life contexts and if the relevance of tasks to immediate or recognizable future needs is demonstrated, students are likely to find learning more motivating. They are also likely to be more successful in gaining control over target genres and to see the possibilities for variations in these texts, how they relate to other genres, and their connections to the contexts students have to work in.

It is also worth bearing in mind that genres do not occur in isolation in the real world but in sequences of written and spoken texts that are interrelated as "genre systems." As well as knowing *how* to use a genre, writers also know *when* to use it, and in many contexts, one genre will set up the successful conditions for the use of another. Thus, an expository essay is likely to be preceded by note-taking, sifting through web pages, and discussions with friends, just as a business report may be embedded in a network of research and consultation genres. These genres can be integrated into a course in the same way as they are integrated in real life, with opportunities for participation in a range of spoken and written genres that give learners a realistic understanding of their use. An understanding of these needs and systems can thus provide an authentic basis for determining what is to be learned, how these elements will be sequenced in the writing course, the kinds of writing tasks that will be required, and what counts as having learned the genre for assessment purposes.

Genre-Based Teaching Is Supportive

A fourth advantage of genre-based writing teaching is that it provides support for writers as they gradually develop control of a genre. Many genre-based pedagogies are underpinned, either explicitly or implicitly, by Vygotsky's (1978) emphasis on the interactive collaboration between teacher and student, with the teacher taking an authoritative role to "scaffold" or support learners as they move toward their potential level of performance and the confidence to independently create texts. This scaffolding is most evident at the early stages of learning a genre where the teacher intervenes to model and discuss texts, deconstructing and analyzing their language and structure. Language activities are selected to relate closely to the ways they are used in specific kinds of texts and domains to help students create meanings for particular readers and contexts. This support is gradually reduced until the learner has the knowledge and skills to perform independently. This makes the approach particularly valuable to students of beginner and intermediate proficiencies, but it is equally important to any student who is seeking to develop the skills required to write a new genre.

Genre-Based Teaching Is Empowering

Fifth, genre pedagogies offer the capacity for initiating students into the ways of making meanings that are valued in English speaking communities. L2 learners commonly lack knowledge of the typical patterns and possibilities of variation within the texts that possess "cultural capital" in particular social groups. Genre approaches are committed to a redistribution of literacy resources to help learners to gain admission to particular discourse communities; to operate successfully in them; and, in the long run, to develop an informed creativity in using these discourses.

Valued genres are those that determine educational life chances; regulate entry into professions; restrict passage through career pathways; and have symbolic value in institutions, signifying the competency or status of their users. Typically, these are the genres that L2 students wish to control and use. The study of such target texts assists learners to manage the appropriate linguistic and rhetorical tools to gain access to the powerful genres of mainstream culture, revealing *why* writers make certain linguistic and rhetorical choices and *how* to use these genres effectively. It provides the means to reveal writing as relative to particular groups and contexts and help students unpack the requirements of their target communities.

Genre-Based Teaching Facilitates
Critical Understanding

Because they make all these things possible, genre approaches also have the potential for aiding students to reflect on and critique the ways that knowledge and information are organized and constructed in written English texts.

Genre perspectives stress the view that a text is constructed in response to context and therefore only comprehensible because of its relationship to a context, the ways it builds its meanings through a specific set of linguistic choices. With educational genres, these contexts are typically located in the academic institutions or professional bodies to which students are trying to gain access. An understanding of the genres of the powerful not only provides access to those genres, however; it also allows users to see how they represent the interests of the powerful. Understanding how texts are socially constructed and ideologically shaped by dominant social groups reveals the ways that they work to represent some interests and perspectives and suppress others. By focusing on the literacy practices writers encounter at school, at work, and at university, genre pedagogies help them to distinguish differences and provide them with a means of understanding their varied experiential frameworks. What appear as dominant and superior forms of writing can then be seen as simply other practices and therefore become open to scrutiny and challenge.

Genre-Based Teaching Assists Teacher Development

Finally, genre pedagogies not only address the needs of ESL writers but also draw teachers into considering how texts actually work as communication. Knowledge of genres has an important consciousness-raising potential for teachers, with significant implications for both their understanding of writing and their professional development. By fostering an understanding of how texts are effectively shaped to meet writers' goals in particular contexts, teachers are in a better position to reflect on their own writing and that of their students, offering them a means to understand, deconstruct, and challenge texts.

In a genre-based writing course, teachers are confronted with the need to understand how language is used as a communicative resource. They have to categorize the texts they ask their students to write, consider how these texts are similar and different, identify the purposes they serve for writers, analyze the forms that structure them, and understand the contexts they are used in. Coming to terms with these issues makes teachers better discourse analysts, and this in turn helps make them better teachers, more attuned to the ways meanings are created and more sensitive to the specific communicative needs of their students. A reflective teacher is therefore also a more effective teacher. A person who understands how texts are typically structured, understood, and used is in a better position to intervene successfully in the writing of his or her students, to provide more informed feedback on writing, to make reasoned decisions about the teaching practices and materials to use, and to approach current instructional paradigms with a more critical eye.

Reservations about Genre Instruction

Genre approaches have not been uncritically adopted into L2 writing classrooms, and reservations have been voiced by those who favor situated learning, by those influenced by theories of critical pedagogy, and by exponents of process approaches. These will be discussed below.

Genres Should Be Taught "In Situ" Rather than in an ESL Class

From a situated learning perspective, genres are too complex and varied to be removed from their original contexts and taught in the artificial environment of the classroom. Modern social practice theories, such as that of Lave and Wenger (1991), see learning as gradually increasing "legitimate participation" in social communities through "broad access to areas of mature practice." Learning is an integral aspect of activity in and with the world, and the knowledge that is acquired always undergoes transformation in use. In other words, situated learning proponents argue that we learn through engaging in real-world tasks, and we learn to write the genres we need in the contexts in which we need them.

This argument has been taken up by some proponents of the New Rhetoric approach to genre (e.g., Dias & Pare, 2000; Dias, Freedman, Medway, & Pare, 1999), who argue that writing is always intimately part of the goals, occasions, and contexts that bring it about. In real-world settings, writing is a means to accomplish larger goals and often involves non-linguistic actions. For these thinkers, the disjunction between situations of use and situations of learning is unbridgeable, and studying genres in the classroom is an artificial exercise that can never provide the experience of improvising with the social, material, and experiential resources that are used in practice. Teaching genres in the classroom can only teach classroom genres. Teachers cannot, therefore, hope to reproduce authentic cultural and community contexts in the writing class and so can only provide instruction in general writing skills rather than a specific understanding of vernacular genres.

Situated learning theory seems to have considerable explanatory potential. It offers a persuasive account of how learning takes place in occupational settings and a way of seeing how apprentices become established as fully literate members of disciplinary or workplace groups. But it is difficult to see a clear role for writing teachers in this perspective, while situated learning theory has little to say about the fact that writers from non–English speaking backgrounds are often at a considerable disadvantage in such naturalistic contexts. This kind of learning presupposes and builds on a complex array of social and discoursal understandings—of work practices, genre patterns, social relationships, and so on—with which students from other cultural backgrounds may be unfamiliar. Genre-based writing teaching can provide learners with the confidence and skills to participate more effectively in such apprenticeship contexts by short-cutting the long processes of natural, situated acquisition. This is assisted in ESP teaching environments that seek to identify and reproduce these contexts in the classroom.

Genre Teaching Reinforces Dominant Discourses and Hierarchies

Genre teaching has also come under attack from critical pedagogy. Unlike situated learning theories, this view admits the effectiveness of genre teaching as a means of helping learners to gain access to the dominant genres of our culture but doubts the political wisdom of doing so. Critical theorists argue that facilitating control of such genres does nothing to change the power structures that support them or to challenge the social inequalities that are maintained through exclusion from them (e.g., Benesch, 2001). This view, therefore, poses questions about ideology and about the fact that genres embody the values, attitudes, and "ways of doing" of the dominant culture. It asks whether students typically master the genres they are taught or are mastered by them (e.g., Coe, Lingard, & Teslenko, 2002). Luke (1996, p. 314), for example, writes:

A salient criticism of the "genre model" is that its emphasis on the direct transmission of text types does not necessarily lead on to a critical reappraisal of that disciplinary corpus, its field or its related institutions, but rather may lend itself to an uncritical reproduction of discipline.

Thus, by teaching genres, we may be "accommodating" students to powerful interests—simply reproducing the dominant discourses of the powerful and the social relations that they construct and maintain.

This is an important and legitimate argument that will be examined in more detail in Chapter 2, but it is worth noting here that a similar charge could be leveled at most other pedagogies, including those that fail to provide students with better access to powerful genres (e.g., Hasan, 1996). In fact, learning about genres that have accumulated cultural capital in particular professional, academic, and occupational communities does not rule out critical analysis but provides an essential foundation for their critical evaluation.

Genre Teaching Stifles Creativity

Finally, genre teachers have had to defend themselves against proponents of process methods and the charge that genre instruction inhibits writers' creativity and self-expression. In fact, this is probably the most contentious area of genre teaching and has sometimes polarized teachers into those who emphasize the importance of form as a resource for expressing meanings and those who give more importance to the writer and the act of writing. A group of language teachers from a variety of countries surveyed by Kay and Dudley-Evans (1998), for example, expressed the view that genre-based pedagogies carried the danger of prescriptivism and the possibility that students might expect to be told exactly how to write certain types of texts, rather than learning for themselves.

Genre pedagogies assume that L2 writing instruction will be more successful if students are aware of what target discourses look like, and so teachers provide students with opportunities to develop their writing through analyzing "expert" texts. It is, however, this reproductive element that many teachers have been suspicious of. They argue that the explicit teaching of genres imposes restrictive formulas that can straightjacket creativity through conformity and prescriptivism; that genres might be taught as molds into which content is poured, rather than as ways of making meanings (e.g., Dixon, 1987).

Obviously, this is a fundamental concern that cannot be brushed lightly aside. The dangers of a static, decontextualized pedagogy are very real. This is certainly true if inexperienced or unimaginative teachers fail to acknowledge variation and choice and apply what Freedman (1994a, p. 46) calls "a recipe theory of genre" so that students see genres as a how-to-do list. But there is nothing *inherently* prescriptive in a genre approach. There is no reason why providing students with an understanding of discourse should be any more prescriptive than, say, providing them with a description of a clause, the parts of a sentence, or even the steps in a writing process.

The key point is that genres *do* have a constraining power that restricts creativity and places limits on the originality of individual writers. Once we accept that our social and rhetorical goals are best achieved by, say, writing a postcard, a lab report, or a five-paragraph essay, then our writing will occur within certain expected patterns. The genre does not dictate that we write in a certain way or determine what we write; it enables choices to be made and facilitates expression, but our choices are made in a context of powerful incentives where choices have communicative and social consequences. Genre pedagogies make both constraints and choices more apparent to students, giving them the opportunities to recognize and make choices, and for many learners, this awareness of regularity and structure is not only facilitating but also reassuring. As Christie (1989) points out, choice is enhanced by constraint. We might add that the ability to create meaning is made possible by awareness of the choices and constraints that the genre offers.

Genre-Process Connections

In fact, despite a long antagonism between proponents of the two approaches, process and genre are not mutually exclusive. Indeed, they can usefully be seen as supplementing and rounding each other out. Writing is a sociocognitive activity that involves skills in planning and drafting, as well as knowledge of language, contexts, and audiences. As Tribble (1996, p. 45) observes:

> While a process approach will certainly make it possible for apprentice writers to become more effective at generating texts, this may be to little avail if they are not aware of what their readers expect to find in those texts.

Genre pedagogy is based on the belief that learning is best accomplished through explicit awareness of language, rather than through experiment and exploration, but this does not mean replacing learner-centered practices with teacher-centered ones. Few teachers would deny that planning, drafting, and editing are important aspects of writing, but it is now clear that these are only part of the process. Genre simply requires that these be used in the transparent, language-rich, and supportive contexts that will most effectively help students to communicate their meanings. There is nothing in genre pedagogies that excludes the familiar tools that many writing teachers use every day.

Genre pedagogies insist that instead of addressing grammar at the end of the writing process as an extemporized solution to learners' writing difficulties, teachers should ensure that students possess this central resource for constructing meanings from the outset. Students should have clear guidelines for how to construct the different kinds of texts they have to write. Process methods can therefore be combined with genre-based teaching to ensure that learners develop understanding and control of:

- the **processes** of text creation;
- the **purposes** of writing and how to express these in effective ways;
- the **contexts** within which texts are composed and read and that give them meaning.

Summary

In this chapter, we have seen that genre is a socially informed theory of language offering an authoritative pedagogy grounded in research of texts and contexts. Many genre teachers are also strongly committed to empowering students to participate effectively in writing situations. The main implications for writing teachers are that genre-based teaching:

1. Allows teachers to identify the kinds of texts students will have to write in their target academic or occupational contexts and to organize their courses around these needs.

2. Enables teachers and learners to see how texts are related to particular contexts
3. Helps teachers and students to see that texts are purposeful and patterned to serve writer and community purposes
4. Provides teachers with a principled means of supporting the development of student writing
5. Shows how some texts are valued more than others within a community
6. Provides students with a means of understanding, using, and critiquing these texts
7. Encourages teachers to integrate grammar, process, content, and function

However, genre is a rapidly growing area of study, and, as with any developing field, there is more than one way into it. While this diversity is a healthy sign of growth, it may also be confusing for those new to the area, and for this reason, this chapter has deliberately glossed over the differences among theorists about how genres should be described and what these differences mean for the classroom. Chapter 2 looks more closely at these different perceptions of genre and at the various tensions that the term embodies.

Tasks and Discussion Questions

1. Reflect on your own experiences as a writing teacher for a moment. (a) What are the most important things you want students to learn from your classes? (b) What kinds of activities do you use? (c) Do you think your students could become better writers with an understanding of genre? (d) Why or why not?
2. The concept of genre is based on the idea that we usually have little difficulty in recognizing similarities in the texts we use frequently and that this helps us to read, understand, and write them relatively easily.

List the written genres that you use regularly in different social settings, at work, at home, and elsewhere. Which are you most comfortable with writing? Or reading? List some written genres that you only use occasionally.

3. "*It is not enough to equip students with the strategies of good writers and step back to let them get on with it. Providing students with the freedom to write may encourage fluency, but it does not liberate them from the constraints of grammar and form in public contexts of writing.*" To what extent do you agree with this quote from the chapter? How might you persuade a process adherent of the potential advantages of providing students with grammatical and text information about the texts they are asked to write? Are you persuaded by these reasons? At what stages and in what ways might grammar best be introduced?

4. The process and genre approaches to writing are often presented as polar extremes. Can you think of ways that they might be seen as complementing each other rather than as being incompatible?

5. Do you agree with the view that genre-based teaching only reinforces dominant discourses and social hierarchies? What arguments would you use to counter this view?

6. What do you see as the most important advantage of genre-based instruction for you personally as a teacher? What would you need to do to introduce genre teaching into your classes?

7. Take a text that you have used recently in class or are thinking of using. What genre would you categorize it as? Who is it written for? What is the writer's purpose in writing it? How is it organized, and what do you think its main language features are?

Chapter 2

Perspectives on Genre

Genre approaches to writing instruction are based on the idea that every successful text displays the writer's awareness of its context and the readers that form part of that context. Individuals draw on their experiences of what has worked well in the past in similar contexts when they write and can be assisted to write more effectively if they are taught to recognize such similarities and differences among texts. As a result, in many classrooms around the world, students are encouraged to examine text features and to use this knowledge to process and write texts. Yet, despite its attractiveness, Swales (1990, p. 33) warns us that the term *genre* is "extremely slippery." We find major differences lurking just below the surface concerning precisely what it means and its relevance for writing teachers. This chapter explores the different ways that genre is understood and the implications these understandings have for teaching multilingual writers.

Approaches to Genre

It is customary to identify three broad, overlapping approaches to genre (Hyon, 1996; Johns, 2002). While it is possible to overemphasize the differences among them, these approaches differ in the educational contexts to which they have been applied, their intellectual roots, and the weight they give to either context or text. The three orientations are associated with:

1. the Australian work in the tradition of *Systemic Functional Linguistics;*

2. the *New Rhetoric* studies developed in North American composition contexts;
3. the teaching of *English for Specific Purposes.*

Genre as Social Purpose: Systemic Functional Linguistics

The approach to genre influenced by *Systemic Functional Linguistics* (SFL) is perhaps the most clearly articulated and pedagogically successful of the three orientations and for this reason will be discussed first and in greater detail than the other approaches. Known in the United States as the Sydney School, this model of genre emerged from linguists and teachers working to create a genre-based pedagogy consistent with the theoretical work of Michael Halliday (Halliday, 1994; Halliday & Hasan, 1989). Halliday's conception of linguistics as a set of systems for creating meanings in social contexts is far wider than most linguistic theories as it is concerned with the ways we use language as a resource for communication rather than with rules for ordering grammatical forms. Language is a system of choices by which writers can communicate certain functions, allowing them to express their experiences of the world, to interact with others, and to create coherent messages.

The SFL View of Genre

Genre in SFL is seen as "a staged, goal oriented social process" (Martin, 1992, p. 505), emphasizing the purposeful, interactive, and sequential character of different genres and the ways that language is systematically linked to context. Genres are social processes because members of a culture interact to achieve them; they are goal-oriented because they have evolved to achieve things; and they are staged because meanings are made in steps, and it usually takes writers more than one step to reach their goals. SFL research has therefore stressed the importance of the social purposes of genres and of describing the rhetorical structures that have evolved to serve these purposes. Broadly, when a set of texts shares the same purpose, they will often share the same structure, and thus they belong to the same genre.

Martin (2000, p. 120) describes the importance of genre like this:

> In functional linguistics, genre theory is a theory of how we use language to live; it tries to describe the ways in which we mobilize language—how out of all the things we might do with language, each culture chooses just a few, and enacts them over and over again—slowly adding to the repertoire as needs arise, and slowly dropping things that aren't much use. Genre theory is a theory of the borders of our social world, and thus our familiarity with what to expect.

We cannot, in other words, communicate without using genres. They provide the basis for what we expect to find in a text, contributing to what we see as its coherence and the options available to us for creating meanings.

Theoretical Framework

The relationship of texts and contexts is central to this framework as interactions can only be understood by seeing them against their social setting. Each context is seen as having the possibility for a range of possible texts, or what Hasan calls *Generic Structure Potential,* which is the verbal expression of the context. Texts are seen as being connected to particular contexts at two levels: register and genre. When people create a text they first make choices in *register* along three broad dimensions:

- ***Field***—the social activity in which people are involved and what the text is about
- ***Tenor***—the relationships of the participants in the interaction
- ***Mode***—the role of language (wholly written, written and spoken, illustrations, etc.)

These three elements have consequences for the language choices writers make so that some registers, such as those in legal or scientific fields, for example, are likely to contain texts with fairly predictable features of lexis and grammar, while more personal and informal registers tend to be more open, with texts containing a less restricted range of meanings and forms. Register variables basically explain our intuitions that we do not use language in the same ways to write or speak, to talk to our boss or talk to our lover, to talk about writing or talk about fishing. The second level of text-context interaction is *genre,* where linguistic choices are influenced by the writer's social purpose in using language, what he or she sets out to do.

A student who is given the task of writing a class assignment on, say, environmental pollution has many of these choices made for him or her. He or she knows that it will be written (*mode*), that the teacher is likely to be the only reader and that certain relations of power and solidarity will come into play (*tenor*), and that the topic or focus of the activity will draw on a certain vocabulary (*field*). The student will also need to make genre choices, deciding on the best way to structure the essay to best achieve his or her goals—whether to craft the paper to report a particular situation, to explain the reasons for it, to argue for certain solutions, and so on. So, while the notion of register refers to broad fields of activity that often overlap, genre is a more concrete expression of field, tenor, and mode, involving conventions for organizing messages so readers can recognize our purposes.

Building on Halliday's views of language, the concept of genre in SFL has largely emerged from the work of theorists such as Martin (1989, 1992), Christie (1991), and Rothery (1996). Extensive analysis of writing has shown that different types of texts are distinguished by distinctive patterns of vocabulary, grammar, and cohesion. These patterns structure the texts into stages, and in turn, each stage supports the purpose of the genre. For SFL theorists, then, all texts can be described in terms of both the functions they serve and how component elements are organized to express these functions.

SFL Genres

The SFL approach to genre has been motivated by a commitment to language and literacy education, helping teachers to view linguistics as a practical tool that they can use in their classrooms. Unlike the other two approaches to genre discussed here, SFL attempts to provide a framework that will help explain genre use at all educational levels rather than just the post-secondary one. Genre pedagogy in Australia, in fact, began with the study of writing by primary school students (Rothery, 1996) and later expanded to include secondary school subject classes, adult migrant programs, academic disciplines, and professional workplaces (see Feez, 2001).

The fact that SFL conceptions of genre have emerged within a linguistic framework has meant that those working in this tradition tend to characterize genres in terms of broad rhetorical patterns such as *narratives, recounts, arguments,* and *expositions.* For SFL theorists, genres represent groupings of texts that are similar in terms of their discourse patterns. They are defined by internal linguistic criteria, rather than by the regularly occurring activities that we typically regard as genres, such as *job applications, film reviews,* and *recipes.* Defining genre elements linguistically allows analysts to see how these elements combine in different ways to make up the genres that are found in a range of different contexts and activities.

Genres such as *narration, description,* and *exposition* are sometimes referred to as *text types* (Biber, 1988), which can be used in creating many different kinds of genres. While SFL does not distinguish between genre and text type, the term *macrogenre* is sometimes used to refer to larger, more complex genres that combine more basic *elemental genres* (Martin, 1992). Thus, a macrogenre such as a newspaper editorial might be composed of several elemental genres such as an exposition, a discussion, and a rebuttal. In the same way, elemental genres can contribute to more than one kind of macrogenre. So, scientific lab reports, instruction manuals, recipes, and directions for self-assembly furniture can all consist of descriptions and procedures. As will be discussed further in Chapter 3, this approach is helpful in discovering how genres blend and overlap. It also helps us to understand how elemental persuasive genres such as expositions and opinions are increasingly found in information texts such as government reports, university prospectuses, and research articles.

Genres in SFL, then, are the rhetorical structures fundamental to various forms of communication in a culture. Some core educational genres are listed in Table 2.1, showing their social purpose and some possible "locations" or macrogenres where they are likely to be encountered.

One way in which this kind of classification is useful to teachers is that it provides a means of understanding how genres differ in the demands that they make on students. Descriptions of key genres show that *expositions* and *explanations,* for example, contain more complex forms and are consequently more difficult for learners to write than *recounts*

TABLE 2.1. Some Example Genres

Genre	Social Purpose	Social Location
Recount	To reconstruct past experiences by retelling events in original sequence	Personal letters, police reports, insurance claims, incident reports
Procedure	To show how something is done	Instruction manuals, science reports, cookbooks, DIY books
Narrative	To entertain and instruct via reflection on experience	Novels, short stories
Description	To give an account of imagined or factual events	Travel brochures, novels, product details
Report	To present factual information, usually by classifying things and then describing their characteristics	Brochures, government and business reports
Explanation	To give reasons for a state of affairs or a judgment	News reports, textbooks
Exposition	To give arguments for why a thesis has been proposed	Editorials, essays, commentaries

Source: Butt, Fahey, Feez, Spinks & Yallop, 2000; Martin, 1989.

and *procedures.* A *procedure,* for instance, consists of a series of steps that shows how to achieve a goal and at lower levels may be based around simple imperative clauses using familiar action verbs and everyday objects. *Explanations,* on the other hand, are more demanding because they typically require students to use sequential, causal, and conditional conjunctions. Each genre in the table moves writers further from their own experience to more generalized events and objects outside their experience. Not only are these kinds of meanings valued more highly in academic and professional settings, but the structures and features students need to draw on to write them effectively become more complex and demanding.

The classification is also useful as it helps teachers to see how particular genres can be expressed using increasingly complex forms. This means that as students become more proficient in their use of English and in their control of the genre, they can be exposed to more sophisticated ways of expressing the genre. More specialized and technical *procedures,* for example, go beyond simple instructions and may include steps that specify constraints that have to be met to carry them out, perhaps expressed as conditional clauses. Similarly, more advanced *explanations* go beyond the resources needed to discuss specific and familiar people and things, as in "why my essay was late," to more general phenomena such as "how a telephone works."

To sum up, in the second language writing class, an SFL view of genre allows teachers to:

- Group like texts into families in terms of their principal social functions or contexts of use
- Plan a sequence of genres for a writing course or unit of work based on the relationship between genres and an understanding of a progression of difficulty and complexity
- Assist learners to see similarities and differences in texts in terms of their genre structures
- Develop writing skills by recycling elemental genres in gradually more complex macrogenres

- Reveal how genres are related to other genres, both written and spoken, in the real world
- Help students understand the structure and relationships of valued genres in order to control them and use them creatively

Genre Descriptions

In addition to specifying key genres that students are often asked to write, SFL researchers have identified the typical features and stages of these texts. Beginning with the purposes for communicating and then moving to the features of a text that can express these purposes, teachers can help students to distinguish between different genres and to write them more effectively. So, for example, when teaching simple recounts and descriptions, teachers may find it useful to highlight the key grammatical differences between these two genres as:

- Descriptions tend to use present tense, and recounts use past simple tense.
- Descriptions make use of *be* and *have* while recounts usually contain more action verbs.

In more prestigious and complex information genres, such as reports or explanations that contribute to high school or university essays, researchers have identified clusters of style, lexis, and other rhetorical features that writers use to remove their texts from the here-and-now to more conceptual levels of expression and understanding. This is mainly achieved by:

- A high use of abstractions—particularly abstract nouns and "virtual" entities that refer to more intangible objects rather than to personal and concrete ones
- An increase in the proportion of content words over grammar words—a feature known as "lexical density." Casual conversation typically has about two content items per clause, and this increases with more specialist written genres.
- A higher frequency of conditional conjunctions such as

unless, if, and *because,* as opposed to temporal relations expressed through words like *and, then, as,* etc.
- A greater use of nominalization, the process that freezes events or properties as objects (Halliday, 1998). Thus, actions (e.g., *it measures*) or properties (e.g., *it is soft*) are not represented as verbs and adjectives but as nouns (*measurement, softness*). This allows writers to control the information flow of their texts by packaging complex events as a single thing so that *atoms bond rapidly,* for example, can be presented as an object, *Rapid atom bonding,* at the beginning of a sentence in order to say more about it.

Genres can also be described in terms of the stages that a text moves through to express the writer's purpose. A great deal of work has gone into analyzing key academic genres as a sequence of obligatory and optional elements or stages. The notion of text structure is essentially a linguistic one, with stages identified according to their function or the writer's rhetorical purpose. The approach follows Halliday's systemic grammar (Halliday, 1994) and involves combining units of the same size to form larger ones in much the same way that words combine to form groups that make clauses and so on. For example, the argument genre, often found in college essays, typically opens with a *thesis* stage that introduces the proposition to be argued, followed by a *claim* that discusses and supports the grounds for the thesis, and ends with a *conclusion* that reaffirms the validity of the thesis (Hyland, 1990).

The structures of some established genres are set out in Table 2.2 in their typical sequences (Lock & Lockhart, 1998).

By describing the typical stages and features of valued genres, teachers can provide students with clear options for writing, both within and beyond the sentence, to help them create texts that seem well-formed and appropriate to readers. This approach is also valuable for teachers as it helps them to identify why weak texts seem incoherent and to suggest clear remedies to assist learners in addressing the problems they may be having. In the classroom, model texts can be annotated for their stages and distinctive language features pointed out and practiced as a way of supporting student writing in the

TABLE 2.2. Some Genre Structures

Genre	Stages	Purpose
Recount	Orientation ^	Provides information about a situation
	Record of events ^	Presents events in temporal sequence
	(Reorientation)	Brings events into the present
Procedure	Goal ^	Gives information about purpose of the task—in title or intro
	Steps 1–n ^	Lists activities needed to achieve the goal in correct sequence
	(Results)	Presents final state or "look" of the activity
Narrative	Orientation ^	Gives information about characters' situation
	(Complication)	Presents one or more problems for the characters to solve
	(Evaluation) ^	Evaluates the major events for the characters
	Resolution	Sorts out the problems for the characters
Description	Identification ^	Defines, classifies, or generalizes about a phenomenon
	Aspect^n ^	Describes attributes of each category of the phenomenon
	(Conclusion)	Sums up the description
Report	Problem ^	Identifies a problem
	Reason^n ^	Gives possible reasons for or consequences of the problem
	(Conclusion) ^	Makes suggestions for solving the problem
	Recommendations	Presents measures to be adopted as a result of the report

Note: ^ = is followed by; ( ) = optional stage; n = stage may recur

early stages of producing a new genre. Figure 2.1 shows texts produced by primary learners that are used as examples of written factual genres in the Australian English syllabus.

SFL Genre Pedagogy

Within SFL, a rich and sophisticated methodology has developed to provide both first and second language learners with access to socially valued genres through an explicit grammar of linguistic choices. In the writing classroom, this pedagogy has drawn on the work of the Russian psychologist Lev Vygotsky (1978) and his argument that learning occurs best when students are engaged in tasks that are within their *Zone of Proximal Development* (ZPD), the area between what they

Exposition		Recount	
Stage	**Example**	**Stage**	**Example**
Thesis	A good teacher needs to be understanding to all children.	**Orientation**	On Tuesday we went on a harbor cruise.
Argument	He or she must be fair and reasonable. The teacher must work at a sensible pace. The teacher also needs to speak with a clear voice so the children can understand.	**Events in chronological order**	We went underneath the harbor bridge and then we went past some submarines. When we got to Clifton Gardens we had a picnic. After we had finished we played on the climbings. Then Mr. Robinson came over and said Mr. Moses was giving out frozen oranges. Then after we finished that we went home.
Reiteration	That's what I think a good teacher should be like.		
		Personal comment (optional)	It was a nice day out.

Fig. 2.1. Some factual genres (English K–6 syllabus) (Board of Studies, 1998, p. 287)

can do independently and what they can do with assistance. Learning to write is thus seen as a result of interacting with a more knowledgeable person. This means that the teacher has a central role in "scaffolding" student development through a cyclical process:

- Contextualizing the genre through activities such as prediction tasks, problem-solving activities, site visits, etc., that reveal the purpose of the genre and the situations in which it is found
- Modeling appropriate rhetorical patterns of the genre to reveal its stages and their functions (comparing texts, sequencing activities, etc.)
- Providing guided practice in writing the genre through role plays, information-gap tasks, group construction or completion activities, etc.
- Withdrawing to allow students to write independently (planning, drafting, and editing texts; peer critiques) in realistic contexts

We will return to these techniques in Chapter 5, but it can be seen that the genre classroom seeks to offer students a supportive environment. It is also characterized by talk, by many kinds of writing, and by the development of a linguistic *metalanguage* by which students can describe and control the structure and grammatical features of the texts they write.

Genre as Situated Action: The New Rhetoric

The second main perspective on genre differs considerably from SFL. Not only does it take a different view of what a genre is and how it should be studied, but it also questions the value of genre in the writing class. This perspective does, however, raise some interesting issues for teachers wishing to apply genre pedagogies, and these will be addressed here.

The New Rhetoric View of Genre

While both SFL and New Rhetoric (NR) recognize the importance of context and the social nature of genres, New Rhetoricians diverge from the Sydney School in following Bakhtin's notion of *dialogism*. This is the view that while genres involve regularities and conventions, they are nevertheless much more "flexible, plastic, and free" (Bakhtin, 1986, p. 79) than SFL would allow. Because of this, there is a greater emphasis on the dynamic quality of genres, the ways that they develop and exhibit variation, and this leads to a far more provisional understanding of the concept. They are represented as "stabilized-for-now" forms of action that are open to change and subject to negotiation. In sum, genre is seen as a form of social action that is "centred not on the substance or the form of the discourse but on the action it is used to accomplish" (Miller, 1994, p. 24).

Theoretical Framework

It can be seen from this definition that, in contrast to SFL, NR perspectives of genre are not informed by a linguistic framework. Rather, they draw on postmodern social and literary theories (especially Bakhtin, 1986) and on North American research into L1 rhetoric and composition (e.g., Freedman & Medway, 1994). The values and arguments of this group therefore emerge from ideological and social perspectives derived from cultural and rhetorical studies and only occasionally from detailed analyses of texts. New Rhetoric actually embraces a number of perspectives that address the issue of how people know how to write what they write, only some of which focus on texts. The collection edited by Bishop and Ostrom (1997) gives an idea of the variety of such approaches. In general, however, NR research has generally been less interested in describing the linguistic similarities of texts for teaching purposes. Instead, it has devoted more attention to investigating the ways that such similarities are related to regularities of social activity (Dias & Pare, 2000).

For New Rhetoricians, then, understanding genres involves not only describing their lexico-grammatical forms and rhetorical patterns but also investigating their social, cultural, and institutional contexts. Through these contexts, we can understand the circumstances in which creativity is employed in writing and how meanings are negotiated. Textual regularities are not ignored in this approach, but they are regarded as evidence of how people respond to routine situations in ways that differ by culture and by community.

New Rhetoric Studies of Genre

This view of genre as a flexible instrument in the hands of expert community users has meant that the use of texts in the classroom or by novice writers has not been a major feature of NR research. Instead, publications have focused on how "expert" users exploit genres for social purposes and the ways genres are created and evolve. Thus, research has examined such issues as the historical evolution of genres (Atkinson, 1996); the processes of revising and responding to editors and reviewers in writing scientific articles (Myers, 1990); the social impact of transferring genres into new contexts with different purposes (Freedman & Adam, 2000); and the study of genres in the workplace (Pare, 2000; Dias et al., 1999).

This work has also tended to employ ethnographic rather than linguistic research tools. In particular, researchers have made use of participant observation, interviews, and descriptions of physical settings, as well as analyses of texts, to develop "thick descriptions" of the contexts that surround genres. In these ways, analysts study the attitudes and values of the communities that employ particular genres.

The Importance of Context and Power

NR researchers are therefore principally interested in the contexts in which genres are used, and an important dimension of these contexts, often neglected in writing textbooks, is that of power. By providing writers with socially authorized ways of communicating, genres also promote the interests of those with the power to authorize these genres. In other words, genres incorporate the interests and values of particular social groups in an institutional and historical context and work to reinforce particular social roles for individuals and relationships between writers and readers.

Obviously, the complexity or inaccessibility of some genres can work to exclude many individuals, preventing their access to, say, the benefits of academic success or membership in professional bodies. By the same token, the fact that prestigious genres often come to be associated with precedent and proper procedure means that they can be symbolic bastions of the status quo, serving to represent an elite of expertise and power. For this reason, New Rhetoric theorists argue that the SFL agenda of extending access to valued genres is fatally flawed. Teachers who facilitate such access may believe they are improving the life chances of their students, but they are not changing the system because they do not subvert the power of such genres. Genres, in other words, function to empower some people while oppressing others, and if writing teachers ignore this dimension of genres, they simply reproduce power inequalities in their classrooms.

Instead, New Rhetoric urges teachers to ask critical questions, such as:

- How do some genres become respected, and how are they granted esteem?
- In whose interest is this?
- What kinds of social organization are created and maintained by such prestige?
- Who is excluded, and who benefits?
- Does a particular genre have negative effects beyond the immediate context?
- What representations of the world does a genre entail?

By widening the concept of genre to the institutional and societal levels of discourse and investigating the ideological, social, and physical surroundings in which genres are used, New Rhetoric encourages a different stance on genre. It reminds us to consider the ways that genres position and influence individuals within specific situations, as well as the opportunities they offer people for effective communication. Freedman and Medway (1994, p. 15) put the case succinctly:

> We need to commit ourselves to critical examination of at least the following specific issues: what we might call the "labour process of genre"; the nature of the sanctioned representations, and their implications for people's lives and experience, moral and material; the degree of accessibility of a genre to potential users, as common resource or as means of exclusion; and genre maintenance as power maintenance.

Genre and Classroom Applications

Another distinctive feature of the New Rhetoric view of genre is its attitude to classroom applications. Because NR sees genres as guiding frameworks or rhetorical strategies rather than as recurring linguistic structures, there is a perceived instability about genres that makes some NR theorists skeptical about their pedagogic possibilities. Freedman and Adam (2000), for instance, stress that classroom genres differ from those elicited in real-world contexts in terms of the goals, roles, learning methods, and types of evaluation they engender. More broadly, NR assumes that genres can only be taught if they are static, as it would make no sense to teach flexible entities that are perpetually subject to change and reshaping by individual users. Thus, genres cannot be transferred to the writing classroom because this seeks to make solid what is actually shifting and variable.

A second reason why many New Rhetoric theorists reject the possibility of teaching written genres is that the classroom is seen to represent an inauthentic context for acquiring an understanding of writing. Like the Social Learning theorists discussed in Chapter 1, NR scholars believe that learning involves co-participation in community activities, and neither writing nor learning to write can be removed from its local historical and cultural contexts. Freedman (1999, p. 766), for example, asks:

> Because genres are dynamic, fluid and blurred, is it possible to extrapolate rules and regularities from one context (or situation type) to another? Even more significantly, can the complex web of social, cultural, and rhetorical features to which genres respond be explicated at all or in a way that can be useful to learners?

Studying and teaching genres in isolation from such communities, therefore, removes them from the contexts in which they have meaning and cannot reveal the writer's acquisition, reproduction, and manipulation of their conventions. In such circumstances, genres become artifacts for study rather than resources for communication. Worse, genre teaching can be positively harmful as overanxious L2 learners can misapply rules in their writing. All teachers can hope to do in these circumstances is to establish facilitative environments that expose students to relevant expository genres and limit their teaching of genres to "overall features of format or organisation . . . and a limited set of rules regarding usage and punctuation" (Freedman, 1994, p. 200). Coe (1994), however, admits that genres can provide students with a useful heuristic process to guide their writing, encouraging them to ask questions such as "what is my thesis statement?" or "have I oriented the reader?" in relevant genres.

Genre Change and Manipulation

In response to these NR views, I think it would be a mistake to overestimate the flexibility of genres and the constraints this places on teachability. After all, genres change relatively slowly while the extent to which individuals are able to manipulate established forms is relatively inhibited. If teachers had to wait for knowledge and practices to stabilize before they could be taught, then a great deal of what is taught in the science and technology curriculum would be out of bounds.

Moreover, the issue of manipulation avoids the support current patterns receive from powerful interests. Within every culture, social ideologies and power relations are played out through language and systematically work to advantage some people and disadvantage others. The fact that some genres have accrued value in society means that they are supported by vested interests to help sustain power differences. This seriously restricts the extent to which such genres are freely manipulable and negotiated. Valued genres represent the entrenched interests of insiders; this is precisely how insiders are able to exert such power. While individual writers can exercise a degree of creativity, the fact remains that rhetorical decisions have social consequences. The control we exercise over genres when we write is a signal of our status, education, expertise, and so on, and it is unclear how far modifications of genres will be either tolerated by readers or recognized as effective.

It is not usually the novice, and certainly not the L2 writer, who is best served by genre flexibility. Nor is it usually the L2 writer who is best able to make use of it. Indeed, many learners prefer the security of familiar structures to develop their meanings. Chang and Swales (1999), for example, found that their L2 graduate writing students exhibited "a palpable sense of unease" with the use of informal features of academic writing such as the use of first-person pronouns, questions, and the sentence-initial *but*. More significantly, the use of appropriate genre conventions is an important means of demonstrating membership in and identification with a group and the most effective way of being heard as competent within it.

When writers manipulate established forms, this is usually a subtle redrawing of a genre, confined within the boundaries of what is recognized as conventional practices. It also involves a good grasp of the resources for creating meanings and the confidence to depart from the conventional. As Bakhtin (1986, p. 80) has suggested, writers must be able to control the genres they use before they can creatively exploit them. So, while an important dimension of belonging to a community is the knowledge of when to follow and when to innovate, neither the knowledge nor the right to do so is equally distributed. The point is well made by Bhatia (1997, p. 359):

> Unfortunately, however, this privilege to exploit generic conventions to create new forms becomes available only to those few who enjoy a certain degree of visibility in the relevant professional community; for a wide majority of others it is more of a matter of apprenticeship in accommodating the expectations of disciplinary cultures.

In other words, the power to bend conventions is principally in the hands of the powerful themselves. Part of what it means to be powerful is the power to transform genres, precisely because challenging genres means challenging cultures, and the powerful are in the best position to do this.

Genres and Critical Literacy

Given the visibility and importance of valued genres, the extent to which the development of an effective critical literacy in English depends on control of mainstream literacy practices is a pressing question. Both SFL and ESP approaches to genre propose that providing students with more equitable access to such genres is a crucial aspect of writing instruction, not least because it is students from non–English speaking backgrounds who are among the most disadvantaged by lack of such access. They also argue that learning about genres does not preclude critical analysis but, in fact, provides a necessary basis for critical engagement with cultural and textual practices. As Christie (1987, p. 30) argues, "Learning the genres of one's culture is both part of entering into it with understanding, and part of developing the necessary ability to change it."

Hammond and Macken-Horarik (1999, p. 529) make the point forcefully:

> Systematic discussion of language choices in text construction and the development of metalanguage—that is, of functional ways of talking and thinking about language—facilitates critical analysis. It helps students see written texts as constructs that can be discussed in quite precise and explicit ways and that can therefore be analysed, compared, criticised, deconstructed, and reconstructed.

Highlighting variability thus helps undermine a deficit view that sees writing difficulties as learner weaknesses and that misrepresents writing as a universal, naturalized and non-contestable way of participating in communities. While teachers may wish to tread carefully when drawing on genre models in their writing classes, to fail to provide learners with what we know about how language works as communication denies them the means of both communicating effectively in writing and of analyzing texts critically.

New Rhetoric provides us with serious food for thought, emphasizing the crucial role of discourse communities, text dynamism, and individual manipulation of genres. Most important, perhaps, it cautions teachers against regarding genres as materially objective "things" and against employing pedagogies that reduce text descriptions to fixed templates. But while we can recognize that genres evolve to meet the changing needs of communities, technologies, and specific situations and that individuals take liberties with text conventions, the mechanisms by which such changes occur and the extent to which such manipulation is possible remain central unresolved issues of genre studies.

Genre as Professional Competence: English for Specific Purposes

Researchers in English for Specific Purposes (ESP) are interested in genre as a tool for understanding and teaching the kinds of writing required of non-native English speakers in academic and professional contexts. The ability to function competently in a range of written genres is often a central concern for ESL learners as it can determine their access to career opportunities, positive identities, and life choices. As a result, ESP investigates the structures and meanings of texts, the demands placed by academic or workplace contexts on communicative behaviors, and the pedagogic practices by which these behaviors can be developed. It thus addresses a cross-cultural and L2 dimension of writing instruction that is often lacking in SFL and NR work.

The ESP View of Genre

Although ESP is regarded as a separate approach to genre studies, it is not easy to clearly identify a distinctive ESP perspective on genre. This is partly because of the pragmatic diversity of the field, which, while acknowledging a commitment to linguistic analysis and contextual relevance, has always based teaching and research on local needs as far as possible. Separating ESP from other theoretical strands is also difficult because some ESP scholars draw from both SFL and NR (Johns, 2002, p. 7). A good example of this is the work of John Swales, the doyen of ESP genre studies, whose major published contributions to the field are a seminal work on the linguistic-rhetorical features of academic genres (Swales, 1990) and a closely detailed ethnographic description of the contexts in which some of these genres are created (Swales, 1998).

ESP theorists generally agree on seeing genre as a class of structured communicative events employed by specific discourse communities whose members share broad social purposes (Swales, 1990, pp. 45–47). These purposes are the rationale of a genre and help to shape the ways it is structured and the choices of content and style it makes available (Johns, 1997). At the heart of ESP perspectives, then, are the concepts of community and social purpose. Neither of these ideas has proved to be as straightforward as first imagined, but they enable ESP to maintain a narrow concept of genre that allows researchers to distinguish similar texts in terms of the purposes recognized by members of a relevant community.

Theoretical Framework

This approach draws from an eclectic theoretical foundation. Principally, ESP is based on a commitment to research-based language education through needs analysis, and genre analysis, and to revealing the constraints of social contexts on language use and the ways learners can gain control over these. In fact, ESP approaches to genre tend to steer between the two positions discussed earlier. Like NR, ESP employs notions of dialogism and contextual situatedness, but it also draws on SFL understandings of text structure and, more sparingly, on SFL principles of pedagogy. But while it tends to favor a more top-down approach to genre and a synthesis of different models of learning and discourse, the ESP approach is more linguistic than NR and more oriented to the role of social communities than SFL.

ESP Genres

ESP differs significantly from SFL in the way that it conceptualizes genres. Unlike the Australians, ESP analysts do not see genres as linguistic strategies for achieving general rhetorical goals in a culture, such as *narrative, argument, recount,* and so on. Their interest in the communicative needs of particular academic and professional groups leads them to what it is those groups use writing to do. ESP researchers look to the specific practices of groups and the names group members have for those practices. Genres are the purposive social actions routinely used and recognized by community members to achieve a particular purpose, written for a particular audience and employed in a particular context. Genres are therefore the property of the communities that use them rather than the wider culture.

The close relations between communities and their genres is described by Swales (1998, p. 20) in this way:

> Discourse communities evolve their own conventions and traditions for such diverse verbal activities as running meetings, producing reports, and publicizing their activities. These recurrent classes of communicative events are the genres that orchestrate verbal life. These genres link the past and the present, and so balance forces for tradition and innovation. They structure the roles of individuals within wider frameworks, and further assist those individuals with the actualization of their communicative plans and purposes.

Although Swales goes on to show how matters may be more complex than this, the idea that people acquire, use, and modify the language of written texts in the course of acting as members of occupational groups is an attractive one. It helps to explain the ways that we learn to become members of such groups through situated practice, how we display our competence and expertise as members of such groups, and it shows us one way in which we can demarcate the boundaries between those groups. It also offers teachers a powerful way of understanding the writing needs of their students.

Some genres that have been identified and explored by teachers for use in ESP classrooms are shown in Figure 2.2. Because these genres are rarely found in isolation in the real world, ESP research has also recently begun to explore the relationships between genres in workplace and academic settings. The idea of "genre sets" or "systems," originally discussed by Devitt (1991) and Bazerman (1994), is a useful way of understanding social contexts and how spoken and written

Academic	Professional
Research articles	Direct mail letters
Conference abstracts	Business faxes
Book reviews	Engineering reports
Grant proposals	Legal cases and briefs
Undergraduate essays	E-mail memos
Ph.D. dissertations	Company annual reports
Textbooks	Charity donation requests
Reprint requests	Letters of recommendation

Fig. 2.2. Some academic and professional written genres

texts cluster together to form routine social practices. We can see, for example, that genres may be networked in a relatively fixed sequence, as in the case of those that contribute to a successful job application (e.g., Paltridge, 2001):

> Read advertisement → Research employer through company documents, etc. → Write a curriculum vitae → Write a covering application letter → Read response letter → Attend oral interview → Write acceptance letter

Alternatively, genres may more loosely associate as a "repertoire" of options in a particular context; students might, for example, be able to choose among several genres for finding information (e.g., Swales, 2000), as shown in Figure 2.3.

An ESP approach to genre teaching offers teachers and students the following advantages:

- An efficient way of identifying the texts learners will need to write in a particular context
- A means of sequencing and grouping texts
- A description of the typical features of key genres that

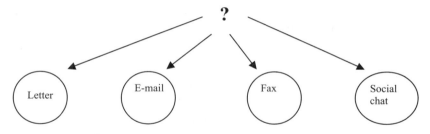

Fig. 2.3. A repertoire of mode and genre options for finding information

    students can draw on for their own communicative pur-
    poses in their professional or academic lives

- An ability to understand what happens in real-world interactions and a means to participate in these interactions
- A way of seeing how genres are interrelated in real life
  and an authentic context for developing skills in a range
  of spoken and written genres
- An understanding of the roles and purposes of writers and
  readers—why someone would write and read the genre

Genre Descriptions

Genre analysis in ESP is often associated with the kind of
move analysis exemplified by John Swales (1990) in his seminal description of research article introductions. This approach describes the rhetorical patterning of a genre or
"schematic structure." This kind of analysis is very similar to
the "stages" of SFL analyses discussed earlier. It involves
identifying the series of moves that make up the genre from a
representative sample of texts. Each move is a distinctive
communicative act designed to achieve one main communicative function and can be further subdivided into several
"steps." Both moves and steps may be optional, embedded in
others, repeated, and have constraints on the sequence in
which they generally occur.

    A recent example is Yakhontova's (2002) study of confer-
ence abstracts in applied linguistics, which provides a useful
model for graduate students. The description is based on the
writer's purpose to persuade the conference committee to ac-

cept the abstract by establishing the importance of the research and situating it within the discipline. Abstracts are seen to have a five-move structure, as shown in Figure 2.4, although only Move 2 occurred in all abstracts in Yakhontova's sample.

These kinds of analyses of text structures have proved extremely useful in L2 writing teaching by raising student awareness of the ways genres are organized to express certain purposes. In addition, however, ESP studies have also identified key features of particular genres. McKenna (1997), for example, shows that engineering reports are dominated by sentence subjects that refer to real world entities and processes, often restated as analytical concepts:

- *The alarm sensors* operate on . . .
- *Composting* may be an appropriate . . .
- *Bracing systems* allow us to . . .

This feature distinguishes reports from more interactive genres such as research articles and contributes to the way engineers represent the world. Similarly, Bhatia (1993) shows

Move structure	Rhetorical strategies for realizing the move
Move 1: Outlining the research field	a. Referring to established knowledge
	b. Referring to previous research
	c. Asserting the importance of the area
Move 2: Justifying the research study	a. Indicating a gap in the previous research
	b. Making a counterclaim
	c. Raising a question about the previous research
Move 3: Introducing the paper to be presented	a. Stating the purpose of the paper (aims)
	b. Stating the focus of the paper (content)
Move 4: Summarizing the paper	a. Giving an overview of the whole paper
	b. Giving an overview of its parts in sequence
Move 5: Highlighting outcomes	a. Reviewing the most important results of the study
	b. Stating the implications or applications of the resul

Fig. 2.4. A move analysis of conference abstracts in applied linguistics (Yakhontova, 2002)

how legal documents are characterized by a high frequency of complex prepositional phrases such as

- *for the purpose of*
- *in respect of*
- *in accordance with*

This kind of information can provide practical information for students about writing effective engineering reports and legal cases.

In a genre that is perhaps closer to home for many writing teachers, Hyland and Hyland (2001) draw attention to the high use of interpersonal strategies in teachers' feedback comments on L2 student essays. In this highly specialized genre, teachers are able to tone down criticisms and moderate what might be seen as over-directive interventions by combining criticism with praise, using modal verbs, responding as ordinary readers through personal attribution, and using questions. This previously unremarked feature of a neglected genre might prove useful in teacher education programs, particularly as teachers need to balance the need for clear and intelligible feedback with an appropriate interpersonal tone.

ESP Genre Pedagogy

Like the SFL tradition, ESP genre studies are motivated by teaching outcomes. Researchers analyze genres to see how a particular aspect of the real communicative world works in order to translate these understandings into the classroom. In contrast to SFL approaches, however, ESP has tended to adopt a more eclectic set of pedagogies and to write applications for more specific populations, usually adults, with particular communicative needs. Most activity has focused on translating research findings into materials for L1 and L2 tertiary students and professionals (Swales & Feak, 1994; 2000), and curricula differ considerably across such groups. These pedagogies, however, are becoming increasingly explicit and coherent. In particular, there is a strong emphasis in ESP pedagogies on offering students a variety of genres and rhetorical experiences and requiring them to reflect on their genre practices. Methods therefore tend to stress rhetorical consciousness raising through classroom analyses of the genres students need to write, often by comparing texts and producing mixed-genre portfolios (e.g., Johns, 1997; Swales & Feak, 2000).

Summary

Each of the three conceptions of genre discussed in this chapter sees language as a central feature of human behavior. Language, through genres, helps to construct meaning and social context, rather than being merely a tool for transmitting ideas. The three traditions also share the common goal of analyzing the relationship of writing to particular contexts. They differ, however, in their intellectual frameworks, their educational settings, their focus, and their use of genre in the classroom. Table 2.3 summarizes these differences.

To the teacher who turns to genre in search of answers to the very real dilemmas and difficulties of the L2 writing class, these perspectives may seem to offer depressingly contradictory advice. Do we focus on texts or contexts? Should we identify broad rhetorical genres or the needs of specific learners? Ought we to emphasize consciousness raising, composing heuristics, or linguistic scaffolding? Probably the answers to

TABLE 2.3. Perspectives on Genre

Orientation	Primary Focus	Intellectual Roots	Pedagogy	Education Context	Sample Genres
SFL	Discourse structure and features	Systemic linguistics	Vygotsky (ZPD) teaching-learning cycle	L1 schools, adult migrants	Narrative, report, recount
NR	Social purposes, context	Post-structuralism	Heuristics, general formats	L1 university composition	Political briefs, patents, medical records
ESP	Discourse structure and features	SFL, CLT, Pragmatics	Consciousness raising, needs analysis	Occupational and academic training	Article, memo, sales letter

these questions depend very much on the particular interests of the teacher, the needs of his or her students, and the local circumstances of instruction.

Despite these differences, however, there is general agreement on a number of key assumptions of genre-based perspectives which can be summarized as follows (see also Berkenkotter & Huckin, 1995, p. 4; Kress, 1989):

1. Genres develop as a result of the recurrent ways people get things done in their social groups.
2. Because these groups are relatively stable, the genres produced in and by institutions achieve a certain stability over time, helping to give coherence and meaning to social experience.
3. Genres have specifiable linguistic characteristics that are not fully determined by the context or the genre but are not fully under the control of individual writers either.
4. Texts are not simply produced by individuals expressing inner meanings but are influenced by communities or cultures—in terms of both products and processes— and so change in response to changing needs.
5. An understanding of genre embraces both form and content, including a sense of what is appropriate to a particular purpose and context;
6. The language of texts should always be taught together with the functions texts usually perform for writers in specific contexts.
7. Genres have social origins, and so different genres carry different degrees of power and status.
8. Knowledge of text characteristics and of their social power should form part of any writing curriculum.

It is certainly true that genre pedagogies are more complex and demanding than earlier approaches to composition, but they also offer greater direction and situational focus. Chapter 3 takes up some of the key issues introduced here in greater detail. In particular, it looks at how we can characterize genre knowledge and what this means for teaching L2 writing.

Tasks and Discussion Questions

1. Summarize the main points of similarity and difference among the three approaches to genre discussed in this chapter. Which of these do you think has the most to offer the teacher of second language writing, and why?

2. Select one of these approaches, and consider its main advantages and disadvantages for you as a writing teacher. How could you exploit the advantages and overcome the disadvantages?

3. Explain the difference between macrogenres and elemental genres, and give examples of each. Which of these do you think you would feel most comfortable teaching, and which would be most useful to your students?

4. We all belong to several communities or groups that share certain communicative purposes and common genres. Note down one community that you belong to, and list the genres that it uses. Why are these genres important to this community?

5. Draw up a list of texts relevant to a group of students that you are familiar with. Can you group these into families or "genre sets"? What principles did you use to do this, and how could this be useful in offering a way of sequencing the genres for teaching purposes?

6. Look at this list of genres, partly taken from Cook (1989, p. 95). Can you see any similarities and differences among them? Try to group them into categories in different ways, for example, spoken vs. written, similar purposes, type of audience, main grammar patterns, key vocabulary, formality, etc. You will find that genres often have things in common but are distinct in various ways.

sales letter	notice	informal letter
inventory	warrant	advertisement
essay	menu	manifesto

biography	label	jingle
abstract	note	will
prescription	postcard	sign
anecdote	consultation	memo
report	manual	seminar
toast	editorial	novel
sermon	poem	article
lecture	chat	conversation
telegram	song	film review

7. Select a written genre from the list above, and find an example of it. Describe the main features of the genre according to its likely audience, purpose, context, structure, and main grammar and vocabulary. How might this description be useful in teaching L2 students to write this genre? Consider how you would approach it in class, and sketch out a lesson plan that includes an appropriate authentic context, a model text, main instructional points, and writing activities.

8. The explicit teaching of grammar in teaching writing is a controversial issue. What are your own views? When do you think it is appropriate to focus on language, and how can this be done most effectively?

9. Look at the key assumptions of genre-based writing teaching listed in the summary. Which of these offers the most important insight about writing for teachers and students? Why?

Chapter 3

Genre Knowledge

The different views discussed in Chapter 2 all recognize that the ability to see texts as similar or different, and to write or respond to them appropriately, is vital to achieving literacy in a second language. Berkenkotter and Huckin (1995, p. ix) refer to this as *genre knowledge,* "an individual's repertoire of situationally appropriate responses to recurrent situations," and it is useful for writing teachers to have some understanding of what the term means in order to apply genre methods in their classes.

The notion of genre knowledge is important to L2 writing teachers for a number of reasons, but two stand out:

1. It stresses that genres are specific to particular cultures and communities, reminding us that our students may not share this knowledge with us.
2. It urges us to go beyond structures, vocabulary, and composing to incorporate into our teaching the ways language is used in specific contexts.

This chapter explores what genre knowledge means, focusing on what writers need to know to produce effective texts and pointing out the implications of this for second language writing classes.

What Is Genre Knowledge?

To be part of any social event, individuals must be familiar with the genres they need in that event. But although genres are recognized types of communicative actions, they are, in reality, just abstract ideas because what we see are *texts,* not *genres.* As a result, our knowledge of genres is often only vague and schematic, particularly when it comes to those genres we encounter only rarely. In some cases, we may have a great deal of trouble deciding what kind of genre a particular text belongs to, a fact that is often exploited by devious mail advertisers, for example, who disguise sales messages as "good news" announcements. More significantly, without adequate genre knowledge, we may find it very tricky to write an unfamiliar genre, such as an accident report for an insurance claim or a poster for a teachers' conference. In sum, unless we use a genre regularly, our knowledge is likely to be partial and poorly remembered.

Genre Knowledge and Schema

Genre knowledge only develops with repeated experiences. We gradually gain control of a genre by using it, remembering how it is set out to help us express what we want to say. This kind of knowledge is sometimes referred to by literacy theorists as a *schema,* or a system for storing and retrieving past knowledge. Originally a cognitive perspective on reading comprehension, schema theory suggests that we can only engage with a text effectively if we are able to relate it to something we already know. This is why teachers often develop writing assignments from readings and use pre-writing activities like brainstorming and focused freewriting. These help to stimulate student ideas for writing and to develop recall of the topics and vocabulary students will need to create an effective text.

A more socially enriched view of schema, however, goes beyond what we know about content and background to include the contexts and purposes of genres. Genre knowledge is not simply grammatical competence but involves the ability to understand how to participate in real-world communicative events. It implies that a writing or reading task will evoke not only expectations for particular text features but also assumptions about how a genre is used, the contexts it occurs in, and the roles and values associated with it (e.g., Johns, 1997; Swales, 1990).

The fact that individual and cultural experiences help shape schemata means that the genre knowledge of our L2 students may be very different from our own, and this can influence the genres they select and how they write them. It also means that teachers need to help students not only to understand the conventions of organization, grammar, vocabulary, and content associated with a genre but also to see how these are tied to wider regularities of activity: locating genres in the cultures and institutions within which they are used. Skilled writers are able to create successful texts by accurately predicting readers' background knowledge and anticipating what readers are likely to expect from a particular piece of writing. Growing familiarity with a genre, therefore, develops knowledge that is partly cognitive, based on our prior knowledge and familiarity with similar texts, and partly social, shared with other text users in particular circumstances. This means that although few rhetorical situations are exactly alike, we are able draw parallels with related purposes and texts that we have experienced while modifying and evolving our use of them for new situations.

Genre knowledge is therefore knowledge of the culture in which writers, readers, and texts are found, and the following sections explore the main components of this knowledge:

- Knowledge of the communicative purposes that the genre is commonly used to achieve
- Knowledge of the appropriate forms that are needed to construct and interpret texts
- Knowledge of content and register
- Knowledge of the contexts in which a genre is regularly found

Knowledge of Shared Communicative Purposes

The notion of a shared communicative purpose is central to most ideas of genre. Purposes provide the rationale for a genre and exert a constraining influence on what it typically contains and how it is written. That is, in employing a given genre, we see it as representing the most efficient and economical way of achieving a particular goal, whether this is persuading people to buy a brand of toothpaste or wishing someone a happy birthday. Genres are therefore often defined by the jobs they are said to achieve. The concept of purpose also allows us to distinguish the *means* of communication, such as a letter or e-mail, which lack any ascribable purpose, from more specific *acts* of communication, such as *complaint* letters or *sales* emails. It also allows us to help users to differentiate between otherwise similar texts, such as advertisements presented as offers and the real thing.

Multiple Purposes

The last point underlines the fact that purpose is not always an easy and obvious way of identifying a genre. Recipes and self-assembly instructions may be straightforward procedure texts, but it is not hard to imagine them written as poems or perhaps recycled in our classes as language teaching materials. Nor is it hard to see how political biases can be insinuated into so-called objective news reporting or how advertisements might be woven into narrative texts. Fairclough (1995), among others, for example, has discussed how we increasingly find promotional purposes intruding into texts that we often think of as having purely informational goals, such as undergraduate prospectuses and job announcements. Figure 3.1 shows one way that promotional and informational purposes can be combined in a single text, in this case a recent advertisement for an academic post in Hong Kong.

Perhaps less obviously, writers often have unacknowledged "private intentions" that they seek to achieve through

THE UNIVERSITY OF HONG KONG

The University of Hong Kong, as a pre-eminent international university in Asia, seeks to sustain and enhance its excellence as an institution of higher learning through outstanding teaching and world-class research so as to produce well-rounded graduates with lifelong abilities to provide leadership within the societies they serve.

Professor: Chair of Speech and Hearing Sciences

Applications are invited for appointment as Professor: Chair of Speech and Hearing Sciences in the Division of Speech and Hearing Sciences of the Faculty of Education tenable from September 1, 2004, or as soon as possible thereafter.

Fig. 3.1. Mixed purposes in a job advertisement genre

a strategic use of the socially recognized "public purposes" served by a genre (Bhatia, 1999). So, while book or article acknowledgments, for example, seem to be an unselfish and personal dedication of thanks for help, they also provide writers with a rare opportunity to display their well-connectedness, flatter the powerful, and promote themselves. The praise for a mentor here, for instance, reflects on the positive character of the author as much as the recipient:

> To the extent that this book is informed by a love of life, a desire to reach a broad and non-professional audience, and a determination to recreate the teeming diversity of a vanished world in all its exuberant abundance, I am deeply indebted to the example and inspiration of Sir John Plumb. (D. Cannadine, *The Decline and Fall of the British Aristocracy*)

Broad and Narrow Purposes

Clearly, trying to identify a *single* social purpose may not always provide teachers with a clear-cut means of identifying a genre, but nor is it obvious how *broad* a coherent notion of purpose should be. In Australian schools, for example, teachers emphasize a set of purposeful text categories such as *recounts, narratives, explanations,* and so on that students can use to construct a range of everyday texts. Grabe (2002), on the other hand, draws much broader boundaries to identify *narrative* and *exposition* as two overarching macrogenres that occur in different contexts and employ dissimilar patterns of organization. Alternatively, ESP theorists look for purposes in the goals of social groups, so that the *term paper,* the *lesson* plan, and the *five-paragraph essay* are familiar purpose-driven genres to most writing teachers. More confusingly, however, even these genres have been lumped together. Bhatia (1993), for instance, groups *promotional letters* and *job application letters* into the same genre because both have the purpose of promoting something—whether a company, person, or product.

Each of these understandings of purpose has obvious strengths and attractions. A view that focuses on "elemental" rhetorical actions (such as *recounts* and *discussions*) has enormous teaching value as it enables students to create a wide range of texts from a limited group of key purposes. It is not, however, always clear how these purposes combine and interact with one another to produce a text we are able to recognize as a *newspaper article, term assignment,* or *annual report.* The broader perspectives, on the other hand, offer students insights into the ways purposes can link together, but they violate our sense of what genres are, collapsing what we see as different rhetorical acts into single mega-categories.

It might be useful here to keep in mind a distinction originally made by Miller (1994) between purposes that are *similar* as rhetorical actions, that is, texts that *look* alike, and those she calls *typified* rhetorical actions, or those we recognize as similar because they involve similar types of situation, participants, and rhetorical forms. An expert's genre knowledge thus goes beyond form to embrace the wider events and participants associated with a text.

Purposes and Writer-Reader Roles

Selecting a genre to communicate our social purposes also makes a number of roles available to achieve these purposes. A job applicant, for example, may adopt a role as a "viable candidate" in a letter by representing him- or herself as someone who is articulate, conscientious, and qualified, yet respectful and modest, recognizing the reader's power in the exchange. The recognized social purpose of the genre therefore influences the role the writer adopts through his or her choice of content and language.

The ways that purposes, roles, and forms may relate can be illustrated with the example of the introductory textbook genre. A main purpose of textbooks is to assist students to a new competence. While there are several ways writers can approach this purpose, they often draw on a classroom model by adopting the role of an "expert knower" who sets out and explains material to a novice audience. This audience, in turn, studies, remembers, and perhaps sometimes critiques this material. Adopting this role helps explain why textbook authors tend to make heavy use of features such as:

- **Imperatives.** "As *you* read this excerpt, *pay* particular attention to the use of tenses."
- **Second person pronouns.** "Imagine that *you* are about to buy a product in that category."
- **Rhetorical questions.** *"Can you guess what happened next?"*
- **Unhedged assertions.** "This tendency *obviously* reflects the preponderance of brand-image advertising."

These features give an impression of authority and confidence and imply a writer in full control of his or her topic—and readers. This can be seen in an example from a biology textbook:

Are there fungi which specialize in exploiting dung? And if there are, how do they gain access to this substrate when it becomes available? The answers may surprise you. About 175 genera of *ascomycetes* are largely or exclusively found on dung. The extremely advanced and successful agaric genus *Coprinus* has many species that occur exclusively on dung. There are also many specialized dung-inhabiting *zygomycetes,* among which *Pilobolus* is the most important, and there is no doubt that a specialized *mycota* of dung-inhabiting (*coprophilous*) fungi exists. But how do they compete successfully for this substrate? The answer here may be a little unexpected, but it is nevertheless perfectly logical if you give it some thought. (E. Moore-Landecker, *Fundamentals of the Fungi* [3rd ed.])

In student academic essays, on the other hand, these knowledge roles are usually reversed as students try to demonstrate their understanding of the topic—and an appropriate degree of intellectual independence—to expert readers. A "good student" role requires a display of content knowledge and a perspective on it that is appropriate for the discipline—and this is usually the teacher's perspective. Moreover, power and authority often lie behind these roles. In a course that is graded and where the teacher is the primary audience for the text, the reader's role is an evaluative one, giving the reader greater power than the writer. Writers may then see it as an advantage to take on a more modest and unassertive role, perhaps toning down their confidence in expressing ideas, adopting a more tentative voice, avoiding challenges to valued ideas, and so on. In other genres, the writer has more power than readers, so that teacher written feedback and class reports, for example, give their writers considerable authority.

This is not to say that writer-reader roles and relationships are *determined* by the social purpose of a genre. Obviously, begging letters or job applications can be written with varying degrees of assertiveness and using any number of writer roles from humble supplicant to insistent claimant, perhaps moving between these within the text itself. In the writing classroom, ESL teachers often try to take the sting out of the "expert evaluator" role that the genre of feedback on student writing offers them, avoiding direct criticism and softening the force of their comments using various mitigation strategies, as in Figure 3.2 (Hyland & Hyland, 2001).

The use of these strategies helps moderate the teacher's dominant role and tone down what might be seen as over-directive and prescriptive interventions in student writing. But while the teacher's role can be adjusted, it is not removed. Roles are closely associated with purposes and are a central aspect of genre knowledge, influencing the content, expression, and interpersonal relations in a text.

Paired comments   Combining criticism with either praise or a suggestion

Vocabulary is good, but grammar is not accurate and often makes your ideas difficult to understand.

This is a very sudden start. You need a more general statement to introduce the topic.

Hedged comments   Using modal verbs, imprecise quantifiers, etc., to soften criticisms

Some of the material seemed a little long-winded, and I wonder if it could have been compressed a little.

Your conclusion was a bit weak.

Personal attribution   Responding as ordinary reader rather than as expert

I'm sorry, but when reading this essay I couldn't see any evidence of this really. Perhaps you should have given me your outline to look at with the essay.

I find it hard to know what the main point of each paragraph is.

Interrogative form   Expressing doubt or uncertainty in the comment

The first two paragraphs—do they need joining?

Have you used quotations here? Some of it sounds like it might be.

Fig. 3.2. Mitigation strategies in feedback comments

Some Key Points for Teachers

There are four main points for teachers to take away from this brief look at purpose:

1. Teachers should take the purposes that texts serve as the starting point of a genre so that students can understand how the social purposes of a text are expressed through its structure.
2. Teachers should encourage students to see that texts are organized in terms of stages, each having a conventional purpose and contributing to the overall purposes of a text.
3. Text features should always be taught in relation to whole texts to help students understand the ways that

roles and purposes can influence the content and argument of a text.

4. Classes should help equip students with a range of writing experiences in English to help them select a genre that best supports their goals. While "personal experience" assignments can offer learners meaningful topics to write about, students also need exposure to the more formal and abstract writing they will encounter in other contexts.

Knowledge of Text Conventions

While the communicative purpose of a genre may not be immediately obvious, its form always is, and because of this, genre knowledge is often regarded by teachers as knowledge of text structure. This aspect of genre knowledge refers to a shared sense of the conventions of grammar, vocabulary, content, organization, and so on, which allows us to write and read texts with ease and confidence. Certainly, there are features that emerge with some regularity in a genre, and readers expect to see these familiar features when approaching a text, generally noticing if there are variations or absences. For this reason, genres are said to have a "reality" for readers (Devitt, 1997): the expectations are often so strong that violations can have consequences. So the student who omits an Orientation in a recount or a literature review in a research paper may regret it when receiving his or her grade.

Choices and Constraints

This is not to say that genres are strictly rule-governed systems that dictate uniformity. Not every aspect of every text is laid down by genre constraints. Experienced users are often able to select from a range of options to represent the identities and values they feel comfortable with while still conveying their meanings effectively. But while genres allow a great deal of individual choice, these choices are not unlimited.

Both choice and constraint are necessary components of genre—each is made possible by the other, and both are essential to expression (Christie, 1987). *Where there is no constraint there can be no meaning.* Genre knowledge thus comprises an awareness of possible variation—an understanding that deviations are acceptable to the extent that they do not cancel out function or appropriateness. Expectations are an important part of our genre knowledge, and while users recognize that they have choices and that genres will change over time, they anticipate a fairly stable range of features when they come to communicate.

In other words, genre knowledge includes our sense of genre boundaries. We have an idea of how far we can bend the constraints before a text becomes unrecognizable as an example of the target genre. The form of a genre can differ in relation to culture, historical period, social community, and communicative setting. Not only has the scientific research article, for instance, changed its form and purpose over the last 200 years (Atkinson, 1996), but it can also look quite different in different disciplines (Hyland, 2000). Despite this, however, a user's genre knowledge embraces knowledge of roughly where the edges of a genre are and of the extent to which writers can exploit the conventions while still hoping to achieve their goals.

Teachers should recognize the possibilities of genre variation to avoid dogmatic assertions. We need to encourage a sense of exploration and experiment among our students so they can come to see the possibilities of expression that lie open to them. Equally, however, most genre manipulation is realized within the broad limits of a genre and is often very subtle. We have to ensure that students see that taking liberties with formal constraints is often risky and can result in readers' failing to recover their meaning and purpose. Writers, therefore, need a good understanding of genre forms and constraints before they decide to manipulate the conventions, but even this may not be enough to get such manipulations accepted by readers. This is because L2 students are not in the best position to initiate changes. Innovations are, in fact, gen-

erally accepted only if they are backed by stability or authority. Kress (1987, p. 42) points this out clearly:

> That is why childish innovations fail; not because they do
> not constitute perfectly plausible solutions to particular
> textual/cognitive problems, but because they are supported
> neither by a stable social occasion, nor by "authority." This
> latter is of course the case where a writer of "authority" cre-
> ates a new generic form, which, seemingly because of the
> writer's authority alone, succeeds in establishing a new
> generic convention.

Manipulation and Prototypicality

Manipulating genre features is possible because genres vary
in their prototypicality. One way of understanding genre
boundaries is to see genres as comprising features that must
be present for a text to be an example of a particular genre.
With this definitional approach, we use our genre knowledge
to check whether a genre contains key features and to compare one genre with another. This has the advantage of showing us where genre boundaries lie and how closely some genres relate to each other. Thus, as Figure 3.3 suggests, *recounts*
and *narratives* have numerous features in common, as do *arguments* and *discussions,* while still remaining distinct from
each other (e.g., Feez, 1998).

Looking at genres in this way allows teachers to group genres that have similar purposes, structures, and language forms
into families of genres. They can then use these similarities to
provide scaffolding for students as they progress from one
genre to another (see Chapter 4). It also helps us in providing
feedback on student writing, identifying what students need
to do to improve the effectiveness of their texts. While attractive, however, this does not really allow us to clearly see the
variations that are possible within genres (Cope & Kalantzis,
1993).

Swales (1990) offers a different way of looking at genres by
drawing on the notion of "family resemblance." He argues

Category	Genre	Purpose	Structure	Main features at intermediate level
Story text	Narrative	To deal with problematic or unusual events To entertain	Orientation—Complication —Evaluation—Resolution	Series of clauses in past tense linked with conjunctions Vocabulary related to characters, contexts, and events
	Recount	To retell events in order To entertain or inform	Orientation—Events — Reorientation and/or Coda	Sequencing conjunctions Some 2-clause sentences Past tense and markers
Persuasive text	Argument	To argue for a viewpoint	Thesis—Argument— Reinforcement	Cumulative argument Specific information and supporting statements Writer's position
	Discussion	To argue for two or more points of view	Issues—Points of View— Conclusion	Organized information "Objective" information and supporting statements

Fig. 3.3. Common features and families of genres (NSW AMES, 1998)

that what holds similar texts together as a genre is not a fixed set of defining features that has to be applied to all cases but a looser kind of relationship in which texts can be characterized in terms of similarities to prototypical cases of a particular genre. Texts are thus spread along a continuum, from core examples that display all the features we typically associate with the genre—"best examples" of a genre—to those further from the core, which are seen as atypical by readers although still belonging to the genre. The further a text may be from the prototype of one genre, the more it might resemble a text from a nearby genre.

In some cases, texts may be non-prototypical in their structure. For example, in a study of university genres written by Hong Kong students, Lock and Lockhart (1998) found several texts that did not conform to the typical structures they had identified. Thus, the majority of *reports* had this pattern:

Problem   ∧   Consequence ^{n} (Conclusion)
∧   Recommendations   (∧ = follows and ^{n} = recursion)

However, one text identified as a report began by specifying the rising crime rate in Hong Kong as a problem, then went on to detail the dire consequences of the problem, then listed recommendations for solving it. So far so good, but it also contained two stages that simply described two kinds of crime, armed robbery and smuggling, which seemed more like stages in a *description* genre, giving the text this structure:

Problem ∧ Consequence ^{n} *Description*
∧ (Conclusion) ∧ Recommendations

While these two stages were atypical aspects of a report genre, Lock and Lockhart were still able to recognize and classify the text as an example of a *report* because of its clear overall purpose in offering a solution to a problem.

In other cases, non-prototypicality may lie in specific features of the text. For example, one of Lock and Lockhart's problem student texts began by identifying an issue (euthanasia) without signaling a stance toward it. The writer then presented views for and against euthanasia and ended with a short summary of the opposing views. Lock and Lockhart saw this text as a *discussion* with a prototypical structure of

Issues ∧ Points of view ^{n} ∧ Conclusion

However, in distancing herself from the *"anti"* position by using projecting clauses (e.g., "they believe that," and "doctors feared that") and using strongly evaluative and emotive language in presenting the pro-euthanasia section (e.g., "the indignity of prolonging life," "to die lonely and frightened in cramped hospital wards"), the writer signaled a standpoint. While the text was still recognizable as a discussion, this language violated the more neutral expository purpose of the genre and pushed the text toward an argument that had a more partisan stance.

Students often try to convey seriously held ideas in their writing but lack an understanding of the means to do this effectively. By focusing on the consequences of armed robbery and smuggling, the first student could have successfully made his interests more prominent, while the second writer may have been able to express her pro-choice views more clearly by selecting an argument rather than a discussion genre. An explicit interventionist pedagogy can provide students with the choices available to extend their incipient control over these genres so that they can exploit conventions more effectively.

Grammar in the Writing Class

An understanding of grammatical options and the limits of their constraints is central to genre knowledge and therefore to writing instruction. Many writing teachers do teach grammar, but often this takes the form of tasks that are disconnected from writing activities or set as supplementary work to address persistent errors. The forms students need often remain elusive as they cannot make connections between the grammar they study and the meanings these items express in the context of a particular genre. Teaching writing must involve increasing learner awareness of genre conventions to help learners produce texts that seem well formed and appropriate to readers, and to do this we have to see grammar as more than a set of rules applicable across contexts.

We need to develop student understanding of these conventions by showing their relationship to whole texts as ways of creating cultural meanings, not as isolated "grammatical knowledge." This idea of treating form as a way of creating meanings, rather than as labeling parts of texts, is clearly set out in Knapp and Watkins's (1994, p. 8) description of a "genre-based grammar":

> Grammar is a name for the resource available to users of a language system for producing texts. A knowledge of grammar by a speaker or a writer shifts language use from the implicit and unconscious to a conscious manipulation of language and choice of appropriate texts. A genre-based grammar focuses on the manner through which different language processes or genres in writing are codified in distinct and recognisable ways. It first considers how a text is structured and organised at the level of the whole text in relation to its purpose, audience and message. It then considers how all parts of the text, such as paragraphs and sen-

tences, are structured, organised and coded so as to make the text effective as written communication.

This is grammar with a purpose: introduced in relevant contexts and when students need it to construct genres effectively.

This knowledge of the conventional ways used to create texts also relates closely to knowledge of the social purposes of a genre. Swales (1990, p. 53) illustrates the connection between purposes and genre features by using the example of "good news" letters and "bad news" letters. While the purposes behind such letters may appear sufficiently similar to constitute a single genre, say, *responses to applications,* the rationales are very different. In "good news" letters, the assumption is that the information is welcome, and so it is usually conveyed early with the following text smoothing the way for a positive response. In contrast, however, the "bad news" letter is written to take the edge off unwelcome information and to minimize personal resentment. As a result, it typically opens with a 'buffer' to prepare the recipient for the news and works toward an understanding that communications have ended, implying that the decision has been made by an impersonal body over which the writer has no influence and against whom appeal would be fruitless.

Form and Parody

The formal characteristics of texts might seem a reliable way of introducing students to genres. Halliday and Hasan (1989), in fact, dispense with the idea of purpose altogether and regard a text as an instance of a genre if it includes obligatory formal elements—what a text must have to qualify as an example of a specific genre. These elements are determined by field, tenor, and mode: what the text is doing, what the relationship between participants is, and the medium of communication. But this seems to overconstrain writers and carries the danger that students may fail to see genre patterns in similar texts if they do not contain "obligatory" elements. The absence of a friendly salutation does not transform a personal letter into another genre, for instance. More problematically, a purely formal knowledge of genre does not allow us to distinguish texts that have been repurposed for literary, humorous, or dishonest reasons. Parodies, satires, frauds, and spoofs are successful precisely because they impersonate the form of a genre while subverting its function (e.g., Bex, 1996, p. 136). Take this example from Laurie Taylor's *Times Higher Education* Problem Page (Taylor, 1994, p. 80):

LETTERS TO THE EDITOR

Sir, I wonder if you can help me. I'm a happily married 45 year old man at present employed as a lecturer in a respected university department. According to my head of department I am extremely likely to be promoted to senior lecturer in the very near future. My problem is this: in the last few years I've found myself simply longing to dress in women's clothes. Quite frankly, I would like nothing more than to turn up for work tomorrow wearing a dress or a skirt. What do you advise?
Yours faithfully
(name and address supplied)

(Nurse Linda Lovejoy says: *Under no circumstances whatsoever must you turn up to work in a British university looking like a woman. All the available statistical evidence suggests that this would seriously jeopardise your promotion prospects.*)

This letter looks real enough, and all the surface features of the genre have been adequately met. We approach the text with expectations based on encounters with similar "problem page" or advice letters, guided by the title, the format, the salutation, and the introductory orientation; we perhaps only begin to suspect a trick when the problem is introduced, and this is confirmed by the response from Nurse Lovejoy. Once we realize the deception, we *read* the text differently, but the success of the text as a parody depends on our recognition of it as a problem letter and on our association of the form of such a letter with its conventional purpose. Parody must parody something, and this implies that readers approach written texts with expectations formed by previous examples of the genre.

Parody, therefore, suggests that genre knowledge must encompass more than an ability to reproduce discourse forms. Going further, we can say that if students only understand genres through their forms, they will have great difficulty in identifying the situations where they can appropriately use the genre, the tolerance readers might have of variation in the way they write it, or even the reasons for selecting it in the first place. Genre knowledge restricted to the production of accurate forms is a sterile and asocial knowledge that does not allow us to see how the genre is used or to understand the meanings it has for a community.

Some Key Points for Teachers

The formal dimension of genre knowledge is relevant to writing teachers for a number of reasons:

1. Students need to have a clear understanding of the system of choices and constraints for creating meanings through texts. So, writing teachers cannot avoid issues of grammar and form.
2. Genres should always be taught with the functions they usually perform for writers so that students can learn to understand the ways that form interacts with purpose and context.
3. Teachers should be aware that not all differences in L2 texts result from students' inability to write a genre effectively. Some may be attempts to negotiate the conventions and exercise creativity, and learners may need assistance in recognizing where the borders of effectiveness lie.
4. Teachers need to help learners see that grammar is about choices for making meanings rather than rules

to be learned. This involves linking forms to functions and showing the meanings that different patterns can express in particular genres.

5. Teaching should give attention to whole texts rather than to isolated grammatical forms to help students see the purposes of genres more easily.

Knowledge of Content and Register

In addition to a shared awareness of formal aspects of texts, students also need to understand the kinds of topics appropriate to a genre and the possible register options for expressing these. What the text is about, how this content is conveyed, and the assumptions about readers' prior knowledge are key factors in creating and understanding texts.

Knowledge of Content

A knowledge of the kinds of content appropriate for a given genre is important in localizing genre knowledge, making it specific to the requirements of a particular situation and writing task. As mentioned earlier, schema theory suggests we can think of content as general background knowledge of a topic together with more specific sets of knowledge stored as units that we are able to access when we write or read.

A **schema** is a frame for understanding and producing written content. The idea suggests three key points about content for writing teachers:

- Students will write more when they are writing on a topic they are familiar with, a view supported by research with L2 students (e.g., Freidlander, 1990).
- Like genre knowledge itself, the background knowledge writers draw on to create content is partly shaped by cultural experiences.
- Content knowledge is cognitive and social, as it draws on both individual and community knowledge.

One of the biggest challenges that content presents to students is that their previous learning experiences may not have prepared them for the kinds of topics and assignments they encounter in our classrooms. This comment from one of Leki and Carson's (1997) ESL students, for example, echoes the views of many learners:

> There are sometimes subjects you never think to write about those. For example, they say write about a custom or an important value. I never thought about writing about them.

We also need to bear in mind that cultures attribute different meanings to events and human relationships, and these cultural frames influence *what* students write about and *how* they write about it. Religion, politics, status, death, and sex can be taboo topics, while writing about personal or family issues may seem intrusive to some learners. In academic writing classes, not all students may be comfortable when asked to adopt a position or take a critical stance in an essay. Nor can L2 students always catch up quickly on the background of an assigned topic, often complaining about the time it takes them to read as they struggle to make sense of the texts they are given.

Equally important, schema theory also points to the value of achieving a sense of what is shared in a community and what is new. Content knowledge is as much social as cognitive as it depends on an understanding of "what everyone knows." Obviously, readers do not want to be told what they already know, nor do they want to struggle to relate unknown content to their background knowledge. A good understanding of what one's readers will consider as news is a key factor in successful journalism, for example, but it is no less important in academic writing, where novelty drives both research and the reading patterns of academics (Berkenkotter & Huckin, 1995).

Unfortunately, L2 students do not generally have a clear understanding of their readers' knowledge base and so are often unsure of what to include and what to omit in their essays. This problem is particularly acute in subject classes, where part of the purpose is to display knowledge that the reader already has, rather than to make judgments concerning what a reader will find new or novel. The ability to judge the understandings and needs of an audience and to manage specific disciplinary or professional knowledge is an essential element of genre knowledge and often crucial to students' academic success.

Field Choices

A key aspect of creating appropriate content is the writer's ability to make suitable register choices. As mentioned briefly in Chapter 1, this involves fitting the text to its immediate context through the use of particular lexical and grammatical features. These choices contribute to the style and meanings of writing and allow us to distinguish texts found in a courtroom, a classroom, and a boardroom. Thus, *field* is concerned with systems of activity, what the text is about, including descriptions of the participants, processes, and circumstances surrounding the activities. Field choices enable us to discuss activities and relate them to each other by linking participants with processes and with circumstances in recognizable ways. So, for example, when we read that

> The NASDAQ took another battering as Wall Street fell for the fifth straight day yesterday

we know that the field of finance is being discussed.

Tenor Choices

Writers must also ensure that they adopt the right interactive *tenor,* presenting themselves and their ideas in ways that readers are likely to find sympathetic and persuasive. This mainly involves selecting language that will convey an appropriate relationship with readers, the right degree of social intimacy and relative power. These interpersonal meanings are expressed through various kinds of evaluative language

(Hunston & Thompson, 2000) that allow writers to convey a range of feelings or opinions toward the topic and so build a relationship with the reader. Martin (2000b) calls the system of choices for expressing evaluative meanings *appraisal,* which he subdivides into three systems of meaning:

- *Affect:* words for expressing emotions (*happy, sad, angry, like, laugh, surprise, trust,* etc.)
- *Judgment:* words for expressing moral assessments (*lucky, pitiful, tragic, stupid, brave,* etc.)
- *Appreciation:* words for expressing aesthetic judgements (*lovely, beautiful, exciting, shallow, reactionary,* etc.)

Unfortunately, these features of language do not always get the kind of attention they deserve in L2 writing classes, particularly in courses geared to academic or professional genres. It is clear, however, that students' control over these features and their ability to express an appropriate degree of commitment to them are important parts of writing competence.

Mode Choices

In terms of *mode,* writers need to be able to discuss the content of their text with an appropriate sense of "semiotic distance." This means they need to write in ways that recognize that, unlike conversation, writing is separated in time and space from reading so that there is also a separation between the social activity and the language used to talk about it. Studies of student writing suggests that L2 writers often have considerable difficulty with this kind of distance and tend to overuse features that are more typical of spoken face-to-face conversational English (e.g., Granger, 1998; Hinkel, 2002). This is not to say that teachers should see mode differences as a simple cut-and-dried opposition between speech and writing. Actual instances of writing are often a complex mix of "oral" and "written" features (e.g., Biber, 1988). But most L2 students are generally expected to write expository and narrative genres that demand the use of more reflective, spatially and temporally distant language than usually occurs in casual conversation.

Unlike in face-to-face conversations, writers cannot rely on the immediate context of composing to ensure that readers are able to recover their meanings. They have to take care in how they employ deictics, or "pointer words" such as *this, that, there,* etc.; their choice of personal pronouns; and the ways they link ideas together. Perhaps more important, they also have to work harder to create a shared context for interpretation. Because writing generally lacks immediate feedback, writers have to be more explicit about what is new and what can be taken for granted, carefully monitoring their writing to ensure that it is accessible to their readers.

Some Key Points for Teachers

The key points relating to content and register for writing teachers are:

1. Teachers should be aware that writers from other cultures have different content schema and may apply different standards to decide what can be "talked about" in writing.
2. Developing content in writing classes involves not only providing students with texts and background materials but also developing an understanding of readers' interests and knowledge.
3. Teachers can use field, tenor, and mode differences to identify the meanings, words, and structures their students need to control in target situations.
4. Teachers can help students to develop strategies for recognizing and analyzing varieties of language appropriate to different contexts.
5. Students will better understand register differences if they are given a range of writing tasks on different topics and are able to experience both spoken and written texts.

Knowledge of a Cultural Context

This final aspect of genre knowledge actually embraces all the others as it concerns a shared knowledge of the contexts in which genres are repeatedly produced and processed. The notion of context refers not only to a physical place where the genre is found, such as an office or classroom, but to various non-linguistic factors and events influencing the writer. Interest in context therefore shifts student focus from the features of an isolated text toward the ways the text functions as an instance of human activity.

Contexts of Composing and Contexts of Use

When considering context, it is useful to distinguish between the environment in which composing occurs, such as the tasks and situations that writers deal with as they write, and the understanding that writers have about the purposes and uses their completed text may eventually fulfill.

Most teachers are aware of the impact that the immediate context of writing can have on a student's understanding and performance of a writing task. There are various physical and emotional factors that can shape writers' approaches to an assignment, such as their attitude to the topic, the time and space they occupy while writing, the degree of stress created by the situation, and the kinds of resources available. In addition, the teacher's goals and values, as well as various acts of reading, talking, observing, acting, thinking, and feeling, will also influence the ways writers represent their purposes and the kinds of writing they do (Prior, 1998).

While these local factors are important, a writer's understanding of context also includes his or her projection of the likely beliefs and understandings of potential readers. In other words, effective writers not only draw on a stock of writing strategies and text knowledge but are also able to see when these are needed. They are able to look at a writing situation and compare it with earlier writing experiences to select and write genres that readers are most likely to understand. Both writers and readers are therefore influenced by their previous experiences of a genre and the meanings it has in certain institutional, social, and cultural contexts. Brown and Duguid (1989) refer to this knowledge of past contexts as "situated cognition," an understanding of texts that is always developing and evolving as we participate in the activities of our culture.

This ability to recognize contextual demands develops with (1) the user's knowledge of the community of readers and writers who will make use of the text, (2) the relationship of the text to other similar texts, and (3) the way the text is used in communicative activities.

1. The Genre's Relationship to Users: The Idea of Discourse Community. The idea of a discourse community is important to genre knowledge as a way of joining writers, texts, and readers together. For teachers, it highlights the fact that genres are used and evolve in social groups whose routine activities influence the kinds of writing that is done and how it is understood. For students, the concept helps them to see how the genres they are learning are relevant to them and how they relate to their everyday lives.

The notion of community is not easy to pin down, however, and it is often unclear how broad or abstract a community is. Should we see a community as comprised of people interacting together in face-to-face groups? As a more large-scale configuration of mutual interests? Or as any group temporarily engaged in a project of some kind? Is it all teachers? All teachers in a school or department? All writing teachers? L2 writing teachers? Or contributors to an Internet user list? More problematically, such groups have sometimes been seen as rather utopian and deterministic, as places where members conform to institutional goals and share agreed values and conventions that they simply reproduce in their texts (see Swales, 1998, for a discussion). Clearly, a useful idea of community must avoid the view of a monolithic and all-powerful influence on writing. Instead, it must relate to real people and the cultural understandings that have meaning for them.

Essentially, the idea of community is helpful as it reflects our experience that social groups tend to develop their own "insider" ways of using language. This is sometimes because "ordinary" usage isn't precise enough or doesn't give its users sufficient prestige, but generally it is because members need efficient ways of dealing with regular events. The jargon of the wine connoisseur and the argot of the surfer help them express repeated meanings, and over time, these ways of saying often become normative, providing a model for group practice. Writing, therefore, develops from a shared history of previous writing practices and displays a certain continuity over time, so that doctors come to write like doctors and lawyers like lawyers. Because of this, active members of a discourse community have an enormous amount of genre-specific competence, an ability that is increasingly seen as a measure of expertise in many professions.

One result of this specialized usage is that community members give names to the genres they use regularly and recognize as serving recurring uses (Swales, 1990, p. 54). Writing teachers, for example, may share genre knowledge of *portfolios, research assignments,* and *class essays.* Students who are regularly assigned the five-paragraph essay will understand the purpose of the genre, how long it should be, its formal conventions and how far these can be safely manipulated, and what is required to get a good grade. These communally held names thus offer a shorthand way of referring to the genres that are important to them. As Swales points out, however, these tend to be institutional labels rather than descriptive ones and don't really tell us what these genres look like or how they change. They are also quite general: something called a *term paper, in-class essay,* or *research paper* will differ considerably across courses and lecturers so that students allocated such a writing task are likely to require a lot more information and assistance before they are able to produce a text that suits a particular teacher and situation.

2. The Genre's Relationship to Other Texts: The Idea of Intertextuality. The concept of intertextuality refers to "the web of texts against which each new text is placed or places itself, explicitly or implicitly" (Bazerman, 1994, p. 20). It concerns the extent to which our texts echo other texts in their similarities and variations and originates with Bakhtin's (1986) view that writing is always an ongoing dialogue between a writer and a reader as we draw on and incorporate ideas and forms from our past experiences of texts. The fact that texts are at least partly created out of other texts and, in turn, are able to potentially influence future texts links writers, readers, and meanings together. It also allows writers to write coherently because they have knowledge of other texts and of readers' abilities to recognize coherence through their own experiences.

Intertextuality is central to genre knowledge because it is the concrete way that writers are able to share repeated contexts, genre names, social purposes, and experiences of forms and content with readers. All texts reflect traces of other texts upon which they build and take into account, and they do this in two main ways (Fairclough, 1992, p. 117):

- *Manifest intertextuality*—the use of *explicit bits* of other texts that the writer merges into the current text through quotation, paraphrase, reference, irony, and so on. This allows writers to agree with, dispute, or supplement what has been said elsewhere.
- *Interdiscursivity*—the use of *conventions* drawn from a recognizable genre, including format, structure, style, use of visuals, patterns of grammar and lexis, interpersonal tone, and so on, that link a text to a wider institution or community.

Virtually all genres that L2 learners will encounter in their studies depend on other texts in some way, although exactly how experiences with former texts are exploited depends on the genre and the writing task. Students need to see that an argumentative essay, for instance, cannot exist in isolation but must anticipate a reader's possible objections and respond to a discussion already in progress, in newspapers, TV documentaries, conversations, and so on. It will probably incorporate quotes and citations and will try to address the possible rebuttals and objections of readers. Similarly, when creating narratives, students must write in ways that not only employ a recognizable structure but engage readers by portraying and exploring common experiences and understandings. Teachers can help students to see that their texts do not stand alone but must be understood against a background of other opinions, viewpoints, and experiences on the same theme.

Our knowledge of intertextuality also contributes to the ways that genres change, develop, and are transformed for new contexts and purposes. The growth of the Internet, for example, has seen the emergence of a considerable number of new genres, but it has mainly developed from the migration of familiar paper and video texts. Initially, these tend to faithfully replicate existing genres and only later evolve to exploit the technical capabilities of the new medium (Shepherd & Watters, 1999). Crowston and Williams (1997), for instance, identified 48 different Internet genres, classified by their purpose, from a random sample of 1,000 web pages and found that over 60 percent were directly reproduced from familiar paper formats and another 30 percent simply added minor technical changes.

Type of genre	Characteristics	Example	Percentage
Reproduced	Existing unchanged genre	Essays, course descriptions, minutes	60.6
Adapted	Existing genre with added links	Vitae, tables of contents, genealogies	28.6
Novel	New web genre	Homepages, hotlists, search engines	5.3
Unclassifiable	Unable to identify	(Midway genres, mixed or incomplete)	5.6

This evolution is occurring gradually because new forms require social acceptance and users are more comfortable dealing with familiar genres. The intertextual knowledge we bring to the new environment creates expectations about form, content, and purposes that help us to grasp the function of the genre and to interpret it quickly. The fact that transformation is always shaped by social as much as technical factors has led designers of corporate and commercial web sites to make extensive use of surveys and interviews to discover users' genre knowledge (Fucella & Pizzolato, 1998).

3. *The Genre's Relationship to the World: Genre and Activity Systems.* Part of the writer's genre knowledge also relates to the ways that written and spoken activities link together into communicative systems and chains, how they offer users menus of alternative options, and the kinds of constraints these imply (Bazerman, 1994). Genre systems are important because they allow teachers to relate texts to real-world activity sequences. They highlight the fact that the activities we frequently engage in are often composed of many linked genres—oral, written, and electronically mediated. Expert users know that only certain genres may appropriately follow each other. For example, a research essay is generally the culmination of a student's trail through a series of texts, notes, webpages, and conversations to uncover and collect material for the finished product. Drawing up event sequences related to the contexts in which our students will operate enables us to see the written texts we need to teach our students and offers a way of organizing a writing syllabus.

Exploring these activities offers a number of advantages to language teachers:

- Teachers can focus on what participants are doing (following the actors) or on what features and conventions are used (following the texts).
- Teachers can foreground what is communicatively important and relevant in particular situations to provide learners with a more concrete idea of contexts.
- Teachers can create courses that logically sequence learning by ordering related genres.
- Teachers are able to demonstrate the interrelatedness of spoken and written texts so they can see what they need to learn to participate in real-world activity sequences outside the classroom.
- Teachers are able to integrate reading and writing activities in ways that relate to authentic activity sequences,

such as planning a trip and writing an itinerary using maps, tourist websites, guidebooks, etc.

Some Key Points for Teachers

Some relevant points for writing teachers that emerge from a consideration of context include:

1. Teachers should encourage students to reflect on their previous experiences of a genre in order to approach writing in parallel contexts with greater confidence.
2. Teachers can use genre naming to begin a discussion of texts that can lead to reflections about what students know about them in terms of purposes, formats, choices, and constraints.
3. Teachers should offer students a variety of writing contexts and audiences, rather than just a teacher audience alone. This will help students develop a sense of the ways contexts are similar and different and help them decide what they can apply from past situations and what they can temporarily discard.
4. Students can discuss and reflect on the ways they use library resources, lectures, webpages, textbooks, and notes to write essays in order to understand the interrelationship of texts in networks.
5. Teachers or students can list the event sequences in a relevant situation and list the texts arising from this sequence in order to reflect on what students need to know and to encourage them to participate in the design of a teaching unit.

Summary

This chapter has emphasized the importance of genre knowledge in writing to unpack the various factors that allow us to create situationally appropriate texts. These aspects of genre knowledge can be summarized as follows (see also Berkenkotter & Huckin, 1995, pp. 2–25; Johns, 1997, pp. 23–37):

1. Knowledge of the personal, institutional, and social communicative purposes a genre is routinely employed to accomplish
2. Knowledge of the roles, or general positions, that particular genres typically make available
3. Knowledge of the ways texts are typically formed and structured to relate to purposes and meanings and how far manipulation and variation are feasible
4. Knowledge of appropriate topics and how these are developed and presented
5. Knowledge of the bundles of lexical and grammatical features that together create appropriate register choices
6. Knowledge of the recurring contexts in which genres are composed and used
7. Knowledge of the values and beliefs of the audiences and communities that frequently use the genre, the names they use for genres, and the meanings genres have for them
8. Knowledge of a text's dependence on other texts that it draws on, including the ways texts form chains and connections in human activity sequences

This perhaps seems a daunting list, and teachers may feel it is unrealistic to expect their students to manage all these aspects of genre knowledge. In reality, of course, these elements cannot easily be separated out, and genre knowledge should be seen as a unified understanding of the regularities of purpose, form, and social action occurring in a given context. For writing teachers, there are advantages to picking out these threads of genre knowledge as this helps reveal the factors that make writing a relatively smooth experience for skilled users and foregrounds the kinds of difficulties that many L2 writers can face if they do not share these understandings. Part of developing students' genre knowledge involves helping them to see what they already know from previous situations and then providing them with strategies for using this knowledge for their immediate purposes. At the heart of this is the teacher's role in offering explicit instruction in the ways language is used to write effective texts. This will be discussed in greater detail in Chapter 4.

Tasks and Discussion Questions

1. What do you understand by the term *genre knowledge,* and why might the idea be useful for teachers of L2 writing?

2. What do you think is the most difficult aspect of genre knowledge that second language writers face in successfully developing competence in a genre? What kinds of teaching and learning activities would you use to help students to gain greater familiarity and understanding of this aspect?

3. A major problem for many second language learners is that they often bring different schema to a writing task, either because the particular target genre is used differently in their own culture or perhaps because it does not exist. In what ways can cultural factors influence the ways students write and learn to write? Select one language group you are familiar with, and consider some of the difficulties its members might experience in using a particular genre. Suggest some activities that might work successfully with this group.

4. Knowledge of conventional ways to create texts interacts closely with knowledge of the recognized social purposes of a genre. Select one genre, and consider how you might help students to understand the relationship between the language choices in the text and the social purposes they are used to express.

5. To what extent do you think that the idea of mixed purposes, or the strategic use of "public purposes" for "private intentions," may be confusing for students?

What steps could you take in the writing class to overcome these difficulties?

6. *"Where there is no constraint there can be no meaning."* Do you agree with this statement? How can teachers help students gain an awareness of both genre boundaries and the variations that are possible in genre patterns so that they do not just see genres as templates for writing?

7. Knowledge of text conventions is obviously an important component of genre knowledge and the student's ability to control a genre, but there is often a temptation to focus on this aspect of genre knowledge at the expense of others in the writing class. Do you think this kind of focus is justified? How might you ensure that students receive a more balanced view of genre that includes other elements of genre knowledge?

8. Find several instances that seem to you to be prototypical examples of a genre. Now find one that is not. How would you deal with this in the classroom?

9. How could you use genre naming to focus student attention on a familiar genre? Think of a genre that your students are familiar with, and sketch out how you could encourage reflection on what they know about it in terms of purposes, formats, choices, and constraints.

Chapter 4

Organizing a Genre-Based Writing Course

Up to this point, we have focused on identifying what genre is, why it is a useful idea, and what it means to be able to use a genre. This chapter looks at more concrete issues for writing teachers and concentrates on the role of genre as an organizing principle in L2 writing instruction. Careful course and lesson planning is important, especially for new teachers, as it provides a framework for a coherent sequence of activities and learning. It also means that the teacher can let students know what to expect from the course and where it will take them, making both the goals and the approach of the teaching explicit. This chapter will therefore discuss what genre principles can offer teachers in designing an L2 writing course, exploring key concepts such as student needs, course objectives, target context analysis, and sequencing genres in a course.

Principles of a Genre-Based Writing Course

Writing teachers work in a range of teaching situations—in schools, colleges, universities, corporate training divisions, and language institutes—and with students of different motivations, proficiencies, language backgrounds, and learning needs. But while this means that teachers can rarely pull a course off the shelf to fit all circumstances, there are a number of principles that underpin all genre-based teaching. These principles include understandings about language, about writing, and about learning that can be translated into syllabus goals and teaching methodologies. I have touched on these ideas in the more theoretical chapters of this book (Chapters 1–3), but it is worth recapping them here to show how they relate to genre-based writing teaching more directly.

1. *Writing Is a Social Activity.* Fundamental to this approach is the idea that communication always has a purpose, a context, and an intended audience, and these aspects can form the basis of both writing tasks and a writing syllabus. Writing always involves making choices about how best to get one's meanings across effectively to particular readers by writing in ways they will recognize and understand. Because of this, students need to engage in a variety of relevant writing experiences that draw on different purposes and readers. These purposes and readers can be openly discussed, analyzed and investigated to help students see how texts relate to particular contexts and to particular ways of using language.

2. *Learning to Write Is Needs-Oriented.* Effective teaching recognizes the prior learning and current proficiencies of the students, together with their aspirations and the constraints of the learning situation in terms of time, resources, and so on. In a genre-based course, however, effective teaching also means, as far as possible, identifying the kinds of writing that learners will need to do in their target situations and incorporating these into the course. While these future needs might not always be easy to identify, students often have general purposes for learning to write, which can help structure a course. One of the teacher's main goals is to help students achieve their own goals, so they can write effectively in their target contexts.

3. *Learning to Write Requires Explicit Outcomes and Expectations.* A third basic observation is that learning occurs more effectively if teachers are explicit about what is being studied, why it is being studied, and what will be expected of students at the end of the course. Explicitness refers to helping students to understand how texts are patterned in distinctive ways to achieve particular goals, representing what

Bernstein (1990, p. 73) calls a "visible pedagogy." To make texts clear to students, teachers therefore have to go beyond simply monitoring input. They have to identify what is to be learned and assessed and to provide learners with the resources to achieve specific outcomes. Genre-based teaching is therefore clear about what an individual will be able to do as a result of teaching and learning and provides a basis for the attainment and demonstration of explicitly negotiated and specified knowledge and skills.

   4. *Learning to Write Is a Social Activity.* Learning to write is a social activity, involving collaboration and support so that the learner is seen as a social constructor of knowledge. This is a significant step away from Piaget's "lone scientist" view of the learner acting and reflecting on an environment. It is also where genre approaches to writing contrast most starkly with process approaches. These often take the view that too much teacher intervention stifles the individual's motivation and self-expression and removes his or her sense of responsibility for learning. A genre approach doesn't mean domination of the student by the teacher, however, but negotiation and collaboration between them. Both need to have a shared understanding of the context and the meanings being created, and these meanings may be best supported within predictable and familiar routines, or cycles of activity, and by linking new contexts and understandings to what students already know about writing. In these ways, teaching is always a series of scaffolded developmental steps in which teachers and peers play a major role.

   5. *Learning to Write Involves Learning to Use Language.* By working with others in activities that have a purpose, students come to see that the target language is a resource they can use to make meanings when they write. They learn that to communicate effectively in writing they must make choices from grammar and vocabulary that relate to their particular purposes and contexts. In a genre-based writing course, grammar is integrated into the exploration of texts and contexts rather than taught as a discrete component. This allows writers to draw on relevant knowledge about text structure and context to predict the language they are likely to need. Moreover, in learning the language, students not only begin to understand how to create meanings and interpret reality but also develop an understanding of how language itself works, acquiring a vocabulary they can use to talk about language itself and its role in texts.

This chapter will discuss the practical applications of these principles. First, it will outline some possible starting points for a genre-based writing course and then go on to set out the main stages involved in course design.

Starting Points for a Genre-Based Writing Course

A genre approach to writing instruction suggests two possible starting points for teachers:

1. *Theme-based:* genres are selected and sequenced by learner needs and the demands of the theme.
2. *Text-based:* genres are selected and sequenced according to those found in a relevant real-life context or according to increasing levels of abstraction or difficulty.

Theme-Focused Courses

All language, including that of the writing class, must be about something. Themes are a useful way to organize course content, especially where student needs cannot be specifically identified or the focus of the course is quite broad. Themes are best seen as real-life activities or situations in which people do specific things through writing, rather than grammatical structures or functions. Themes can be approached as either situations or topics that provide potentially relevant and motivating ways into writing while unifying a set of genres and activities. The choice of themes should relate to the needs and interests of the learners as far as possible to allow them to draw on their personal experiences and prior knowledge.

General topics such as *health, pollution, work relationships,* or *crime* can be a useful way to contextualize research and report writing skills, although they can also stimulate other kinds of writing. The topic *technology,* for example, suggests a factual description (explaining how something works), a narrative of personal experience (an encounter with a computer helpline), an argumentative essay (pros and cons of on-line chat rooms), and so on. As they progress, learners are better able to discuss a greater range of topics in more abstract ways, using genres that are increasingly complex in their structure. Situational themes can be familiar or personally relevant to learners and allow them to rehearse concrete types of interactions that draw on their prior knowledge or future goals. Situations such as *applying for a job, responding to customer enquiries, writing a feasibility report,* and *enrolling at university,* for instance, suggest focused target contexts requiring specific genres.

Text-Focused Courses

Where students' language-using contexts can be defined fairly clearly, teachers usually draw on the students' target genres as the main principle of course design. Texts and writing tasks are selected according to learners' needs and then sequenced according to one of a number of principles:

- By following their use in a real-world series of interactions
- By increasing levels of difficulty, from easiest to most complex
- By determining the most critical skills or functions relevant to students' immediate needs
- By estimating the rhetorical demands of the task and moving from least to more complex

A vocationally oriented writing course, for instance, may be organized around the range of oral and written genres needed in a particular workplace. A class of laboratory technicians working in a pharmaceutical company may have to keep inventories of materials, receive written and verbal instructions from scientists, take notes during experiments, produce written reports, and collaborate in producing project proposals. It might be possible to grade these genres according to their rhetorical demands or their immediate value to learners and then sequence them to reflect this priority. Rhetorical complexity can similarly be employed as an organizing principle where one genre is the focus of the course, as in Swales and Lueb's (2002) intensive course for Asian doctoral students in social psychology, where the sections of the research which were sequenced according to their perceived order of increasing writing difficulty: *methods, abstracts, results, introductions,* and *discussions.*

While teachers may like to design their courses around themes or texts, this is a convenience rather than a rigid prescription. More important is that a genre-based course should offer an explicit understanding of the ways texts are organized and the language choices that contexts make available. But this does not imply a single exclusive focus throughout the course as a teacher may teach one unit from one perspective and then shift to another.

Stages in Genre-Based Course Design

The stages involved in designing a genre-based *speaking* course from a text-focused perspective have been outlined by Burns and Joyce (1997) as follows:

1. Identify the overall contexts in which the language will be used.
2. Develop course goals based on this context of use.
3. Note the sequence of language events within the context.
4. List the genres used in this sequence.

5. Outline the sociocognitive knowledge students need to participate in this context.
6. Gather and analyze samples of texts.
7. Develop units of work related to these genres, and develop learning objectives to be achieved.

While presented as stages for greater clarity, these steps are often more simultaneous than sequential. Steps 3 and 4, for instance, are generally undertaken concurrently as it is difficult to distinguish the language events in a context from the genres that comprise them. Burns and Joyce (1997) give the example of a university preparation course to show how this works (Fig. 4.1).

The extent to which a teacher has the freedom to make such course decisions obviously depends on the situation. In some cases, the direction of the course may be pre-specified in a syllabus document or course book. Often, however, teachers have the flexibility to select the materials, tasks, and contexts through which students will work toward general learning outcomes. For example, the curriculum might simply specify a broad process objective such as the ability to brainstorm, draft, and polish a paper. Where such a course is being offered in a vocational situation, teachers can contextualize this outcome through genres such as reports or essays, while in community contexts, they may focus on formal letters or completing forms. Building on Burns and Joyce's skeletal outline, I elaborate on the key stages in designing a genre-based writing course in the remainder of this chapter.

Identifying Contexts of Learning and Contexts of Use

Although not explicit in the model presented earlier, course design always begins with what the students know, what they are able to do, and what they are interested in learning to do. Teachers working on a genre-based course then ask, "Why are these students learning to write?" They seek to answer this by,

Step	Example
1. Identify the context	University: focus on preparing students for study at university
2. Develop an aim	To develop spoken and written language skills for university study
3. Note event sequences	These could include: —enrolling at university —discussing course selection —attending lectures and taking notes —attending tutorials —reading reference materials —writing essays —writing reports —taking exams
4. List the texts required	These could include: —enrollment forms —lectures and tutorial discussions —reading texts: library catalogs; discipline-specific books, articles, and reports —writing texts: discipline-specific essays, critiques, and reports —exam papers
5. Outline sociocultural knowledge	Students need knowledge of: —academic institutions —academic procedures and expectations —the role of the student —classroom practices and genre knowledge
6. Gather text samples	Written texts: essays, catalogs, journals, textbooks, etc. Spoken texts: record authentic or scripted interactions, find recordings
7. Develop units of work and unit objectives	Coherent units with classes sequenced to provide learners with: —relevant ordering of tasks —explicit input —guided practice —opportunities to perform independently

Fig. 4.1. Designing a course from texts. (From *Focus on Speaking,* by A. Burns and H. Joyce, copyright © 1997. Reproduced by permission.)

as far as possible, identifying the competencies that will be required of students in target contexts. Helping students move from their current proficiencies to these target proficiencies therefore becomes the purpose of the course, influencing the objectives, materials, and tasks it employs. The idea of student *needs* is, as we have seen, a central principle of genre-based teaching and refers to the fact that literacy acquisition does not occur in a vacuum. It is a concept that seeks to ensure that learning to write is seen in both the context in which it occurs and the contexts in which these skills will be used. This involves the teacher and learner in a collaborative analysis of the *present* and *target situations.*

Present Situation

Most teachers are aware of the importance of "starting where the students are" by discovering the current proficiencies and ambitions of the students and the constraints of the learning situation in terms of time, resources, and equipment. *Present situation analysis* refers to information about learners' current abilities, their familiarity with writing processes and written genres, their skills and perceptions. It explores what they are able to do and why they are taking the course. Teachers need to discover as much about learners as possible, and this kind of information can be both objective (age, proficiency, prior learning experiences) and subjective (self-perceived needs, strengths, and weaknesses). Some key factors are illustrated in Figure 4.2.

In addition to assessing learner issues, teachers need to ensure that their course will operate successfully in the local context, acknowledging the opportunities and constraints

Who are the learners?	How do learners learn?
Age/sex/nationality/L1	Learning background and experiences
Subject knowledge	Concept of teaching and learning
Interests	Preferred learning styles and strategies
Sociocultural background	Methodological and materials preferences
Attitudes to target culture	
Why are learners taking the writing course?	**What do learners know about writing?**
Compulsory or optional	L1 and L2 literacy abilities
Whether obvious need exists	Proficiency in English
Personal/professional goals	Writing experiences and genre familiarity
Motivation and attitude	Orthographic knowledge and skills
What they want to learn from the course	Familiarity with target genres

Fig. 4.2. Some factors involved in a present situation analysis

presented by the situation in which the course will run. By analogy with needs analysis, this is sometimes referred to as *means analysis* and involves consideration of the teachers, methods, available materials, facilities, and the relationship of the writing course to its immediate environment.

Target Situation

Often it is possible to identify the contexts in which students will use the language. Sometimes this is a specific site, such as a particular workplace or academic discipline, but equally often it may be a general context based on a broad communicative need like "further study," "writing a thesis," or "job hunting." The target situation analysis thus concerns the learner's future roles and the linguistic skills and knowledge required to perform competently in writing in this context. This involves mainly product-oriented data: identifying the contexts of language use, observing the language events in these contexts, noting the sequences of these events, and listing the genres employed (Fig. 4.3).

One way of identifying a context is to draw up a communications network (Burns, Joyce, & Gollin, 1996). This can be completed by the students alone, as a language awareness activity, or by the teacher working with the students, but essentially it helps identify the people, the registers, the modes of

Why does the learner need to write?	**What will the content areas be?**
Study, work, exam, promotion, etc.	Academic subject, professional area, personal, secondary school, craftsperson, manager
What genres will be used?	**What is the structure of these genres?**
Lab reports, essays, memos, letters, etc.	Move patterns, realizations of social purposes, key features, combinations of elemental genres
Who will the learner communicate with?	**Where will the learner use the language?**
Native or non-native speakers	Physical setting: office, school, hotel
Reader's knowledge—expert, layperson, etc.	Linguistic context: overseas, home country
Relationship—colleague, client, teacher, subordinate, superior	Human context: known/unknown readers

Fig. 4.3. Some factors involved in a target situation analysis

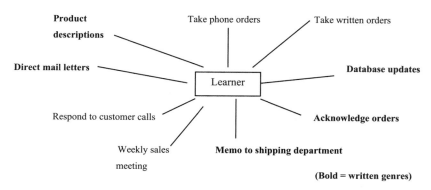

Fig. 4.4. A communication network for a sales class

communication, and the types of texts that learners will need to work with. A simple network to discover the communicative needs of employees working in the sales office of a small company is given in Figure 4.4. Here students need to produce written product descriptions and direct mail promotion letters, take and acknowledge orders, and send written instructions to the shipping department.

Collecting Needs Information

In almost all cases, the identification of an appropriate context and recognition of its main features involve close collaboration among teachers, learners, and other stakeholders and interested groups. Information about present and target contexts can be collected in a variety of ways and is discussed in greater detail in Hyland (2003) and Dudley-Evans and St. John (1998). Some common procedures are set out in Figure 4.5.

The choice of procedures will obviously depend on the time and resources available and on the proficiency of the students. Different methods address different areas, however, and it is always a good idea, if possible, to collect information from several sources (called *triangulation*) to achieve a more reliable and comprehensive picture. A simple example of a context analysis is shown in Figure 4.6, illustrating the kinds of information that can provide an informed basis for course design.

Information	Collection methods
Personal goals and priorities Learning preferences	Brainstorming, group discussions, individual interviews, student diaries interviews, group discussions, questionnaires, observations
Student information (age, gender, prior learning, immigration status, L1, L1 literacy, occupation, years in country)	Enrollment documents, individual interviews, questionnaires, observations
Current L2 proficiency (English literacy and writing experiences)	Placement or diagnostic tests, individual interviews, classroom observations, portfolio of prior work, international certification
Target behaviors	Interviews with learners, interviews with "experts," literature reviews, genre analyses, examinations of tasks, observations of target sites, questionnaires, case studies

Fig. 4.5. Some needs data collection methods (Hyland, 2003)

Determining needs is actually a continuous process since teachers modify their teaching to better accommodate their students as they come to learn more about them. They may recognize that original goals were unrealistically high or that the students have more knowledge of target genres than was supposed. In this way, needs analysis actually shades into *evaluation*—the means of establishing course effectiveness— and into course improvements.

Present situation

Who? (profile of students)	22 newly recruited Cantonese L1 marketing staff (male and female), 25–30 years old with lower-intermediate English proficiency and little sales experience; highly motivated
How? (profile of course)	Intensive, four-week face-to-face and self-study course
What with? (profile of resources)	No textbooks or print resources; unlimited use of multimedia lab and photocopier; access to authentic examples of target texts and to we site; experienced group of writing teachers

Target situation

Who? (profile of context)	Large international telecom company seeking to break into new local broadband and mobile phone markets
What? (genres and tasks)	Written workplace genres, particularly letters to customers, sales reports to middle managers, internal e-mails to dispatchers
Who with? (interlocutors)	Native English speakers and non–native English speaking senior staf and customers with both lay and specialist knowledge
Where? (sites of use)	In Hong Kong; mainly in branch offices

Fig. 4.6. An example context analysis

Some Reservations about Needs

While it is important and necessary to identify a communicative context that is relevant to student needs, this is not always a straightforward exercise. To begin with, it is not always easy to see what constitutes a "context" as studying target genres often only tells part of the story. Participant interviews, observations, and a range of other activities may be needed to reach the underlying linguistic competencies and sociocultural understandings that will allow teachers to identify the relevant communicative repertoire. More seriously, there will often be a conflict between the views of different stakeholders and the personal and career goals of students themselves, which can make it awkward to prioritize competing needs. It may be, for example, that students want to write for very different reasons than those required by their academic discipline, their employer, or their parents, and course objectives may be an uneasy compromise between these competing views.

The question of prioritizing needs also raises important issues of power and influence. Needs are often described in terms of language needs, the genres students need to survive or thrive in some English-using context. But as a number of writers have observed (e.g., Benesch, 2001; Pennycook, 1997), people also have other kinds of needs that do not always coincide with those of the institutions in which they want to participate. Immigrant learners, for instance, obviously have urgent language needs to help them get established in their new environments, but they also have social needs that relate to healthcare, housing, schools, and ways of addressing exploitation in the workplace. While these needs can only be met through effective use of target genres, they are seldom given priority in writing courses.

Similarly, students in university contexts often have needs that go beyond passively carrying out the tasks and assignments that will initiate them into an academic community. Their needs also relate to understanding and questioning the communities they are becoming a part of. Benesch (2001), for instance, argues that EAP teaching can be more effective by being less "accommodationist" to the needs of the disciplines and by encouraging students to question classroom activities and engage in academic life. In this way, students can not only perform their best but also shape the education they are being offered. To parallel needs analysis, Benesch therefore introduces the term *rights analysis* as a way of highlighting power relations and seeing teaching as more than initiating students unquestioningly into particular discourse communities. In addition to collecting information about target requirements, rights analysis is "a framework for studying power relations, building community, organizing students, and bringing about greater equality between language and content teachers" (Benesch, 2001, p. xviii).

Clearly, teachers cannot see needs as unproblematically accommodating students to the requirements of the target situation. Teaching writing is not a simply a neutral transfer of skills or competencies, and while it may have desirable social and career payoffs for learners, the needs that are addressed should go beyond those of the institution. Identifying a relevant context and the genres that students will need to understand and use in that context does not stop at the interactions that occur in it. Genre-based teaching can help reveal to students the assumptions and values that are implicit in those genres and help them understand the relationships and interests in that context. Identification of a relevant context is therefore a means of considering writing in a wider frame and a basis for both developing the skills students need to participate in academic or professional communities and their abilities to critically understand those communities.

Developing Goals and Objectives

Having identified a context and the activities and events that go on in it, teachers then need to develop broad goals, or aims, concerning the purposes of the course and objectives, or particular knowledge and skills that learners will be expected to know or perform at the end of it. These are the global target outcomes around which the course is organized given the students' purposes and abilities, their target needs, and institutional requirements. Writing objectives, therefore, involves a process of referring back and forth between information about the learners' current proficiencies and data collected about the communicative demands of the target context. Often, goals are stated before the course begins so that students can see if it meets their needs.

Objectives break goals down into smaller, achievable units of learning that can provide the basic framework of the course and a coherent learning program for students. In a genre-based course, goals often describe the competencies that the learner will be expected to put into effect using the appropriate knowledge and language features to construct particular kinds of texts. Objectives can vary in the emphasis placed on writing knowledge or skills, but they typically contain elements of both, and while they may not always be easy to separate in practice, it is useful to think about different kinds of objectives in course planning (Burns & Joyce, 1997, p. 75). Some objectives related to these two areas are shown in Figure 4.7.

Figure 4.8 is an example of course objectives adapted from the Australian *Certificate of Spoken and Written English (CSWE)* to achieve a goal of assisting migrant participation in further education.

Collecting and Analyzing Genre Samples

Writing instruction is typically geared toward enabling students to participate in particular contexts with confidence and with some hope of success, and one of the most important elements of these contexts concerns the types of writing that students are likely to meet in them. Collecting and analyzing samples of authentic texts therefore supplies crucial information about relevant content, format, and language for teaching and provides a basis for the choice of appropriate readings, text models, language input, and discussion topics for the course.

Knowledge

- The role of written language in the wider culture or specific discourse community
- Kinds of social situations in the target contexts and the ways they predict certain genres
- Appropriate content areas in particular genres
- The writer and reader roles that particular genres make available
- How target genres are organized to accomplish social purposes
- How grammar functions to convey certain kinds of meanings in writing
- When to use a particular genre and how it relates to other genres in a typical sequence
- The value a genre has for a particular community of users
- The formal aspects that a text requires (e.g., layout, citations, address forms)

Skills

- Specifying a purpose, audience, and format for a given writing task
- Generating ideas and planning writing using brainstorming and freewriting techniques
- Drafting a paper
- Editing a draft for sense, organization, audience, and style
- Evaluating and editing others' writing
- Adopting an appropriate interpersonal tone and authority relations in writing
- Analyzing a specialist text for its structure and characteristic stylistic features
- Writing an essay with a thesis, supporting argument, introduction, and conclusion
- Writing an essay using multiple sources and appropriate citation techniques

Fig. 4.7. Objectives related to knowledge and skills

Collecting Sample Texts

The next step, therefore, is to collect texts that are central to the target context and that represent good examples of the genres employed in it. A good place to start is with the genres that expert text users are able to name and identify as being part of their everyday activities as these evoke in users expectations for particular text features, for certain writer and reader roles, and for certain contexts. While these may be rather loose, even casual labels for the kinds of writing that individuals do, they provide a way into communicative events by offering a shared reference for teachers and students to discuss and discover more about these kinds of writing.

As with context identification, teachers should try to involve students in the collection of target texts so that they can see the task expectations that are required, make assessments

Aim   To assist adult learners of non–English speaking backgrounds to develop the literacy skills required to undertake further education

Objectives

Students will be able to:

• Undertake the roles and responsibilities of a learner in a formal learning environment, accepting a degree of responsibility for learning and participating effectively in learning situations
• Use a range of learning strategies and resources both within and outside class, using computers for writing and establishing an appropriate study pathway
• Write a report of 1,000 words on a topic relevant to the learner using appropriate staging and organizing factual information into coherent paragraphs with appropriate vocabulary and grammatical structures
• Write a discussion of 1,000 words on a topic relevant to the learner using appropriate staging and organizing material into paragraphs that express coherent arguments for and against, including supporting evidence to support claims. The writing will display appropriate conjunctive links, vocabulary, and grammar.
• Write a short formal letter of 100 words using appropriate staging and layout and using paragraphs that express objective information about situations/events, providing information and supporting evidence to substantiate a claim and request action. Texts will display appropriate conjunctive vocabulary and grammar.

Fig. 4.8. Example aim and objectives of a genre-based writing course (NSW AMES, 1998)

of what counts as effective performance, and understand why texts are seen as effective. In addition, learners who are actually from the workplace are often in the best position to gather written texts and record key spoken genres, such as service encounters with customers or oral presentations in business. Obviously, if neither teachers nor learners have access to these contexts or the people who routinely participate in them, then teachers will need to find other ways to discover what goes on. This can involve:

• Conducting a literature search for relevant articles or information
• Studying publishers' catalogs for teaching materials
• Asking colleagues who might have experience with the target contexts
• Contacting institutions that parallel the target site or professional associations

- Joining Internet user lists to check previous discussion threads and ask for advice
- Surfing relevant websites such as professional associations, writing sites, and so on

Some General Patterns in Texts

Teachers then have to look carefully at the written and spoken texts that have been collected to understand the distinct ways meanings are expressed, both at the level of the whole text in relation to its purpose, audience, and message and at the level of how paragraphs and sentences are structured. Analyzing texts for teaching purposes may seem a daunting prospect for many teachers, but it is important to identify the main features of the kinds of writing to be taught. This is often a slow process, as Johnstone (1996) points out: "Discourse analysis is like translation. It involves taking foreign texts (whether in a foreign language or not) and making them meaningful in one's own terms."

Text analysis methods are discussed in greater detail in Chapter 7, but teachers can find considerable help in the literature when trying to analyze texts for the first time. One pattern found in a range of academic, business, and social texts is the *problem-solution* pattern discussed by Hoey (2001). This has four basic moves, each performing a specific function in response to a projected dialogue:

- *Situation:* I am a teacher of ESL writing.

  (What problem arose?)

- *Problem:* My students couldn't express themselves in writing.

  (What did you do?)

- *Response:* I adopted a genre-based approach.

  (What was the result?)

- *Evaluation of response:* Now they can all write beautifully.

Other familiar patterns in English texts are:

- *Claim-justification:* for example, "Genre-based teaching helps improve ESL writing *(c);* just look at the improvement in my students!" *(j)*
- *General-particular:* for example, "There are numerous ways to teach ESL writing *(g),* and a genre-based approach is the one I use." *(p)*
- *Hypothetical-real:* for example, "Some people may be skeptical about a genre-based approach *(h),* but it has certainly helped my students." *(r)*

Because these are common patterns in writing, they tend to occur in many genres and are therefore highly productive teaching items. The fact they can be expressed at different levels of complexity also means that they can be taught to students at different proficiency levels.

Moves and Key Features

When the genres students need to use can be clearly defined, they can be examined for their move structure and key features. An example of a move structure analysis of a common business genre is Bhatia's (1993) description of the *sales promotion letter.* This is an unsolicited letter written with the social purpose of persuading its readers to buy some goods or services. The structure and a gloss of each stage are set out in Figure 4.9.

In some cases, it may not be possible to identify a single structure, and so attention has to be given to what seem to be key features of a genre. Listing the expressions and vocabulary items that recur across most text examples and trying to tie them to their functions in the text can offer useful teaching points. An example is Mulholland's (1999) description of the key features of e-mails sent in preparation for meetings in a Dutch company, shown in Figure 4.10.

Mulholland (1999) found that the reduced features of these e-mails often caused miscommunication as readers were often unsure if the brevity was due to the channel or to deliberate bluntness. Making students aware of the ways these fea-

Stage	Purpose	Sample expressions
1. Establishing credentials	To convince reader of company reputation or achievements	We are expertly aware that financial managers need confidence to . . .
2. Introducing the offer	To describe the offer and its value to the reader	We now provide a training course.
3. Offering incentives	To create interest through promotional offer	There is a discount if six members enr⬝
4. Enclosing documents	To provide information and a way to respond	I enclose a reservation form.
5. Soliciting response	To encourage further communication	Please call if you have any questions.
6. Using pressure tactics	To encourage a quick decision and response	Places are limited so act quickly.
7. Ending politely	To maintain cordial relations with the reader	Thank you for your kind attention.

Fig. 4.9. Structural description of a sales letter (Bhatia, 1993, pp. 46–56)

tures communicated interpersonal as well as business information helped to improve the effectiveness of their workplace communications.

Helping students to analyze and recognize key features of genres is not only limited to the most proficient students. Instruction can still be relevant and motivating to weaker or younger learners if it addresses the contexts and basic features of the key elemental genres that they may eventually have to write. Thus, learners who need to write explanatory genres in their school or workplace can focus on *procedures* and *reports* in their writing classes. *Procedures* can be found in a number of academic genres such as science experiments and technical instructional manuals, while *reports* are familiar aspects of many engineering, business, and social science fields. Through explicit teaching, even very young learners can understand the social purposes of these genres, the ways they

Feature	Examples
Reduced subject-matter representations	Briefly stated or abbreviated content; no capitalization; dashes instead of commas; omission of copulas, personal pronouns, articles, etc.
Brevity in language use	Omission of specific details; qualification of opinions
Use of politeness markers (especially in final place)	Please; grateful; it would be appreciated
Absence of metalanguage	Few reflexive references to the text or linking phrases; sequences; help to the reader in recovering the writer's ideas, thus greater impersonality

Fig. 4.10. Some features of business e-mails (Mulholland, 1999)

	Procedures	**Reports**
Purpose	Tell how to do something	Inform reader about something
Structure	Goal—materials required—steps needed	Identifying statement—description
Grammar	Imperatives; action verbs; describing words; adverbials to express details of time, place, and manner; connectives and sequencers	General nouns, relating verbs, action verbs, timeless present tense, topic sentences to organize bundles of information

Fig. 4.11. Identification of features of procedures and reports at elementary level

are staged, and their significant language features. The New South Wales Syllabus for K–6 ESL students, for example, identifies the features for these two genres, as summarized in Figure 4.11.

Determining the Sociocultural Knowledge Required

Awareness of the connections between different genres is important for L2 writers, but it is also useful if students know something about the sociocultural context in which those genres occur. In particular, the following kinds of sociocultural knowledge are likely to be important to an understanding of genre:

- The institutions in which the genres are used
- The meanings that a genre has for those who use it
- Intertextuality and what elements are borrowed or anticipated from other texts
- What the audience already knows and what it needs to know
- The degree of formality, authority, intimacy, and other interpersonal aspects associated with it
- Who typically uses the genre and who they use it with
- The kinds of purposes that the genre is used to accomplish
- The roles it implies or makes available to writers and readers

Helping learners toward this sociocultural knowledge means equipping them with a schema that they can draw on when they sit down to write. As discussed in Chapter 3, writing does not only mean knowing how to structure papers, what to write about, and how to express ourselves. It also involves knowing what to include and leave out, who we can appropriately use a particular genre with, and when it is appropriate to use the genre at all. Once again, students should be involved in the analysis of communicative events as much as they are in the investigation of genres. By observing activities that occur in the target context and by discussing these with participants, it is possible to piece together a picture of what goes on, who is involved, the roles they play, and the meanings genres have for them. This kind of target situation research involves watching and listening and draws on whatever methods are feasible, but all methods can help students to see how the genres they are learning in their writing classes are embedded in real-world situations. Chapter 7 provides a fuller discussion of these issues.

In addition to providing important information for a genre-based writing course, this kind of sociocultural awareness also has advantages for learners in that it:

- Encourages them to locate texts in their full cultural context, which both assists the development of their genre knowledge and helps them to see that written genres have consequences for users
- Allows students to analyze the events that take place in target contexts so they can understand how genres interact with each other and the part they play in constructing contexts and identities
- Encourages curiosity about and critical engagement with the situations they will participate in, helping them to recognize how written texts are socially specific and how they are underpinned by ideologies and values
- Provides learners with a means for investigating communicative events and cultural contexts, equipping them with the tools to investigate and question what they find there

Sequencing Genres in a Writing Course

Any language course needs a principled way of sequencing learning by integrating written and spoken genres.

Sequencing by Topics

Sequencing genres by topics can depend on the interests of the students or the priority given to their needs. However, it is common to use one of the following principles:

- Begin with topics or situations that are concrete and that relate to learners' prior experiences and everyday life, and gradually move to more applied or theoretical topics.
- Begin with topics that are relatively simple and that allow progress to more advanced activities.
- Begin with topics that meet the most urgent needs of learners. This is particularly relevant to new migrants and ESP learners.
- Begin with topics or situations that are less controversial or that generate simple polar opinions to allow students to develop the confidence to handle and express more varied views.

More familiar or easier topics can be presented first to engage and motivate students; to recycle vocabulary from earlier courses; or perhaps to work with known genres in new registers, using examples where the roles and relationships of the users are different. A similar approach can be adopted when a course focuses on a key genre. A useful approach to topical content is Macken-Horarik's (1996) model of four learning domains, which can help teachers to organize a set of situations or topics. These domains make different demands on students and can be used to recycle topics and genres though different levels of complexity in different registers (Fig. 4.12).

Second language students at elementary levels can begin their writing instruction with themes associated with the everyday domains of home, family, and community while

	Everyday ➔	Applied ➔	Theoretical ➔	Critical
Type of knowledge	Common sense	Practical	Formal education	Informed
Identity and roles	Familiar	Practitioner	Impersonal	Complex
Topics and language	Home, family, community	Work skills, domestic hobbies	Technical and professional	Interpretative, persuasive

Fig. 4.12. Experiential content domains (Macken-Horarik, 1996)

those who bring specific skills to the classroom can be introduced to genres through those skills. More proficient students preparing for further education usually begin with the applied or theoretical domains. Most topics, in fact, can be considered within any of the four domains, allowing students to move from one to another within a single theme or for a mixed-proficiency class of students to work on the same theme in contexts from different domains. The model also allows students to return to the same theme through more complex genres or to approach the same genre at different levels of complexity. So, for instance, a report genre can be introduced in different domains, each providing a greater rhetorical challenge (Fig. 4.13).

Sequencing by Families of Genres

In cases where students have no clear context in which they anticipate making use of their writing skills, a useful approach might be to take a wider perspective and identify

Domain	Topic	Sources	Some Key Language Features
Everyday	A picnic	Personal experience	Active, past-tense action verbs
Applied	An appliance	Advertisements/brochures	Passive, present tense, adjectives
Theoretical	Higher education	Tables and graphs	Range of conjunctions, supporting/elaborating main ideas
Critical	Capital punishment	Multiple written/oral texts	Modality, reporting verbs, conditional

Fig. 4.13. A report genre in different topic domains

broad families of genres. Families of genres help us to see the ways in which elemental genres are similar and make it possible to link one text with the next in a learning sequence designed to scaffold progress through texts that draw on the same general grammatical and rhetorical features to express broadly similar purposes. Figure 4.14, adapted from the Australian *Certificate in Spoken and Written English ESL Curriculum,* illustrates these kinds of relationships.

Through a focus on a particular text family, the social purposes that students are expected to achieve can be made increasingly more challenging as the genres become more complex in terms of their structure and language features. This enables students to make progress in their writing as they review and consolidate much of what they have already learned to engage with more complex social purposes. In this way, the features learners already know help scaffold their learning. In addition, if the course objectives require it, learning could also be sequenced through the *macrogenres* to which *elemental genres* contribute. For example, students could combine *instructions* and *procedures* to write an appliance manual or *descriptions* and *explanations* to compose a geography essay.

Sequencing Using Genre Sets and Repertoires

It is important for students to see that in the real world texts do not occur in isolation but are closely related to other genres, sometimes following each other in a fairly predictable order. A study of the relevant target context will provide an idea of the ways that genres interlock and engage with one another

Text family	Main feature	Sample written genres
Exchanges	Joint construction	Internet chat, personal letters, and e-mails
Forms	Printed, with respondent spaces	Simple and complex formatted texts
Procedures	Steps to achieve a goal	Instructions, procedures, protocols
Information texts	Provide news or data	Descriptions, explanations, reports
Story texts	Retell events and respond to them	Recounts, narratives
Persuasive texts	Argue for/against a thesis	Expositions, discussions, opinion texts

Fig. 4.14. Families of genres

in routine patterns of interaction. These *event sequences* can be helpful in ordering genres and integrating spoken and written texts into a writing course. They provide a way to authentically contextualize what is to be learned and allow the teacher to address the third and fourth principles mentioned earlier: providing learners with explicit expectations and with the language resources they require to communicate. A simple illustration of a linear event may be found in the sequence of genres often required in job seeking (Fig. 4.15).

In other circumstances, the occurrence of one genre may be less dependent on the outcome of another so that an activity unfolds with genres employed more concurrently. An example of this is the genres involved in the process of writing an academic assignment:

Read assignment → Read library catalogs → Read source texts → Write notes → Listen to lectures → Write notes from lectures → Talk to friends and tutors → Write notes from conversations → Search web for information → Write notes from websites → Collate notes, formulate plan, and draft essay

Alternatively, genres may be more loosely arrayed in what Bazerman (1994) refers to as a *system of genres.* These are genres that interact with each other in specific settings, representing the full array of texts a particular group must deal with in a workplace or other context. Some of these genres may depend on others, while some may be alternatives to others; some may be spoken, others read, and some will require written competence. Spears's (1995) analysis of the writing of nurses, for example, shows a range of genres dominated by admission assessments, care plans, notes, and discharge summaries, all of which work to plan, describe, and evaluate client care and ensure its consistency by communicating with other members of the healthcare team. This only represents one side of an interaction, of course, and beyond this the gen-

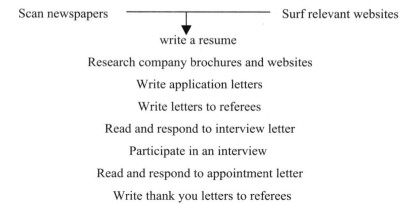

Scan newspapers ——————————— Surf relevant websites

write a resume

Research company brochures and websites

Write application letters

Write letters to referees

Read and respond to interview letter

Participate in an interview

Read and respond to appointment letter

Write thank you letters to referees

Fig. 4.15. A linear sequence of genres for job seeking

res nurses write are responses to other genres in the context, both written and spoken.

Finally, genre sets can present participants with a range of alternative options. This may be the case, for example, where students have to decide how best to collect information from subjects in a class project. Here possible genres may include

Questionnaires	Formal letters	Informal letters	Telephone interviews	Face-to-face interviews

Relations among Reading, Talking, and Writing

Basing writing instruction on the ways genres are sequenced and used in language events not only provides a framework for teaching genres in a way that reflects their real-world use but also reaps the benefits of closely integrating reading, speaking, and writing activities in the classroom.

The role of talk and dialogue in the development of writing abilities has long been a feature of L2 writing instruction. So, while writing classes are often characterized by students engrossed in individual writing tasks, they are just as likely to be noisy places where discussions of group projects, talking in pairs, and consulting teachers provide a basis for the writing that occurs. Writing is always a social experience, and as a result, classroom tasks commonly emphasize "interaction" as a basis for writing. The theoretical foundations for these activities have tended to be argued in rather general ways, however, and only recently has research described the very real and specific advantages of talk around texts (see Wells, 1999). These advantages include the ways that talk can provide writers with a sense of audience, a sense of how coherence is achieved through negotiation, and the cognitive skills needed for communication. The meshing of spoken dialogue and writing through activity sequences is a further argument for the facilitative effects of talk on the development of students' understanding and creation of written texts.

The advantages of linking reading and writing are fairly well understood, and the use of reading as a springboard for writing has long been a staple of writing teachers in both L1 and L2 contexts. In a recent review, Grabe (2001, p. 25) concludes that "one of the most consistent implications of two decades of reading and writing relations is that they should be taught together and that the combination of both literacy skills enhances learning in all areas." By teaching genres in the sequences in which they occur in target contexts, we not only reap the benefits of reading-writing integration but also help students to develop an understanding of context and the ways texts can be employed to realize situated purposes.

Developing Units of Work

After selecting the genres and topics to be taught and then organizing these into an overall sequence, the specific focus for each teaching unit has to be decided and the units designed. Teachers do not generally develop lessons directly from their course objectives but break these down into blocks of several lessons planned around a single focus. Richards (2001, p. 166) suggests that to create a successful unit of work the teacher needs to take five factors into account:

1. **Length.** Material is sufficient but not so long that it creates boredom.
2. **Development.** One activity leads smoothly to the next in a logical way.
3. **Coherence.** The unit has an overall sense of coherence.
4. **Pacing.** Each activity moves along, and no activity is markedly longer than the others.
5. **Outcome.** At the end of the unit, students know how to do a related series of things.

To accomplish this involves deciding on the theme of each unit, how many lessons each unit will comprise, and how they will be sequenced. Unit themes are best seen as real-life activities or situations in which people do specific things through writing, and perhaps the most obvious way to ensure that writing is given priority is to make the focus of the unit one of the following:

- *A written text.* Depending on the focus and objectives of the course, this could be a sales letter, a narrative essay, or a section of a longer genre, such as a problem-resolution stage from a narrative, the discussion section of a post-graduate engineering thesis, or a letter of application for a job.
- *A specific writing strategy.* Again, this will depend on the course objectives, but it could include the collaborative writing of an investigative report, conducting research and planning for an argumentative essay, or the independent construction of a incident report following a workplace simulation.
- *A sequence of genres or part of that sequence.* Depending on the length of the course and students' proficiency and familiarity with the genres in the sequence, a focus of this kind could be developed around the theme of responding to a customer inquiry or assembling a job application portfolio and preparing for an interview.

It is possible to design each unit of work within a course from a different perspective so that one might be based around a topic, such as *environmental pollution,* and the next around a particular genre, such as a *feasibility report* focusing on pollution-reduction measures. Often, however, the real-world sequence of genres discussed earlier provides a convenient and natural means of linking units of work coherently, with each unit focusing on a different genre or stage of the sequence.

Once again, objectives are important to help teachers and students keep on track and to ensure that appropriate learning is achieved. Unit objectives describe the observable behaviors learners will be able to display at the end of the unit; these both relate directly to course objectives and contribute to students' ability to participate in and understand similar events in social contexts outside the classroom. Objectives may relate to:

- **Extending content knowledge**—about people, cultures, events, or topics—particularly in ESP
- **Developing an understanding of genre**—how language works in context
- **Using writing skills**—brainstorming, planning, drafting, editing, polishing, etc.
- **Undertaking some action**—discussing writing, transforming texts, critiquing texts, etc.

Whatever the focus, the objectives for a genre-based writing course are always related to the use of a particular whole text in a social context. Figure 4.16 shows two examples of unit objectives.

The proposed outcomes of these units are stated in terms of student competencies, or behaviors that can be observed and evaluated, using action verbs such as *collect, write,* and *compose.* In addition to having clear outcomes in mind for units of work to ensure that each activity can be justified in terms of what the course is trying to achieve, it is also a good idea to share these objectives with students. As Nunan (1998, p. 79) points out:

By providing learners with detailed information about goals, objectives and learning activities, learners may come

Unit of work	Simple recount for elementary secondary school learners
Goal	Students will be able to independently produce a short factual recount
Objectives	

- Students will collect information on a series of events by completing a worksheet.
- Students will write a recount in the form of a diary.
- Students will use sources to jointly compose a factual recount of a class excursion.
- Individual students will develop the recount by adding in words/phrases to describe people, events, locations, and time in more detail.

Unit of work	Site Inspection Report for first-year Building and Construction BSc undergraduates
Goal	Learners will participate in a situation that calls for a short inspection report.
Objectives	

- Students will be able to draw up criteria for fire safety based on seminar and reading materials.
- Students will be able to discuss key aspects of fire safety.
- Students will be able to make a fire safety inspection at a selected place in the university.
- Students will be able to write an inspection report describing findings and making recommendations for action.

Fig. 4.16. Examples of objectives for units of work from two genre-based writing courses

to have a greater appreciation of and acceptance of the learning experience they are undertaking or about to undertake.

This helps to give students a sense of direction and control over their learning and an understanding of the reasoning behind different activities.

Summary

In Chapter 4, I have described how teachers can go about organizing a course for L2 writers using the principles and understandings of a genre-based approach. While there are numerous ways genre can inform course design, they all depend on the five principles sketched on page 88–89, and they all emphasize that the language gathered from genre examples can provide a resource for writing. The main points made in this chapter are:

1. Genre-based writing courses come in many shapes and sizes, but all assume that learning to write requires social interaction, needs assessment, explicit objectives and expectations, and the deliberate manipulation of language to make meanings.
2. Decisions about what to teach are based on the characteristics and expectations of students and their target writing needs.
3. Texts or topics can provide the starting point for a genre-based course, but target texts are usually favored where students' language-using needs can be clearly defined.
4. Teachers can help students build their genre knowledge and the ability to critique texts and contexts through an understanding of the sociocultural context that surrounds genre uses.
5. Sequencing genres according to the ways they typically occur in the real world helps to integrate spoken and written genres, relate writing closely with reading, and allow students to see the ways genres operate outside the classroom.
6. Genres provide a useful way of developing coherent and relevant units of work that integrate speaking, reading, and other activities in creating writing.

The guiding belief of a genre-based writing course is that literacy development requires an explicit focus on the ways texts are organized and the language choices available to users to achieve their purposes in particular contexts. In the next chapter, we turn to the activities and strategies teachers use to implement a genre-based writing course and the theories that underlie these.

Tasks and Discussion Questions

1. Teachers adopting a genre approach to writing instruction typically use either a theme-based or a text-

based starting point. What, in your view, are the pros and cons of each, and which appeals to you most as a writing teacher? Does the answer depend to some extent on the circumstances of the class?

2. Consider the writing needs of a group of students you are familiar with, identifying the genres they need beyond the classroom. What principle would you use to sequence these genres in a writing course, and why would you choose this method over others?

3. Look again at the stages involved in creating a genre-based course suggested by Burns and Joyce (1997). Use the framework to create a course based on one you are familiar with or that you anticipate teaching in the future.

4. The idea of student *needs* is a central principle of genre-based teaching. What information do you think it is most important to collect about learners at the beginning of a writing course, and what are the best ways of collecting it? How could this information help you in designing your writing syllabus?

5. What is a communications network? Draw up a communications network for your own workplace or study context. List the people, modes of communication, and genres that occur in it. How could you use this to introduce a newcomer to the communication demands of your situation?

6. Consider a group of students you may have to teach. What would be the main problems in identifying their writing needs in English, and how could you overcome these problems? To what extent could you involve the students in gathering materials and sociocultural information on the context?

7. Benesch (2001) refers to *rights analysis* as a way of highlighting power relations and seeing teaching as more than initiating students unquestioningly into particular discourse communities. What kinds of methods

could you use to identify the implicit and explicit regulation in a particular setting? How might you go about including this information in a writing course to provide students with greater access to decision making in their target communities?

8. Why is it important to integrate speaking, reading, and writing in a writing course? Sketch out how you would ensure that there is such an integration in a course you are familiar with or are likely to teach.

9. Choose a text suitable for a particular group of students you are familiar with. Can you recognize its genre? Are there any particular features of the text that suggest this? Can you identify any stages in the text? Are there any features that stand out as being crucial? Compare your responses with those of a fellow student or teacher.

10. How important is it to have objectives for a writing course? Draw up the objectives and sketch out a unit of work for a genre-based writing course that you may have to teach. Show clearly how the tasks relate to achievement of the objectives.

Chapter 5
Texts, Tasks, and Implementation

In addition to providing writing teachers with a way of organizing their courses, the concept of genre also suggests a range of approaches to classroom teaching. Once again, while the students and learning contexts that teachers confront will vary enormously, a genre-based approach to teaching L2 writing *always* involves attending to the texts learners will most need to write beyond the classroom. This means making genres central to teaching: a talking point and focus for analysis to raise awareness of the interdependence of texts, of the resources used to create meaning in context, of the connections between meanings and social forces, and of ways to negotiate the genres of power and authority. This chapter will explore some genre approaches to these issues by looking at key notions such as *scaffolding, collaboration,* the *teaching-learning cycle,* and *consciousness raising,* showing how L2 writing teachers can use these to devise activities and sequence tasks.

Scaffolding and Collaboration

Genre-based writing instruction follows modern theories of learning in giving considerable recognition to the importance of *collaboration,* or peer interaction, and *scaffolding,* or teacher-supported learning. Together, these concepts assist learners through two notions of learning:

- *Shared consciousness*—the idea that learners working together learn more effectively than individuals working separately
- *Borrowed consciousness*—the idea that learners working with knowledgeable others develop greater understanding of tasks and ideas

More specifically, genre-based pedagogies employ the ideas of Russian psychologist Vygotsky (1978) and the American educational psychologist Bruner (1990). For these writers, the notion of **scaffolding** emphasizes the role of interaction with peers and with experienced others in learning, moving learners from their existing level of performance (what they can do now) to a level of "potential performance" (what they will be able to do without assistance). Vygotsky termed this gap between current and potential performance *the Zone of Proximal Development* and argued that progress from one level to the other is not achieved only through input but rather through social interaction and the assistance of more skilled and experienced others. Research shows that students are able to reach much higher levels of performance by working together and with an expert than they might have achieved working on their own (e.g., Donato, 2000; Ohta, 2000).

In other words, teaching anticipates competence and involves a dialogue between teacher and student, rather like an expert training an apprentice. Figure 5.1, taken from Feez (1998), represents the changing nature of this collaboration in response to the learner's progress.

Vygotsky's ideas, therefore, offer a theoretical basis for genre-based writing teaching. The concept of scaffolding is mainly associated with SFL approaches to language instruction in Australia, but it is also implicit in much ESP genre teaching, which seeks to provide learners with the means to understand and then create new texts by a process of "gradual approximation" (Widdowson, 1978, pp. 91–93). Scaffolding takes many forms and can be provided in relation to cultural, social, contextual, and linguistic aspects of a target genre; it

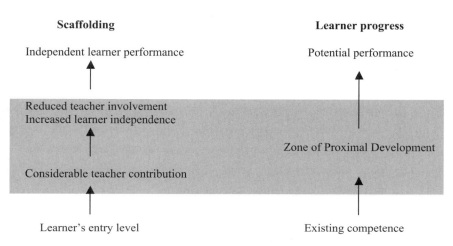

Fig. 5.1. Teacher-learner collaboration (based on Feez, 1998, p. 27)

typically includes modeling, discussion, explicit instruction, and considerable teacher input to assist learners toward competence in a genre. The degree of teacher intervention and the kinds of tasks selected for students to engage with, therefore, play a key role in scaffolding writing, representing a cline of support from closely controlled activities to autonomous extended writing. Figure 5.2 represents a broad characterization of these tasks in the second language writing class.

In SFL approaches, this theory has been elaborated into an explicit methodological model designed to support learning as a social process around the twin ideas of scaffolding and joint construction. As we have seen, *scaffolding* refers to the teacher providing initial explicit knowledge and guided practice while *joint construction* refers to teachers and learners sharing responsibility for developing texts until the learner can work alone. In ESP approaches, we find more varied interpretations of Vygotsky's ideas—utilizing concepts such as *consciousness raising, socioliteracy,* and *gradual approximation* to refer to the ways learners develop an understanding of relevant genres and communities and work toward the creation of their own rhetorically skilled and situationally appropriate texts.

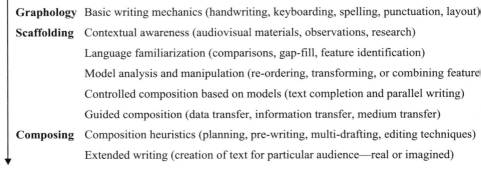

Most support

Graphology	Basic writing mechanics (handwriting, keyboarding, spelling, punctuation, layout)
Scaffolding	Contextual awareness (audiovisual materials, observations, research)
	Language familiarization (comparisons, gap-fill, feature identification)
	Model analysis and manipulation (re-ordering, transforming, or combining features)
	Controlled composition based on models (text completion and parallel writing)
	Guided composition (data transfer, information transfer, medium transfer)
Composing	Composition heuristics (planning, pre-writing, multi-drafting, editing techniques)
	Extended writing (creation of text for particular audience—real or imagined)

Most independence

Fig. 5.2. Tasks and relative support for writing (Hyland, 2003)

While the SFL and ESP approaches to instruction may be realized differently, they are both based on similar principles for effective teaching and learning:

- Learners must have adequate prior knowledge to enable them to learn new things.
- Contexts for learning have to be legitimate and meaningful to learners.
- Teachers need to provide opportunities for group interaction and discussion.
- Students need assistance to develop metacognitive skills and achieve active, conscious control over the knowledge they have acquired unconsciously (Vygotsky, 1978).
- Teachers need to provide support to students in the early stages of learning a new genre in order for them to eventually write it independently.

Chapter 5 will outline some of the ways these principles have been developed and applied in different teaching contexts. Before discussing key ideas from the SFL and ESP approaches, it might be useful to see a simple illustration of how scaffolding devices have been used to help young children develop literacy skills.

Developing Literacy Skills in Children: Writing Frames

One way in which the concept of scaffolding has been applied is through the use of writing frames (e.g., Wray and Lewis, 1997) that are created as flexible and provisional forms of scaffolding to help young children develop a sense of genre when introducing them to non-fiction writing. Often, children have considerable difficulty recognizing the appropriate genre they need for their purposes and produce either *narratives* or *recounts* of what they did, instead of writing an instruction text or a report. This response is largely a result of the well-established and important tradition of getting learners to write about "real experiences," an objective that invites a personal telling. But while it is important for children to write in this way, they also need to be able to deal with the more formal and abstract genres such as *reports, procedures, explanations,* and *arguments,* which they will meet in other areas of the school curriculum.

An important way of assisting students to become familiar with the structures of these non-fiction genres is to encourage them to read and use examples of target texts in the classroom. Discussing children's writing, Meek (1988, p. 12) observes:

> The most important single lesson the children learn from texts is the nature and variety of written discourse, the different ways that language lets a writer tell, and the many different ways a writer reads.

This implicit familiarity with genres, gained through exposure to a range of examples and texts, then needs to be made explicit through teacher modeling and shared writing experiences. This also means asking students to write about things that matter to them, perhaps by writing to the local authorities to complain about litter in the streets or to the school principal asking if they can bring snacks to school. Most important, however, this kind of writing can develop with the support of writing frames.

A *frame* is simply a skeletal outline to scaffold and prompt student writing, providing a genre template that enables students to start, connect, and develop their texts appropriately while concentrating on what they want to say. Frames provide a structure for writing that can be jointly constructed between teachers and learners and revised to suit different circumstances. Frames can therefore take many different forms depending on the genre, the purpose of the writing, and the proficiency of the students. Essentially, however, they mirror the kinds of supportive oral prompting that teachers frequently offer children and that Bereiter and Scardamalia (1987, p. 97) suggest can significantly extend a child's written work. Frames, therefore, provide something of the prompting missing between a writer and a blank sheet of paper and a means of spanning the gap between the kinds of writing children are familiar with and the new genres they are asked to write.

Frames are introduced after the kinds of teacher modeling and explicit discussion of the forms needed for a particular kind of text discussed in the next section. This joint construction of texts means working orally with the class, perhaps using flip-chart versions of frames to talk students through a genre, and arises within the context of ongoing classroom work such as explaining how to do something (procedure) or describing something (report). Framed writing, like all writing, involves planning and drafting stages, and frames can be devised to scaffold this planning. Wray and Lewis (1997) show how frames can be useful for planning a discussion genre (Fig. 5.3) and then a draft (Fig. 5.4).

The draft frame in Figure 5.4 provides students with both a skeletal outline of the genre and the connectives needed to achieve a logical development of their ideas. The frame therefore encourages students to think before they write, provides experience of appropriate connectives, supports their efforts to achieve coherence, and scaffolds the appropriate generic form. Wray and Lewis (1997) suggest that following this kind of drafting, student frames can provide the basis for teacher-pupil conferencing or peer editing before the final version is written.

The issue we are discussing is *School uniform*	

Arguments for	Arguments against
1. *because it is smart* 2. *represents the college* 3. *parents because of washing* 4. *people might turn up to school in hundreds of clothes* 6. *rich children could end up in fancy clothes* 7. *expensive jewellery may get stolen*	1. *school uniform can be expensive* 2. *make you feel the same as everyone else* 3. *people without much money can wear whatever they want and don't have to worry about the right uniform* 4. *won't get into so much trouble if they aren't wearing a jumper or something like that*

My conclusion

I think we should wear whatever we want but not being too outrageous and it is suitable to wear!

Fig. 5.3. A writing frame for planning a discussion (Wray & Lewis, 1997, p. 126)

There is a lot of discussion about whether *smoking should be allowed in public buildings.*

The people who agree with this idea claim that *people have rights and should be allowed to enjoy themselves.*

They also argue that *there are too many laws stopping people to do what they like.*

A further point they make is *smoking is an addiction and people cannot stop easily.*

However, there are also strong arguments against this point of view. *Most of our class* believe that *people shouldn't be allowed to smoke anywhere they like.*

They say that *smoking is dangerous even for people who do not smoke.*

Furthermore, they claim that *it is a bad influence on children and creates pollution and litter.*

After looking at the different points of view and the evidence for them, I think *smoking should be banned in public.*
Because *it is dangerous and dirty.*

Fig. 5.4. A writing frame for the first draft of a discussion (based on Wray & Lewis, 1997, pp. 128–129)

The idea of frames has clear relevance to L2 writing classes as teachers can devise their own frames by drawing on their knowledge of the genres they are teaching and the particular abilities and needs of their students, even creating frames for individual learners. Using these kinds of templates, non-native writers can become increasingly familiar with the generic form being taught. Frames assist writers to envisage what is needed to express their purposes effectively and provide them with ways of anticipating the possible reactions of an intended readership. Frames are not, of course, themselves purposes for writing, nor are they the end of the process. They are used to support writers, not to provide motivation or molds for meanings. Students will need to use them less and less as their confidence in writing and their competence in writing target genres grow.

The Teaching-Learning Cycle: Genre and SFL

The notion of scaffolding receives its most sophisticated expression in the systemic linguistic approach, which is figuratively represented in the *teaching-learning cycle*. The most straightforward representation of this cycle is given by Feez (1998) and is shown in Fig 5.5.

The cycle informs the planning of classroom activities by showing the process of learning a genre as a series of linked stages that provide the support needed to move learners toward a critical understanding of texts. The key stages of the cycle are:

- *Setting the context*—revealing genre purposes and the settings in which a genre is commonly used
- *Modeling*—analyzing the genre to reveal its stages and key features
- *Joint construction*—guided, teacher-supported practice in the genre
- *Independent construction*—independent writing monitored by the teacher
- *Comparing*—relating what has been learned to other genres and contexts

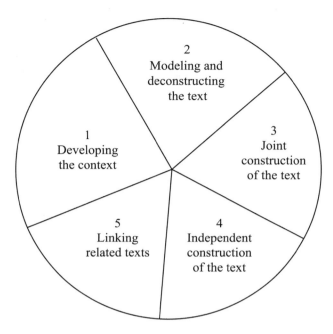

Fig. 5.5. The teaching-learning cycle (Feez, 1998, p. 28)

Each of these stages, therefore, seeks to achieve a different purpose and as a result is associated with different types of classroom activities and different teacher-learner roles.

The cycle is intended to be used flexibly, allowing students to enter at any stage, depending on their existing knowledge of the genre. If they are in-service ESP learners, for instance, they are likely to be familiar with the context in which the genre is used, and the cycle could begin with the modeling stage. When a genre or context is being introduced for the first time, however, students usually work through all the stages. It is also possible that participants may want to return to earlier stages of the cycle for revision purposes or that teachers will decide to go through the cycle again. The model, therefore, allows vocabulary to be recycled and the skills already gained to be further developed by working through a new cycle at a more advanced level of expression of the genre.

The point of the cycle is to draw on the relative knowledge that teachers and students bring to the classroom in order to establish effective Zones of Proximal Development and to scaffold learning. The extent of the scaffolding provided by the teacher or by the materials is reduced according to the learner's development as progress is made around the cycle.

At the beginning of the cycle, direct instruction is crucial as the learner gradually assimilates the task demands and procedures for constructing the genre effectively. The teacher here adopts a highly interventionist role, ensuring that students are able to understand and reproduce the typical rhetorical patterns they need to express their meanings. Grammar tasks are important at this stage to provide learners with the language they need to construct genres and to reflect on what they are doing. At later stages, teacher support is gradually withdrawn as students gain the confidence and abilities to work with more autonomy and to construct genres independently. The final stage gives students opportunities to critique and manipulate the genre and to see it as part of a wider picture of power relations. The main purposes and activities associated with each stage of the cycle are set out below.

1. Developing the Context. One of the most important principles of a genre approach to writing is the emphasis on the functions of language and how meanings work in context. This means that teachers have to understand the key aspects of the sociocultural context and raise student awareness of the institutional and social purposes of the genre. At this stage, then, students are introduced to the social context of the genre to explore the general cultural context in which the genre is used, the social purpose it achieves, and the immediate context of the situation. This allows students to bring their own experiences to the learning process and attempts to create an understanding of the following questions:

- What is the text about?
- What purposes does it serve?
- Who produced the text, and who for (what is the intended audience)?
- What are the writer's qualifications for writing the text?

- What choices does the writer have in formats, vocabulary, topics, etc.?
- What are the roles and relationships of the people using the text, their relative status, power, and level of social involvement?
- What social activity does the genre normally occur in (e.g., job hunting, customer relations, academic essay writing)?
- What does the channel tell us about the text (diary, letter, learner newspaper, website)?

Some of these issues may seem rather difficult, but even young children are able to examine different versions of the same story, such as "fractured fairy tales" (which put a tale in a modern setting or see familiar events from another viewpoint). These provide a stimulus to discuss why changes have been made or to rewrite texts to make different choices. Such activities raise student awareness of the choices made in writing and how these affect the contexts of texts.

Useful context-building activities include:

- Present and discuss the context through pictures, films, documentaries, journalistic materials, realia, site visits and excursions, guest speakers, etc.
- Provide students with analytical tasks requiring learners to interrogate a text to reveal aspects of its cultural context. (Who was it written for? What is the relationship between author and reader? What shared knowledge is assumed?)
- Discuss cross-cultural comparisons of similarities and differences between the target context and similar contexts in the learner's home culture.
- Explore register features of sample texts that make up a genre set in order to raise student awareness of the context.
- Engage students in simulations, role plays, case studies, and other activities that focus on aspects of the target culture.

- Encourage students to conduct research into the cultural contexts and the literacy practices of their target communities through observation of what goes on in the setting, interviews with participants, and analyses of texts (Johns, 1997).

2. *Modeling.* Modeling is an important scaffolding activity that involves teachers and learners discussing and exploring the stages of the genre and its key grammatical and rhetorical features. The purpose here is to focus students on features of the genre. Representative samples of the target genre are analyzed, compared, and manipulated in order to sensitize students to generic structure, alert them to the fact that writing differs across genres, and equip them with the resources needed to produce quality pieces of writing. Learning to write involves acquiring an ability to exercise appropriate linguistic choices, both within and beyond the sentence, and teachers working within a genre-based approach seek to assist this by providing students with an explicit grammar. As pointed out in Chapter 3, the ability to control and manipulate the resources of language is crucial for producing texts.

While an initial assessment of students' language proficiency will provide a more accurate guide to the kinds of help students will need, key issues addressed at the modeling stage are:

- The stages of the text and the function served by each stage
- How each stage contributes to the overall social purpose of the text
- The language features that help to express these functions
- How we know what the text is about
- How social relationships between the writer and reader are encoded
- What the main language features of the genre are

A variety of tasks is used to raise students' awareness of these features and to scaffold their evolving control of the genre. Modeling involves deconstructing a genre at different levels, and here many familiar language-teaching tasks are useful (see also Hyland, 2003).

- *Text-level tasks:*
  - naming stages and identifying their purposes
  - sequencing, rearranging, matching, and labeling text stages
  - comparing texts with omissions, changes, or different structures
  - identifying different and similar sample texts as particular genres

- *Language tasks:*
  - reorganizing or rewriting scrambled or unfinished paragraphs
  - completing gapped sentences or an entire cloze from formatting clues
  - substituting a feature (e.g., tense, modality, voice, topic sentence)
  - using skeletal texts to predict language forms and meaning
  - collecting examples of a language feature, perhaps with a concordancer
  - working in groups to correct errors, circle particular features, match one feature with another, etc.

Clearly, there is a danger of simply concentrating on a model as the one right way of writing a particular kind of text, and this needs to be guarded against by ensuring that students are exposed to a range of readings, texts, and activities to encourage reflection on similarities and differences. Students could, for instance, examine the strategies writers use to open or close their texts or the kinds of paragraph development they use. Comparison activities are also helpful in raising awareness of features such as personal pronouns, politeness markers, or hedges to see how removing or adding these features can alter the style, tone, or presentation of the genre.

The activities, therefore, provide opportunities for students to identify and practice relevant grammatical features, but it is crucial that these activities are related to the genre being studied, the social purpose being achieved, and the meanings being expressed. Too often, however, such activities are employed piecemeal for the purpose of improving students' grammar, rather than scaffolding their writing, and for this reason, they tend to be dismissed by writing teachers as mechanical and boring. But grammar is a resource for making meaning and not an end in itself, and therefore it should always be an integral part of learning to write specific kinds of texts. For this reason, it is a good idea to support learning by working down from the entire text rather than from the bottom up. This involves considering how a text is organized in stages to express a purpose and relate to a particular audience and message, then working on how all parts of the text, such as paragraphs and sentences, are structured, organized and written to make the text effective as written communication.

An example of how a text can be seen in this way is shown in Figure 5.6, taken from an Australian primary school syllabus. A description such as this provides the teacher with a statement of the purpose, structure, and main grammar points of a recount text, which can then be used to select examples and devise tasks to model the genre and guide learners to constructing texts of their own.

3. *Joint negotiation.* At this stage of the cycle, teachers and learners work together to construct whole examples of the genre, with the teacher gradually reducing his or her contribution as learners gain greater control over their writing. Once students know what is required of them, they are in a better position to start writing texts in the genre, but they still rely on the assistance of scaffolded tasks and the guidance of the teacher. Now, however, the teacher focuses less on input and modeling and begins to act as a facilitator for shared writing activities and as a responder to student writing. While joint construction is normally done as a whole-class activity, it can

Social purpose

Recounts "tell what happened." The purpose of a factual recount is to document a series of events and
evaluate their significance. The purpose of a literary recount is to relate a sequence of events so that
it entertains, and this generally includes the writer's expressions of attitude about the events.

Structure

- an orientation providing information about *who, where,* and *when*
- a record of events usually recounted in chronological order
- personal comments and/or evaluative remarks interspersed throughout the record of events
- a reorientation, which "rounds off" the sequence of events.

Grammar

- use of nouns and pronouns to identify people, animals, or things involved
- use of action verbs to refer to events
- use of past tense to locate events in relation to the writer's time
- use of conjunctions and time connectives to sequence the events
- use of adverbs and adverbial phrases to indicate place and time
- use of adjectives to describe nouns

Fig. 5.6. General features of a recount genre (Board of Studies, 1998,
p. 287)

also provide opportunities for more able students to work together in groups while the teacher works with those who need
more help. Scaffolded collaborative writing activities include:

- Teacher-led whole-class construction on blackboard or
  overhead projector
- Collecting information through research and interview-
  ing
- Small-group construction of texts for presentation to the
  whole class
- Completing unfinished or skeletal texts
- Creating a parallel text following a given model
- Creating a text using visual or audio stimulus
- Editing a completed text for meaning, structure, and
  form
- Negotiating an information/opinion gap to construct a
  text

An example of a joint construction activity for a lower-inter-
mediate EFL class is shown in Figure 5.7. The teacher draws

- Ask students what the stages of a descriptive report are, and write them on the left side of the board.
- Tell students that they and you are going to write a report about your college together on the board, stage by stage.
- Ask for suggestions from the students about each stage. As they give their input, correct it in terms of grammar, and highlight differences between their spoken forms and appropriate written expression.
- Get feedback from students on appropriacy and accuracy as you write it up.
- Ask students to extend the ideas they suggest and to organize them into the stages.
- Ask students to check that the text is correct in terms of grammatical features.
- Ask students to work in groups to produce a parallel text on overhead transparencies about the city they are studying in.
- Show group overhead transparencies to the whole class and discuss them.

Fig. 5.7. A joint construction task

on the knowledge students have acquired about the genre from previous stages in the cycle and from their knowledge of the topic to collectively construct an example of the genre. He or she can correct student contributions as they are being written up and focus student attention on the stages, vocabulary, and form of the language used. Creating a number of texts in this way provides support for students when they come to write independently, creates awareness of variations in how the genre can be written, and indicates the potential for creativity and negotiation.

4. Independent Construction. The purpose of this stage in the cycle is for students to apply what they have learned and write a text independently while the teacher looks on and gives advice from the sidelines. All writers, regardless of their proficiency in English, need opportunities to create texts. In fact, independent, extended writing is the ultimate goal of the L2 writing class, for while writers do not learn to write *only* by writing, they cannot learn to write *without* writing. Engaging in an entire writing process gives learners the experience of an independent performance in which they combine a knowledge of content, process, language, context, and genre. At the same time, it provides teachers with a means of determining whether students have achieved a required level of competency in the genre. Independent construction is therefore often seen as the core of writing instruction, although this stage is likely to be more productive if it follows the kinds of scaffolded activities discussed earlier.

It is also likely that students may need assistance initially in the skills required to generate content, draft texts, and revise an extended piece of writing. Scaffolded composing tasks (or writing heuristic activities) to develop strategies for planning, drafting, rewriting, editing, and polishing can therefore be invaluable. Some independent construction activities include:

- Practice a range of pre-writing activities (brainstorming, freewriting, cubing, etc.).
- Outline and draft a text based on pre-writing activities.
- Rewrite a text for another purpose (i.e., change the genre).
- Revise a draft in response to others' comments.
- Proofread and edit a draft for grammar and rhetorical structure.
- Read and respond to the ideas/language of another's draft.
- Research, write, and revise a whole, multi-draft text for a specific audience and purpose.
- Research, write, and revise a workplace/disciplinary text.

5. *Comparing Texts.* This final stage of the teaching-learning cycle provides opportunities for students to investigate how the genre they have been studying is related to other texts that occur in the same or similar contexts, to other genres they have studied, and to issues of interpersonal and institutional power and ideology.

The means to write and understand the target genre provided in the previous stages offer students a potential basis for reflecting on and critiquing the ways in which knowledge and information are organized and constructed. Focusing on genres in the classroom creates familiarity with the text types under study and enables teachers to set up activities that encourage students to see the ways texts often work in sequences, ensuring that they write by responding to other texts in a dialogue. This can involve students in rewriting a text by changing a single variable, such as audience, purpose, or channel, in order to see the impact on forms and meanings. Alternatively, students can observe and interview participants who regularly use the genre to discover the meanings texts have for individuals and institutions in specific contexts. Essentially, comparative and critical reflection on difference and similarity in a range of texts, media, and contexts encourages students to draw on their knowledge of genre and focuses them on reinterpreting how they use and experience genres.

Some key activities here include:

- Comparing the use of the genre across different disciplines, institutions, or cultures
- Studying how the staging of information changes when written for different readers or purposes
- Transforming texts for different media: spoken, print, electronic
- Researching other genres used in the same situation and how these relate to the target genre
- Researching how a key feature or text stage is used in other genres
- Comparing written and speech genres in the same context
- Simulating the impact of using the genre in another context
- Rewriting the text to achieve a different rhetorical purpose
- Interviewing expert text users on their impressions of text meanings and genre practices

Like the activities in the first stage of the cycle, these tasks help to show how genres are more than texts. They go further than this, however. By drawing on students' increased knowledge, they help to show how texts play roles, construct relationships, and are embedded in institutional life. By raising awareness of how texts depend on other texts and the ways they function in context, tasks at this stage reveal the cultural and social forces that shape a genre, reminding students that texts are not autonomous and isolated. Finally, these tasks also help students to see the extent to which institutions and genres can be seen as flexible and negotiated and not entirely unchangeable and imposed.

Linking Cycles of Teaching and Learning

Each cycle is usually based on gaining control of a whole text to use it in a social context. A cycle can constitute an entire course or a unit of work in a course, with each cycle linked to the one before it. Cycles can be chained together to form a course in various ways (see also Feez, 1998, pp. 32–33).

- *To develop the same topic.* For example, the topic may be environmental pollution, and the cycle may focus on a descriptive report of graffiti on the walls around the college. The next cycle may use the vocabulary and content of the topic to practice formal letter writing by having students send a letter to the local government authority to complain about the issue.
- *To introduce a genre from the same context.* For example, students may study a report genre in one cycle relating to a product test and then work toward writing a product description report in the next. Cycles can thereby link sequences of genres or contribute toward learners' greater understanding of the communicative events in a single context.
- *To revisit the same genre in another context.* For example, a unit of work that takes students through a cycle focusing on a personal recount about an overseas holiday written for family members back home may be followed by a personal recount reporting an incident at work for the purpose of an insurance claim.
- *To extend student control over more complex realizations of the genre.* For example, students may learn to

write a simple procedural text in the first cycle, developing use of imperatives, action verbs, and describing words. In the second cycle, the steps in the process may be made more complex, involving branching and conditional clauses (*if the mixture starts to boil, then you must . . .*).

- *To focus on the next stage of a genre.* For example, a series of cycles may explore a complex genre such as a research article, with the first stage focusing on the Methods section, the next cycle devoted to Results, then to Discussion, and then to the Introduction. Each cycle is therefore linked to the others by a growing understanding of the genre and control over these increasingly complex stages.

In sum, the teaching-learning cycle assists learners toward greater understanding and control of a genre in a particular context through a series of sequential steps. These steps scaffold their writing and build on the knowledge and experience they have brought with them from previous steps and from previous cycles. In this way, students move from the known to the unknown, from the supported to the independent, and from the easiest to the more complex, in steps that are explicit and seen as doable. Scaffolding thus provides the pedagogic support that students need and helps them to feel that success is achievable.

Consciousness Raising: Genre and EAP Writing

Scaffolding is also an important aspect of genre-based writing instruction in ESP and EAP, although the teaching approaches adopted in these contexts are far more eclectic than those for SFL and are less dependent on a functional grammar. But while the two approaches may differ in the ways language is described, they agree on pedagogies founded on teacher and peer support and an explicit regard for language.

In university settings, disciplinary knowledge and understanding are largely expressed and rewarded through writing, but L2 students entering tertiary studies are often uncertain about what is expected of them. Although they are generally very successful language learners with high TOEFL or IELTS scores, undergraduate L2 students are often dismayed to find that they are unable to fall back on the English language skills they have painstakingly gained over years of study. The general essay-writing techniques that they have learned at school, for instance, leave them ill equipped to support an argument in anthropology or business studies. As a result, their subject lecturers, who tend to see academic discourse conventions as largely self-evident and universal, complain that these learners don't "write in an academic way." Worse, they are told that it is their own deficit of literacy skills that is the problem and are sent off to the University Writing Clinic/Center/Lab to "fix-up" their grammar: the universal panacea.

Genre teaching in EAP has sought to remedy this demoralizing downward spiral by identifying and analyzing the key genres employed in academic settings and making these clear to students through consciousness-raising and linguistic awareness tasks. In EAP, the writing teacher's goal is to demystify the genres that matter to students so that they understand them and write them effectively. Some of the main teaching practices associated with genre in EAP are discussed in the following sections.

Starting with Academic Registers

Genre analysis has helped to show that the discourses of the university represent a variety of discipline-specific literacies, but it has also shown that some grammatical and lexical features are sufficiently prominent for us to recognize academic writing as a specific register. These concentrations of features, which connect writing to academic contexts, are a good place for teachers to start.

Perhaps the most immediately obvious feature of an academic register, and one that students often find most intimidating, is the comparatively high degree of formality in academic texts. Essentially, this formality is achieved through the use of specialist vocabulary, impersonal voice, and the ways that ideas get "packed into" relatively few words. These features of academic writing break down into three key areas: high lexical density, a nominalized style, and impersonality.

- **High lexical density.** A high proportion of content words is used in relation to grammar words, such as prepositions, articles, and pronouns, which makes academic writing more tightly packed with information. Halliday (1989, p. 61) compares the following written sentence (with three italicized grammatical words) with a conversational version (with 13 grammatical words):

  - Investment *in a* rail facility implies *a* long term commitment.
  - *If you* invest *in a* rail facility *this* implies *that you are going to be* committed *for a* long term.

- **High nominal style.** Actions and events are presented as nouns rather than verbs to package complex phenomena as a single element of a clause. This freezes an event, such as *The train leaves at 5:00 P.M.,* and repackages it as an object, *The train's 5:00 P.M. departure.* Turning processes into objects in this way expresses scientific ideologies that seek to show relationships between entities. In addition, nominalization allows writers to thematize processes, or signal what is being talked about at the beginning of a sentence, in order to say something about them and to manage the information flow of a text as in: *Synthetic peptides reducing the penetration of viruses into human cells* have been tested.

- **Impersonal constructions.** Students are often advised to keep their academic prose as impersonal as possible, avoiding the use of *I* and expressions of feeling. First-person pronouns are often replaced by passives (*the solution was heated*); dummy *it* subjects (*it was possible to interview the subjects by phone*); and what are called "abstract rhetors," where agency is attributed to things rather than people (*the data suggest, Table 2 shows*).

As we shall see, the extent to which subject teachers expect students to use these features in the genres they give them to write depends a great deal on their disciplinary specialization (e.g., Hyland, 2000). However, raising students' awareness of general features helps them to see how academic fields are broadly linked and how language both helps construct and is constructed by features of its context. Using genre-based pedagogies in academic contexts means developing the language awareness of students and encouraging them to notice genres so that they can write them more effectively. Learners also come to understand how academic literacy practices relate to their own writing practices. They see that academic writing is just a way of engaging in different contexts, rather than a superior form of discourse. It is often fruitful to begin where students are, to start with discourses they are familiar with before tackling those they will be expected to read and write. Two ways to do this are by exploring "homely" discourses and by comparing spoken and written modes.

1. Johns (1997, pp. 38–50) recommends introducing students to the concepts of genre and context through "homely" genres familiar to most students, such as wedding invitations and obituaries. Students can then move on to explore pedagogic genres like textbooks and then less familiar academic genres. This helps students to gain an understanding of the ways register features interact with social purposes and cultural forces in known genres before they study academic genres.
2. Raising student awareness of the role of register features in constructing contexts can also be achieved by comparing the ways that conversation and academic writing differ in response to audiences and purposes. While speaking and writing draw on the same grammatical system, written language is not just speech written down; it can encode meanings very differently. It is helpful for

students to see that these differences are the result of different purposes and contexts rather than different channels of communication. Prepared speeches may be more like written than spoken text, for example, and a personal e-mail more like speech. Language always responds to context so that an unscripted lecture looks very different from the coursebook the lecturer based it on (Flowerdew, 1993).

Some sample activities focusing on features of academic registers and genres include:

- Discuss and list the features of conversational and written academic language, and suggest possible reasons for any differences found.
- Plan a series of lessons that move progressively from spoken to written language, drawing attention to the characteristics of the target genre as you progress.
- Use the "homely" discourses of students' everyday lives to introduce students to the concepts of genre and context, and then move on to relevant academic genres, as suggested earlier.
- Write a short description of the context and perspective of a text.
- Explicitly compare two texts on the same topic written in an academic and, say, a journalistic register, and examine the frequency and use of the features listed earlier.
- Focus on one register feature, and see how it is used in a relevant genre in the students' discipline.
- Investigate the connections between language features and academic contexts, noting who the readership is, the setting, the tone, writer-reader relationships, and so on.

Investigating Variability in Academic Writing

Consciousness raising also means encouraging students to reflect critically on how language is used. Subject lecturers,

EAP teachers, and students themselves tend to regard "academic English" as a uniform and transferable set of writing skills, while textbooks generally convey the impression that successful academic writing means following universal rules and skills that are usable in any situation. By exploring these taken-for-granted assumptions about academic writing, teachers can address key register features while raising awareness of the ways they are used in particular contexts.

Ann Johns (1997, pp. 58–64) has drawn up a list of the arguments of three leading composition theorists concerning the nature, values, and features of academic writing (Fig. 5.8).

The kinds of scaffolded writing tasks discussed earlier can help guide students who are unfamiliar with academic writing toward an understanding and control of these key features. In addition, by focusing on real texts and exploring the presence and use of these features in the genres they are expected to write, teachers can sensitize students to how these features are used differently across disciplines. In other words, genre approaches seek to avoid giving the misleading impression that writing is the same in all disciplines. They encourage students to question a monolithic, universal view of academic discourse and heighten their awareness of writing as a situated disciplinary practice. There are a number of tasks that students can do to examine feature variability. Some examples are:

Texts are explicit, with clear discussion of data and results.

Texts follow an inductive "top-down" pattern, with topic sentences and an introduction to help readers see where the text will lead.

Texts contain metadiscourse, such as *to summarize, in conclusion, firstly, secondly,* etc., to help guide readers through the argument.

Texts are emotionally neutral and strive to appear objective.

Texts contain hedges like *probably* and *might* to avoid sounding too confident.

Texts are intertextual, drawing on other texts for their structure, form, and patterns of argument.

Texts adopt the right tone to show appropriate confidence and modesty.

Texts acknowledge prior work and avoid plagiarism.

Texts comply with the genre requirements of the community or classroom.

Fig. 5.8. Features of "academic writing" (Johns, 1997)

- Carry out a survey of the advice given on one of these features in a sample of style guides and textbooks, and write a report on the results.
- Conduct a mini-analysis of a text in a student's discipline using a marker to highlight instances of a feature; count and tabulate results, and compare these with those of other students.
- Discuss the extent to which students feel they have to adopt an English "academic style" in their writing or are able to preserve something of their own academic culture or personal identity.
- Explore the use of one item on Ann Johns's list, and compare it with its treatment in a textbook as a way of raising student3 awareness of its importance and diversity.
- Explore the extent to which a feature can be transferred across genres the students need to write.
- Reflect on how far these features correspond with writing in the students' first academic language.

Comparing Texts and Textbooks

In addition to exploring common assumptions about academic writing, writing teachers may find it useful for students to compare the advice found in style guides and textbooks with the actual practices of academic writers. Published materials play an important part in literacy education in university settings, particularly in the sciences, and students should learn to view their advice critically. Often, these materials rely heavily on intuition and conventional wisdom rather than on the analysis of real language use, and as a result, students can work toward a more informed understanding and appropriate use of language by analyzing texts, considering advice, and discussing uses. This helps students to develop a questioning approach to language and the tools to demystify conventional forms that may otherwise seem strange and arbitrary. These attitudes and understandings lead to more fluent writing practices. Almost any feature can be selected to develop students' writing skills and encourage reflection on language use, but information on hedges seems particularly productive in exploring intuitive advice and actual use.

Hedges—items like *possible, might,* and *perhaps*—are key features of academic writing as they weaken statements by qualifying the writer's commitment. Writers hedge to show doubt and indicate that information is presented as opinion rather than as accredited fact or to convey deference, humility, and respect for the views of readers who may disagree with them. As this example from a physics research article shows, hedges are useful in displaying audience awareness and in weighing the degree of certainty to invest in a statement:

> This <u>suggests</u> that a competition exists between nucleation at the hopper edges and within the hopper, which <u>might account for</u> the narrow temperature range over which these features are observed. Filling <u>appears to</u> develop more from the pit of the hopper than the interior edges.

Hedges are important to students as they draw attention to the fact that academic statements don't communicate only ideas but also the writer's attitude to them and to readers. Hedges have roughly the same frequency in academic research papers as do instances of the past tense or passive voice (K. Hyland, 1998), and their use is much greater in humanities and social science writing. Hedging, however, presents considerable problems for second language students, who often make excessively strong claims (Hyland & Milton, 1997). Yet, despite its rhetorical and pedagogic importance, hedging is not well represented in published materials, with information scattered, explanations inadequate, practice material limited, and alternatives to modal verbs absent (Hyland, 1994). The style guides are even worse, with most authors advising writers to avoid hedges, arguing that they rob writing of its certainty and power and undermine judgments. Lindsay (1984, p. 21), for example, advises:

> If you have no conclusive evidence don't dither around with expressions such as "it may be possible that. . . ." or

(worse) "the possibility exists that . . .," which immediately suggests that you do not believe your own data.

This failure to adequately represent the importance of hedges can therefore mislead students about their use; so activities that analyze texts and textbooks can help in raising learner awareness of how hedges are expressed, why they are used, and what they mean. When analyzing textbook coverage, students can complete a simple table such as the one shown in Figure 5.9 to tabulate their findings, simply putting a check (√) to indicate minimal coverage and √√ to represent fair to extensive coverage (Hyland, 1994). Students can then go on to examine the ways hedges are used in target genres. The class members can then pool their expertise and discuss similarities and differences, compiling the results to write an essay or research paper on the subject.

Other consciousness-raising tasks can involve a comparison of how writers express different degrees of certainty in different genres. Thus, students can be asked to compare two treatments of the same topic, say in a research article and in a textbook or popular science article. This awareness provides students with a simple technique for distinguishing facts from opinions and identifying the assumptions writers make about their audience. Finally, an awareness of the effect of hedges on statements can be approached through the use of scaffolding tasks such as the following:

- Examine a text, and distinguish statements that report facts and those that are unproven.
- Identify all hedges in a text, circling the forms used, and try to account for their presence.

Writing textbooks	Modal verbs	Lexical verbs	Modal adverbs	Modal adjectives	Modal nouns

Fig. 5.9. Table for recording occurrence of hedges in textbooks

- Locate and remove all hedges, and discuss the effect on the meaning of the text.
- Identify hedged propositions in a text, and substitute statements of certainty for them.
- Identify hedging forms, and compile a scale ranking the amount of certainty they express, using this data to assess the accuracy of existing scales in textbooks.

Exploring Student Attitudes

Closely related to the kinds of consciousness-raising activities discussed earlier, EAP teachers often draw on genre studies as a means to encourage students to reflect on their own attitudes to academic writing and to develop an enhanced appreciation of the language used in academic genres. Two excellent examples of this approach are given in a textbook for graduate native and non-native English speakers by Swales and Feak (2000).

The first task offers a simplified summary of the cross-cultural research by drawing attention to aspects of academic writing such as metadiscourse, citations, and argument structure in English and asking students to consider conventions in their own language (Fig. 5.10).

This kind of contrastive reflection is useful for showing practices as specific to particular cultures and disciplines and for identifying how little is actually universal. It moves writers toward a descriptive understanding of research language and encourages students to question a monolithic, asocial view of writing. Moreover, while the points appear to address largely surface features of academic writing, they are underpinned by clear ideologies of disciplinary practices and attitudes to knowledge. It might, therefore, be possible with advanced learners to raise key issues for discussion. This can involve reflecting on the nature of argument structure, reader awareness, community relationships, audience expectations, interpersonal interactions, cultural variability, personal identity, and sociocultural domination. An explicit awareness of all these features is important to successful academic writing.

American academic English, in comparison to other research languages, has been said to:

_____ 1. be more explicit about its structure and purposes

_____ 2. be less tolerant of asides or digressions

_____ 3. use fairly short sentences with less complicated grammar

_____ 4. have stricter conventions for subsections and their titles

_____ 5. be more loaded with citations

_____ 6. rely more on recent citations

_____ 7. have longer paragraphs in terms of number of words

_____ 8. point more explicitly to "gaps" or "weaknesses" in the previous research

_____ 9. use more sentence connectors (words like *however)*

_____ 10. place the responsibility for clarity and understanding on the writer rather than on the reader

Reflect upon your own first academic language. Place a checkmark (✓) before those points where academic writing in your L1 and American academic English differ. If you do not think the difference holds for your language, leave it blank.

Are there differences that you think ought to be mentioned?

If you are writting for an American audience, how much do you think you need to adapt to an American style?

Do you think you need to fully "Americanize" your writing, or can you preserve something of your own academic culture in your academic writing?

Fig. 5.10. Reflection task on cultural differences in academic writing (Swales & Feak, 2000, p. 16)

The second example (Fig. 5.11) is also from Swales and Feak's textbook *English in Today's Research World* (2000) and draws on genre research Chang & Swales (1999) to consider several informal features often used by experienced academic writers but generally forbidden by style guides.

Element	Number of occurrences	Average per paper	Number of authors using element
Imperatives	639	21.3	30
I/my/me	1020	34.0	23
Initial *but*	349	11.6	23
Initial *and*	137	4.6	17
Direct questions	224	7.5	17
Verb contractions	92	3.1	11

Take a photocopy of what you consider to be a good but typical paper from your own specialized area, and with a highlighter, highlight all occurrences of the six informal elements that you find. Count and tabulate your findings.

In general, how does your field compare to those in the table? What explanations for any differences occur to you?

Which of these elements would you feel comfortable using yourself?

Have you come across or been told other prescriptive rules? Do you think such rules have validity?

Fig. 5.11. Informal elements in academic style (Swales & Feak, 2000, p. 17)

The purpose of this task is, once again, to raise student awareness of the conventions and expectations that may exist in their own disciplines and provide material for cross-disciplinary comparisons. This time, however, students are asked to conduct their own analysis of a text. This not only heightens their understanding of actual language use but encourages them to consider issues of formality, to distinguish appropriateness from correctness, and to reexamine the pronouncements of experts in the context of real usage. The activity continues with comments from international students about these informal elements and questions designed to stimulate further reflection and discussion.

Genres and Disciplinary Differences

One of the most important contributions that genre analysis has made to teaching L2 writing in EAP settings is to show that while academic discourse is an identifiable register, language varies considerably across disciplines and sub-disciplines. Research demonstrates that scholarly discourse is not uniform, distinguished merely by specialist topics and vocabularies. Instead, it is the outcome of numerous practices and strategies, where arguments are crafted within specific communities that have different ideas about what is worth communicating, how it can be communicated, what readers are likely to know, how they might be persuaded, and so on. Each discourse community develops its own ways of understanding the world, and these are reflected in the ways they talk about it. The clearest way to express this is to see the disciplines as spread along a cline, with the "hard knowledge" sciences and "softer" humanities at opposite ends, as shown in Figure 5.12.

At one end of the cline, the sciences emphasize their empirical basis as new knowledge develops cumulatively and is accepted on the basis of experimental proof. Science writing reinforces this by highlighting a gap in knowledge, by presenting a hypothesis related to this gap, and then by experiments and findings to support this hypothesis. At the other end, disciplines in the humanities rely more on case studies

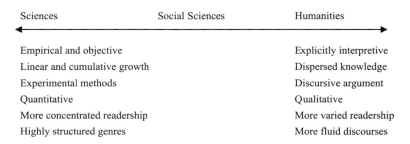

Fig. 5.12. Continuum of academic knowledge

and introspection, and claims are accepted or rejected on the strength of argument. Between these, the social sciences have partly adopted the methods of the sciences, but in applying these to human and therefore less predictable data, explicit interpretation assumes greater importance. For teachers, this means that different disciplines value different kinds of argument and set different writing tasks.

- In the humanities and social sciences, for instance, analyzing and synthesizing multiple sources are important, while in science and technology, skills such as describing procedures, defining objects, and planning solutions are required (Casanave & Hubbard, 1992).
- In post-graduate programs, engineers give priority to describing charts, while business studies faculty require students to compare ideas and take a position (Bridgeman & Carlson, 1984).
- In undergraduate classes, lab reports are common in chemistry, program documentation in computer science, article surveys in math, and project reports in the social sciences (Wallace, 1995).

More problematically, while labels such as *laboratory report, case study, project proposal, essay,* and so on, are familiar in many disciplines and university courses, these often refer to texts that look very different across disciplines. With the increasing popularity of modular and interdisciplinary degrees, students frequently find themselves having to meet the writing demands of very different disciplines.

Examples of how genres in different disciplines reflect different ways of constructing and shaping knowledge are given by Coffin et al. (2003). They identify three genres as being pivotal in each of the three domains of knowledge: *project proposals in the sciences, essays of various kinds in the humanities,* and *reports and case studies in the social sciences.* By describing how these genres are structured as a series of different stages with different purposes and language features, and by drawing on the scaffolded writing tasks introduced earlier, teachers can develop students' ability to write these genres with confidence. Figure 5.13 summarizes the structures of two such genres with descriptions of each stage.

Genre Features in Different Disciplines

As noted earlier, disciplines are also distinguished by choices of register: not only the specialized terminology they use to explain the world but also the interpersonal features they use to persuade their readers of their claims. A good example is the extent to which writers in different disciplines typically employ "self mention." While impersonality was mentioned as a key register feature and "emotional neutrality" occurs in Figure 5.7 as a general trait of academic writing, not all disciplines follow this convention strictly. While science and engineering

Scientific project proposal		Applied social sciences case study	
Title	Concise and accurate indication of project topic	Background	Overview of the organizational or professional context of the study
Introduction	Aims and theoretical background, including literature review and rationale	Analytical framework	For academic reader—provides explanation and rationale of framework
		OR	
Materials and methods	List of materials and apparatus, detailed description of methods and how these will meet aims	Approach to study	For professional reader—provides explanation of the theoretical approach
		Findings	Main findings
Analytical methods	What data will be obtained and how it will be analyzed	Implications	Interpret the findings and show their relevance to the organization under study
References	List of sources the proposal refers to	Recommendations	Suggested action points based on the information collected

Fig. 5.13. Functional stages of two genres (based on Coffin et al., 2003, pp. 50, 69)

research articles still tend to suppress human agency, writers in the humanities and social sciences often make extensive use of first-person pronouns. In fact, *I* and *we* occur extensively in philosophy, applied linguistics, business, and sociology research articles, and there are sufficient cases to suggest that writers have conspicuous promotional and interactional purposes (Hyland, 2001). By exploring these conventions with students, teachers can help them see the options available to them when writing in their disciplines.

As in most pedagogic applications of genre, students can build this kind of rhetorical consciousness by comparing advice with practice, analyzing professional research texts, interviewing experts, or critically evaluating their own writing practices. Subject teachers and graduate students can be an excellent source of data as they are usually willing to be interviewed by novices on their practices and their impressions of the conventions in their fields. By going outside the classroom to observe, question, and learn, students can form and test hypotheses about why people write as they do in their field, how they understand particular features when they see them in texts, the reasons they select certain genres, and why they make certain choices when writing them. Such interviews need to be carefully planned and have clear objectives, but students often benefit enormously from these insider perspectives.

Rhetorical consciousness raising should always involve some kind of focus on texts, and this can be achieved by asking students to conduct mini-analyses of the genres they have to write or of their own writing, identifying where writers have chosen to use or avoid *I* and determining possible reasons for this. A simple task could involve the following steps:

- Mark all occurrences of *I* in a typical paper from your discipline; count and tabulate the findings.
- Compare the results with a classmate (different discipline, specialization, or genre).
- What explanations for any differences occur to you?
- Notice how impersonal and personal forms change in the text. What might be the reason for this?

- Select 5 places where *I* can be replaced with a passive. What effect does this have on the meaning of the sentence?
- What main verbs occur most often with *I* in this text? Can you group them in any way? Do they correspond to the following rhetorical functions?

  - explaining what was done (*We interviewed ten teachers from six schools*)
  - structuring the discourse (*First, I will discuss the method, then present my results*)
  - showing a result (*My findings show that the animation distracted the pupils from the test*)
  - making a claim (*I think two factors are particularly significant in destroying the councils*)

- Now write a report to present and explain your findings.

This section has attempted to show how genre-based pedagogies in EAP seek to correct the autonomous view of academic writing that divorces language from context and misleads learners into believing they have weak language skills. Genre offers teachers a tool to analyze different contexts and present the regularities of structure and form that distinguish one type of text from another, scaffolding students' understanding of academic texts and their ability to write them. While learning the discourses of their fields, learners also come to see that there is no single academic literacy but a variety of practices relevant to and appropriate for particular disciplines and purposes. An awareness of this variation not only makes them better writers but helps them to see texts more critically as community-based artifacts.

Summary

Genre theory tells us that students have greater control over their writing if they are provided with ways to see how different communities employ different genres and how these genres represent writers' social and community purposes. The use of writing frames, the teaching-learning cycle, and consciousness-raising tasks assists students by scaffolding their writing and helping them to focus on how a text works as purposive communication. The main points of this chapter have been:

1. Scaffolding and teacher-learner collaboration are key elements of genre-based writing pedagogy.
2. Scaffolding devices like writing frames provide flexible and provisional means of assisting young learners to develop a sense of genre while planning and drafting.
3. The teaching-learning cycle offers a principled means of organizing learning, selecting tasks, deciding on teacher-learner roles, and sequencing units of work while focusing on genres.
4. Each stage of the cycle—contextualizing, modeling, joint construction, independent writing, and comparing—seeks to achieve a different purpose in supporting learners to new levels of writing performance.
5. Student materials and tasks should address representative samples of the target discourse.
6. Teaching is ideally descriptive and interpretive rather than prescriptive and didactic.
7. Genre descriptions should offer a functional account of the features employed and stress variability and change.
8. Teaching should raise awareness of the rhetorical and linguistic constraints and opportunities involved in participating in different genres.

While I have focused on consciousness raising, scaffolding, and language analysis, activities that take texts and contexts as their starting points, it has to be emphasized that genre methods do not abandon the familiar practices of the process classroom such as pre-writing, peer response, and attention to content. As I noted earlier, while writers do not learn to write *only* by writing, they cannot learn to write without writing at all, and so the tasks discussed here always lead to extended writing activities. In Chapter 6, we turn to the ways that such writing can be responded to and assessed in a genre-based program.

Tasks and Discussion Questions

1. In your view, what makes a good lesson in a writing class? What input should the learners get? What kinds of tasks should be included, and how should they be organized? Should students do a lot of writing in class, or should this mainly be a homework activity?

2. Effective scaffolding requires considerable teacher intervention at early stages of learning to create a new genre. Do you feel this kind of teacher role is necessary in L2 writing development or unhelpfully restrictive? What kind of scaffolding do you currently offer learners, and how could you increase this to good effect?

3. What are writing frames? Do you think these are only useful for younger learners, or do they have a role to play in adult ESL classes? Devise a series of writing frames to help students plan and draft a genre you are currently teaching or may teach in the future. Discuss how you would use them with a class.

4. Consider the strengths and weaknesses of the teaching-learning cycle as a way of sequencing tasks to scaffold L2 writing. In what ways might the use of the cycle depend on the specific teaching context?

5. Plan a unit around an analysis you have made of a genre. Base the unit on the teaching-learning cycle, relating the classroom tasks and writing activities to the key stages of the cycle illustrated in Figure 5.5 (page 129) and showing how these establish a context for the genre, present models, offer opportunities for collaboration and independent construction, and gradually reduce teacher support and move students toward greater independence in writing.

6. Write a critical evaluation of the unit you designed in the previous task. What are you most and least satisfied with? What parts were hardest to create? How do you think a class would respond to the unit, and what would they learn? What did you learn from the experience of designing the unit?

7. What is your view of using models in the writing class? Do you believe they restrict inventiveness and creativity by encouraging imitation, or do they help L2 writers understand how rhetorical and grammatical features are used effectively? Set out your own views, giving reasons for your position and addressing opposing arguments.

8. Select one item on Ann Johns's list in Figure 5.8 (page 145), and compare its use in an academic article in TESOL, composition, or applied linguistics, with the advice given in an academic style guide or writing textbook. How well do they correspond? Devise a task for students that draws on this activity, and discuss its usefulness as a consciousness-raising task.

9. Select a genre that you consider suitable for a particular target group of learners, and devise a task to raise student awareness of a particular key feature of the genre. What difficulties might your learners experience with the task, and how would you address these?

Chapter 6
Genre, Feedback, and Assessment

This chapter explores the role of genre in assessing writing. Essentially, assessment refers to the variety of methods used to collect information about a learner's writing ability, including practices as diverse as timed class tests, short essays, term assignments, project reports, and portfolios. *Assessment* is an integral aspect of the teaching-learning process and central to students' progress toward increasing control of their writing. It is also a practice that happens as a routine part of every classroom day as teachers continually make judgments about the writing of their learners and communicate these to students. These judgments provide information to students about their progress, strengths, and weaknesses and help teachers to evaluate the effectiveness of their tasks and materials and to devise future learning.

Assessment therefore has both a teaching and a testing function, and a distinction is often made between *formative* and *summative* assessment. As a formative process, assessment is closely linked to teaching and to issues of teacher response, or *feedback,* allowing the teacher to advise students, monitor learning, and fine-tune instruction. Summative assessment, on the other hand, is concerned with "summing up" how much a student has learned at the end of a course. The concept of genre has a contribution to make to both types of assessment by providing explicit criteria about what is being aimed at, what is being assessed, and where students need to improve to meet learning goals. Once again, language is seen as a resource for making meaning and writing as involving choices to relate language to contexts. This chapter will discuss what genre can offer in these areas of assessment.

Some Basic Considerations in Writing Assessment

Before looking at genre-based assessments in detail, I will first seek to place them in a wider context by briefly addressing the basic assessment issues of purposes, validity and reliability, and scoring procedures.

Assessment Purposes

Assessments have the general purpose of helping teachers make inferences about language abilities and decisions of various kinds based on these inferences (Weigle, 2002, p. 40). Within these broad purposes, however, there are more specific reasons for assessing students, and the starting point for designing writing assessment tasks is to be clear about these. There are five main reasons for evaluating learners:

- *Placement:* to provide information that will help allocate students to appropriate classes
- *Diagnostic:* to identify students' writing strengths and weaknesses, often as part of a needs assessment, or to spot areas where remedial action is needed as a course progresses
- *Achievement:* to enable learners to demonstrate the writing progress they have made in a course
- *Performance:* to give information about students' ability to perform particular writing tasks, usually associated with known "real-life" academic or workplace requirements
- *Proficiency:* to assess students' general level of competence, usually to provide certification for employment, university study, etc.

In addition to these major purposes, teachers also use assessments to motivate their learners to feel positive about their achievements, to provide practice for international exams, to evaluate the success of their teaching, and to gather information about what to teach next. Writing assessment thus has clear pedagogic goals as it can directly influence teaching, promote learner progress, and inform teachers of the impact of their courses, an effect known as *washback.* In most classroom situations, assessments generally aim for either diagnostic or achievement outcomes, although these often include other subsidiary purposes.

Validity and Reliability

All writing assessment tasks must be designed with *validity* and *reliability* in mind—that is, a test should do what it is intended to do, and it should do it consistently.

There are several kinds of *validity* (see Hamp-Lyons, 2003; Hyland, 2003), although current perspectives see *construct validity* as the most important in writing assessment (Messick, 1996). A construct-valid test is one that appropriately represents the abilities being tested, such as the ability "to write a short report" or "to prepare documents for a job interview." In practice, this requires teachers to understand exactly the domain of writing involved and the behaviors that should be measured and then to devise tasks that indicate the control students display over these aspects of writing. This implies that assessment tasks must be based on a close analysis of target texts to effectively elicit the appropriate rhetorical, cognitive, and linguistic processes required to write in a particular domain. So, a task designed to assess abilities in writing an argumentative essay, for instance, should encourage writers to present and support a proposition, explore points of view and weigh evidence, address an audience appropriately, and draw on relevant topic material. Validity therefore requires a task to assess what it claims to assess and to assess what has actually been taught.

A writing task is considered *reliable* if it measures consistently, in terms of both the same student on different occasions and the same task across different raters. Every effort has to be made to ensure that the same individual will perform equally well on different occasions and tasks. Hughes (1989) argues that there is a greater chance of achieving this through taking a sufficient number of samples, restricting the candidate's choice of topics and genres, giving clear task directions, and ensuring that students are familiar with the assessment format. In addition, student writing must be rated consistently so that all assessors agree on the rating of the same performance and assess the same performance in the same way on different occasions. Unfortunately, raters are often influenced as much by their own experiences and preferences as by variations in writing quality and can differ in what they look for in writing and the standards they apply to the same text. Novice raters, for instance, tend to focus far more on grammatical accuracy and local errors, which tend to be highly visible (Weigle, 2002, pp. 70–72).

Approaches to Scoring

A final major issue in assessing writing is the scoring procedures to be used. These can vary considerably but fall into three main categories: holistic, analytic, and primary trait. The first offers a general impression of a piece of writing; the second is based on separate scales of writing features; and the third judges performance traits relative to a particular task.

A *holistic scale* is based on a single, integrated score of writing behavior. This approach reflects the idea that writing is best captured by a single scale that integrates the inherent qualities of the writing. Yet while this approach is easy to use, reducing writing to a single score means that teachers cannot gain diagnostic information that they can feed back into their teaching to improve the student's performance. *Analytic scoring,* on the other hand, requires readers to judge a text against a set of criteria important to good writing and give a score for each category. This provides more information than a single holistic score by separating and perhaps weighting individual components. Commonly, there are separate scales for content, organization, and grammar, with vocabulary and mechanics sometimes added to these. *Primary trait scoring* involves rating a piece of writing by just one feature critical to that task, such as appropriate text staging, effective argument, reference to sources, and so on. The fact that this approach requires a new scoring guide for each specific writing task makes it very labor-intensive, however, and many raters find it hard to focus exclusively on the one specified trait.

While each scoring method has its advantages and disadvantages (see Cohen, 1994; Hyland, 2003), in all cases, good assessment practice now involves the use of a scoring guide or *rubric,* benchmark scripts, and rater training.

Some Advantages of Genre-Based Writing Assessment

Genre-based approaches bring several advantages to the assessment of L2 writing compared to more general approaches. Genre-based approaches are:

Explicit. They provide explicit criteria for assessment and feedback.

Integrative. They integrate teaching and assessment.

Relevant. They are directly related to learners' writing goals.

Focused on competency. They specify student competencies and genre features.

Focused on preparedness. They ensure assessment occurs when students are best prepared for it.

These advantages will now be addressed more fully.

1. Assessing against Explicit Criteria. Current theories of language assessment emphasize the importance of assessing student writing against a set of clear and agreed-upon performance criteria. This is not only because teachers need to apply consistent standards to judge each task performance fairly but also so that they can communicate these criteria clearly to students. Traditionally, a student's writing performance was judged in comparison with the performance of others, referred to as *norm-referenced* scoring. Today, the quality of each script is usually judged in its own right against some external criteria. Assessing against explicit criteria in this way is called *criterion-referenced* assessment and involves breaking the task into smaller components of skills and knowledge that can be recognized and graded. In genre-based assessment, this is often what is called a *competency-based* procedure. This helps teachers to identify the key features of the target genre in terms of its discourse staging, paragraph organization, cohesive links, interpersonal tenor, contextual appropriateness, and so on. In other words, it utilizes an analytic approach based on the primary traits of the particular genre.

As a result of such explicit criteria, students know how they will be assessed and what they have to do to be successful, and this both makes learning relevant and important and gives students greater confidence to write. It also means that teachers are in a better position to identify the kinds of problems students may be having with their writing, allowing them to target feedback precisely and to plan the remedial interventions needed to assist improvements.

2. Integrating Teaching and Assessment. Genre-based writing programs seek to integrate achievement assessment into the course. This means that students are able to use their knowledge of the purpose, structure, and grammatical features of the genres they have learned to deal with the new or unfamiliar topics or vocabulary that they may find in the assessment task (Paltridge, 2001, p. 104). While it is true that any kind of classroom writing activity requires students to know the kind of text they are expected to produce and how this will be evaluated, they are often uncertain about these issues and can remain confused even when given guidelines or instructions.

A central aspect of genre-based teaching is that assessment provides opportunities for students to demonstrate the knowledge and skills they have developed during the writing course itself. Because such courses focus on the abilities students need to construct particular text types, the features of these texts can be clearly specified, taught, and used to describe a standard of performance. This ensures a direct link between teaching and assessment, giving learners an explicit idea of what is required and enabling teachers to see how far students have gained control of the genre. In other words, genre-based writing instruction encourages teachers to be clear about their purposes in teaching so that students can see what will be tested.

3. Related to Students' Learning Goals. Another feature of genre-based assessment is that the relevance of the test tasks and materials to the learners' goals helps to promote motivation and to provide a more accurate judgment of learners' ability to function in target situations. Because genre-based writing programs are based on an analysis of the students' real-world needs and the kinds of genres they will encounter in future academic, social, or workplace contexts, tests can mimic the ways texts are used in those situations. This means not only drawing on authentic texts such as memos, diagrams, lectures, and so on as input materials but also allowing students to perform tasks independently under conditions that simulate the actual use of the genre as closely as possible. While teachers may be constrained here by institutional requirements for formal exams, such assessment actually means that there is no need for learners to write under timed writing conditions unless those are the conditions under which the genre is used in real life.

4. Allowing Identification of Competencies. By assessing students against explicit criteria and integrating teaching with assessment, genre-based assessment makes clear to students what teachers value in writing and emphasizes exactly what is expected from them in any writing task. In achievement assessment, teachers evaluate a text according to a set of criteria that identifies what each writer should be able to do at the end of a teaching cycle, specifying such competencies as purpose, discourse structure, grammar, etc. Because these descriptions identify the key features of the genre, they also allow teachers to decide whether such features are adequately handled in any particular text and can serve to scaffold student writing in diagnostic assessment, providing teachers with detailed information for teaching purposes. Such competency descriptions provide a clear framework for feedback and revision and allow teachers to target writing weaknesses precisely, with obvious advantages for writing improvement.

Moreover, by teachers introducing these criteria early in the course and reinforcing them explicitly through teaching, students are able to see the properties their teachers value in writing and how their writing will be assessed. This encourages students to view their writing critically and with an understanding of what constitutes an effectively written text in a given situation, bearing in mind the writer's purpose in using the genre, the social context in which it is produced, and the expectations and knowledge of those who will read it.

5. *Ensuring that Students Are Best Prepared for Assessment.* Because genre-based writing courses strongly support and provide scaffolding for students, teachers can ensure that assessment tasks are only administered when learners are ready and likely to succeed. In SFL approaches, for instance, the teaching-learning cycle allows learners to move toward increasing independence in using a particular genre as the teacher gradually removes support. This enables ongoing diagnostic assessments to be made that help teachers to identify areas where learners need extra practice and to target additional teaching to assist them. Achievement assessment can then occur at the end of each cycle, when students are at their most competent in using a particular genre and are most confident and comfortable with their writing. So, the writing abilities of students are gradually stretched until they can achieve successful independent performance in the genre, and this means that teachers can make the transition from teaching to assessment as seamless as possible. This works to establish a writing environment rather than a grading environment in the classroom.

Key Principles of Genre-Based Assessment

While there are a number of different approaches to genre-based assessment, they typically have some general features in common that help them to realize these advantages (see also Macken & Slade, 1993; Feez, 1998):

1. The assessment *criteria* should be made explicit to students in terms they can understand as early in the course as possible. These are then used to scaffold and support students and become achievable target outcomes for the course.
2. The assessment *method* and the conditions under which they will be assessed should be explained to learners. Students should be aware of the number and kinds of writing that they will have to do—timed writing, homework assignments, portfolio, etc.
3. The assessment should employ *criteria-referenced* scales that describe necessary competencies to select and effectively create a genre using appropriate social knowledge and language features. The focus is therefore on learning outcomes—what students can do—rather than on ways of teaching.
4. The assessment should meet conditions of *validity* by being directly related to the genres students have studied, a feature that also implies relevance, usefulness, and a foundation in real-world writing practices.
5. The assessment should be *reliable* in that all assessors are in overall agreement on the criteria and how they will be applied. This implies a degree of rater training, if more than one teacher is involved, to aim at consistent scoring.
6. There should be regular *diagnostic assessments* to monitor progress, identify student strengths and weaknesses, help explain why problems may be occurring, and suggest the teaching intervention that may be needed.
7. Where possible, *students should be involved* in diagnostic assessments so they can develop techniques for critical reflection and for peer and self-assessment. This is most effectively done through assembling a portfolio collection or providing a checklist of criteria for learners to appraise their own performance (or that of their peers) and move toward independent performance.

8. Achievement assessment should take place at the *end of a cycle of learning* or after experience of working independently to create a genre to ensure learners' best performance.
9. Students should receive *feedback* on all assessment tasks in order to point out their strengths, the progress they have made, and what they need to do to improve their performance further.
10. The assessment should be reported in terms that are *understandable* to the potential users of the results (e.g., students, teachers, administrators, employers, parents, etc.).

Perhaps most important, writing teachers should recognize that they are testing knowledge not of formulaic structures but of the underlying mechanisms that enable effective communication to take place. Genre-based teaching is not a prescriptive enterprise—it is a critical and evaluative activity in the creation of more effective communication skills. As a result, a major concern is to make clear to teachers and students how the genre will vary according to topic, purpose, audience, and context.

Some Examples of Genre-Based Assessments

As mentioned earlier, there are several ways that genre-based assessments can be implemented in the second language classroom, and this section briefly discusses a few of these.

Providing Broad Outlines: Writing Frames and Story Plans

At a general level, assessment criteria can provide broad principles for identifying appropriate text structure to ensure that students are effectively incorporating the genre into their independent writing. These criteria are often the guidelines that have been offered to students to help them plan and write the genre during the course and that have served to scaffold their evolving control of the genre. This makes teacher evaluations transparent to learners and helps them to see what improvements are needed in their writing. Here, then, teachers can turn to the writing frames devised by Wray and Lewis (1997) and discussed in Chapter 5 or to the typical genre sequences presented in Table 2.2 in Chapter 2. These are simple means to ensure that students have understood the ways that information can be consciously structured and perhaps assist with their development toward more effective writing. Figure 6.1 gives some examples of such basic frames.

Slightly more elaborate genre descriptions than frames are *story plans.* Figure 6.2 shows a plan for a narrative suggested by Knapp and Watkins (1994) that indicates how narratives are structured to be entertaining and are organized around the ways characters confront and resolve a disruption of their normal events. Once again, these structural plans can be used to provide criteria that can, in turn, help scaffold learning, diagnose student performance, or assess achievement.

Genre	Structure	Example
Recount	Orientation—a scene-setting opening	*I went on a visit to the museum.*
	Sequenced record of events	*I sat with my friend on the bus; we saw . . .*
	Reorientation—closing statement	*When we got back, we wrote about it.*
Procedure	Goal—statement of what is to be achieved	*How to make a fruit cake.*
	List of materials/equipment needed	*Two eggs, flour, etc.*
	Series of sequenced steps to achieve goal	*First grease and line a cake pan.*
	Result—the look of the final state	*The cake will be a rich brown color.*
Discussion	Statement of the issue to be discussed	*Should we wear a school uniform?*
	Arguments for, plus supporting evidence	*Parents think it is a smart way to dress.*
	Arguments against, plus supporting evidence	*It can be expensive for poor families.*
	Recommendation (summary or conclusion)	*I think we should wear whatever we like.*

Fig. 6.1. Brief structural criteria for assessing some common school genres

Theme: *The Fight*
Orientation: *It all started when I was walking home from school.*
    Characters: Descriptions:
      • *Piggy*   *an ugly tough boy*
      • *Kelly*   *his friend*
      •
    Where: *in the street*
    When: *after school*
Complications: *two boys started to call me names*
    Events:
      • *Piggy punched me on the shoulder.*
      • *Kelly grabbed my bag.*
      • *I lost my temper and hit Kelly.*
    Reflection:
      • *This was a silly thing to do as it made me feel stupid.*
      •
Resolution: *The boys ran away.*

Fig. 6.2. A story plan for narratives (Knapp & Watkins, 1994, p. 152)

Systemic Functional Writing Assessments

Teachers using an SFL framework have found this way of look-ing at language to be a useful tool for analyzing texts, both to establish the relevance of a genre to particular groups of stu-dents and to assess student achievement (e.g., Butt et al., 2000). Writing from this perspective, for instance, Macken and Slade (1993, p. 205) argue that "an effective language assess-ment program must be linguistically principled, explicit, cri-terion-referenced, and must inform different types of assess-ment." In an SFL model, the grammar provides explicit criteria for designing writing courses and assessing students' devel-oping control of a genre. The specification of genre features al-lows teachers to conduct diagnostic assessments to determine the genres and contexts that students need and that will guide the course, to offer useful and intelligible feedback on writing, and to form the basis of explicit assessment criteria.

In an introductory book on functional grammar, for in-stance, Butt et al. (2000) provide a number of genre descrip-tions, together with L1 student examples, that are useful for teachers interested in employing genre criteria against which to assess their students' writing. Figure 6.3, for example, shows a detailed description of the narrative genre. Rather than vague descriptors often found in analytic scoring rubrics,

Structural elements	Textual features	Grammatical features	Student sample
Orientation (obligatory) Sets up what is to follow by introducing who, where, when—i.e., setting and narrator	Reference —Looks forward to foreshadow disruption of normal events —Out into the context (*I*) —Time conjunction (*when*)	Dependent time clause (*when I was walking home from school*) with circumstances of place (*home from school*) to build setting Past tense with complete (*happened*) and incomplete (*walking*) aspects	It all happened when I was walking home from school.
Complication (obligatory) —Sequence of events disrupted, creating a problem or crisis for participants —Characters evaluate problematic events to give them significance	References —Track main characters (*two twits, they, I, me,* etc.) —Refers back to sections of text (*this*) Conjunction —Series of clauses in temporal sequence (*while, and, when*) —Signals crisis point (*but*) Appraisal —Repetition to build up suspense —Expression of attitude (*stupid, harmless, sore*)	Clauses combined in different ways, i.e., expansion, projection, non-finite and finite dependent, embedded clauses as participants Main theme participants (*two twits, they, I*) Sequences of past-tense material processes (*rode, kicked, jumped, took off*) Past-tense verbal processes (*started yelling*) Past-tense mental processes (*decided to, didn't mind, made me sore, gave in to my temper*) Past-tense relational processes (*was*) to evaluate events, to slow action, and to build suspense	Two twits from my class decided to pick on me. They started yelling stupid names like spazzo, pigface, etc. I didn't mind this. I also didn't mind Kelly punching me in the shoulder. What I did mind was that Kelly kept me occupied while Matthew (better known as Roberts) rode my bike around the cul de sac of the street. This was harmless. But, still riding, he kicked off my bag and jumped off the bike leaving it to fall. This made me sore. I gave in to my temper. When Matthew saw this he took off.
Resolution (obligatory) Problem resolved; normal events resume	Conjunction —Causal (*so*) signals beginning of resolution of crisis —Temporal sequence (*when, finally, and*)	Sequence of past-tense material processes in quick succession (*chased, caught up, threw, missed, managed to escape, run*)	So it was me and David Kelly to battle it out. I chased him around and around the street. When I finally caught up to him I threw punches galore. Most of them missed. Kelly managed to escape and run home.
Coda (optional) —Shows how characters have been changed by events —Evaluates whole incident	Conjunction —Counter expectancy (*but*)	Mental process (*think*) Relational process to evaluate (*was*) Expressions of attitude (*victor, worth it*)	I think I was the victor, but if I was, I don't think it was worth it.

Fig. 6.3. Description of narrative structure with sample student text (Butt et al., 2000, pp. 225–226)

such as "moderate knowledge of syntax" or "a limited variety of mostly correct sentences," this model offers a clear picture of what counts as evidence for fulfilling basic genre requirements for an effective text. The student example provides a benchmark or "anchor text" that exemplifies features of the criteria, which can contribute to uniform assessment by helping raters to judge texts in the same way.

An SFL genre-based approach underlies the most widely used TESOL curriculum framework in Australia, the *Certificate of Spoken and Written English*. This framework offers a systematic approach to the planning and teaching of English language literacy courses for adult immigrants to assist them in developing communication skills to participate in Australian society. At the heart of this framework is a notion of teaching and assessment based on *competencies*. These are descriptions of learner outcomes, or what students should be able to do at the end of a course, stated in terms of the learners operating in a language context and using knowledge, learning strategies, and linguistic skills. They are statements that help teachers to assess *achievement*. Each competency is expressed in the following terms:

- **Elements**—the essential linguistic features of the genre and context knowledge
- **Performance criteria**—the observable characteristics of performance a student must achieve
- **Range statements**—the conditions for assessment, detailing the length of performance, the degree of teacher assistance, and the resources a student can use
- **Evidence guide**—the kinds of tasks through which students display their competence

Figure 6.4 shows a competency statement for *Can write a report* (NSW AMES, 1998), which is a written competency in the Further Study component of the Level III materials. This statement is designed for adult migrants but can be adapted for other situations quite easily, by either varying the range statements or modifying the competencies, to judge transitional levels of performance.

Elements	Performance criteria	Range statements	Evidence guide
Discourse structure			***Sample tasks***
1. Can use appropriate staging	Structures texts with appropriate beginning, middle, and end	Approximately 200 words Topic relevant to learner	Learners write a factual report on, for example: — an aspect of state/national education
2. Can organize factual information into coherent paragraphs	Writes coherent paragraphs containing factual, clearly organized information	Recourse to dictionary	— own areas of expertise or profession
3. Can use appropriate cohesive links	Links ideas cohesively using, for example, conjunction and reference	Time limit of one hour Learner may draft and self-correct within time limit	— other topic of personal choice, e.g., ecology, accounting, running a business, birdwatching, the migration experience
4. Can use generic reference	Uses reference to refer to general categories as required, e.g., people		
Grammar and Vocabulary		May include a few graphological and grammatical errors, but these should not interfere with meaning or dominate text	
5. Can use appropriate vocabulary	Uses appropriate vocabulary		
6. Can use appropriate grammatical structures	Uses grammatical structures appropriately, e.g., simple present and other tenses as required, passive forms	Access to relevant notes	

Fig. 6.4. Competency statement for *Certificate in Spoken and Written English* (level III) *Can write a report* (NSW AMES, 1998)

Task: Write a factual recount of your visit to the university language center last week. Remember that the purpose of a factual recount is to "tell what happened," so be sure to include the main things you saw and did and who you met. You can use your notes and photographs to help you.

Model structure: Orientation ^   Record of events ^   (Reorientation)

Score	Content	Structure	Language
36–50	Event explicitly stated Clearly documents events Evaluates their significance Personal comment on events	Orientation gives all essential information All necessary background provided Account in chronological/other order Reorientation "rounds off" sequence.	Excellent control of language Excellent use of vocabulary Excellent choice of grammar Appropriate tone and style
26–35	Event fairly clearly stated Includes most events Some evaluation of events Some personal comment	Fairly well-developed orientation Most actors and events mentioned Largely chronological and coherent Reorientation "rounds off" sequence	Good control of language Adequate vocabulary choices Varied choice of grammar Mainly appropriate tone
16–25	Event only sketchy Clearly documents events Little or weak evaluation Inadequate personal comment	Orientation gives some information Some necessary background omitted Account partly coherent Some attempt to provide reorientation	Inconsistent language control Lack of variety in choice of grammar and vocabulary Inconsistent tone and style
1–15	Event not stated No recognizable events No or confused evaluation No or weak personal comment	Missing or weak orientation No background provided Haphazard and incoherent sequencing No reorientation or includes new matter	Little language control Reader seriously distracted by grammar errors Poor vocabulary and tone

Fig. 6.5. A scoring rubric for an elementary-level factual recount

Although criteria for achievement of this kind can assist teachers in making inferences about a writer's ability on an absolute scale, rather than relative to others, it is often necessary to provide more finely grained feedback or to report assessment grades on intermediate levels of performance that fall short of full competency. In such cases, scoring rubrics can be designed to provide separate scores for different features of the relevant task and genre, indicating common problems and levels of acceptable writing for different grades. Figure 6.5 shows an example rubric for assessing a factual recount.

ESP Writing Assessments

Like many teaching approaches in ESP, assessment practices have been greatly influenced by John Swales's (1990) move structure description of academic research article introductions, discussed in Chapter 2 and illustrated by Yakhontova's (2002) analysis of conference abstracts, as shown in Fig 2.6. A further example is provided by Coffin et al.'s (2003) structural description of a common form of writing in undergraduate courses, the investigative project report (Fig. 6.6). Once again, such broad outlines provide a first step in making writing expectations explicit during teaching and assessment. The conventions of particular genres can be illustrated using example texts, perhaps written by previous students, that exemplify good practice and pointing out the features of these examples used to measure students' progress in their writing. A structural description such as the following can also be used to encourage students to take greater responsibility for their learning through self-assessment as it provides explicit criteria that enable them to offer informed comments on their performance when submitting an assignment.

While this kind of structural description can help teachers and learners focus on academic and generic conventions, more detailed analytic criteria can encourage teachers to reflect on specific features of writing quality and to grade papers more delicately. The scoring rubric for an argumentative essay shown in Figure 6.7, for instance, provides criteria that may be more useful as diagnostic and teaching tools as the explicit descriptors provide a clear framework for feedback and revision.

Functional stage	Description
Aims	A full account of what you were trying to find out and why it was important
Literature review	A discussion of the ideas that are relevant to your project. This should show that you understand the relevant background issues and theories.
Methodology	This should be a description of the methods used and will include any alterations that become necessary during the investigation. Your choice of method should be drawn from or build upon the literature review.
Conduct of the investigation	Here you should describe the context in which the work was carried out and give a concise account of what was done. Explain how you addressed any critical issues. It may be written as a first-person narrative or more formally.
Findings	Give the results of the investigation. How do these relate to issues in the literature? Present examples from the data collected to illustrate your points.
Evaluation	Consider the outcome of the project in relation to the initial aims and questions. Are there ways it could be changed and improved if carried out again? What kinds of further investigation could extend the work?
References	A list of all sources quoted or drawn upon in the project
Appendixes	Additional data or analysis that supports your aims and findings

Fig. 6.6. A move structure of the investigative project report (Coffin et al., 2003, p. 23)

Score	Format and content 40 points
31–40 *excellent to very good*	Fulfills task fully; correct convention for the assignment task; features of target genre mostly adhered to; good ideas/good use of relevant information; substantial concept use; properly developed ideas; good sense of audience
21–30 *good to average*	Fulfills task quite well, although details may be underdeveloped or partly irrelevant; correct genre selected; most features of chosen genre adhered to; satisfactory ideas with some development; quite good use of relevant information; some concept use; quite good sense of audience
11–20 *fair to poor*	Generally adequate but some inappropriate, inaccurate, or irrelevant data; an acceptable convention for the assignment task; some features of chosen genre adhered to; limited ideas/moderate use of relevant information; little concept use; barely adequate development of ideas; poor sense of audience
1–10 *inadequate*	Clearly inadequate fulfillment of task; possibly incorrect genre for the assignment; chosen genre not adhered to; omission of key information, serious irrelevance or inaccuracy; very limited ideas/ignores relevant information; no concept use; inadequate development of ideas; poor or no sense of audience

Score	Organization and coherence 20 points
16–20 *excellent to very good*	Message followed with ease; well-organized and thorough development through introduction, body, and conclusion; relevant and convincing supporting details; logical progression of content contributes to fluency; unified paragraphs; effective use of transitions and references
11–15 *good to average*	Message mostly followed with ease; satisfactorily organized and developed through introduction, body, and conclusion; relevant supporting details; mostly logical progression of content; moderate to good fluency; unified paragraphs; possible slight over- or underuse of transitions but correctly used; mostly correct references
6–10 *fair to poor*	Message followed but with some difficulty; some pattern of organization—an introduction, body and conclusion evident but poorly done; some supporting details; progression of content inconsistent or repetitious; lack of focus in some paragraphs; over- or under use of transitions with some incorrect use; incorrect use of references
1–5 *inadequate*	Message difficult to follow; little evidence of organization—introduction and conclusion may be missing; few or no supporting details; no obvious progression of content; improper paragraphing; no or incorrect use of transitions; lack of references contributes to comprehension difficulty

Score	Sentence construction and vocabulary 40 points
31–40 *excellent to very good*	Effective use of a wide variety of correct sentences; variety of sentence length; effective use of transitions; no significant errors in agreement, tense, number, person, articles, pronouns, and prepositions; effective use of a wide variety of lexical items; word form mastery; effective choice of idiom; correct register
21–30 *good to average*	Effective use of a variety of correct sentences; some variety of length; use of transitions with only slight errors; no serious recurring errors in agreement, tense, number, person, articles, pronouns, and prepositions; almost no sentence fragments or run-ons; variety of lexical items with some problems but not causing comprehension difficulties; good control of word form; mostly effective idioms; correct register
11–20 *fair to poor*	A limited variety of mostly correct sentences; little variety of sentence length; improper use of or missing transitions; recurring grammar errors are intrusive; sentence fragments or run-ons evident; a limited variety of lexical items occasionally causing comprehension problems; moderate word form control; occasional inappropriate choice of idiom; perhaps incorrect register
1–10 *inadequate*	A limited variety of sentences requiring considerable effort to understand; correctness only on simple short sentences; improper use of or missing transitions; many grammar errors and comprehension problems; frequent incomplete or run-on sentences; a limited variety of lexical items; poor word forms; inappropriate idioms; incorrect register

Fig. 6.7. A scoring rubric for an argumentative essay

Portfolio Assessment

An approach to assessment well-suited to genre-based writing teaching is the use of portfolios. Portfolios are multiple writing samples, written over time and purposefully selected to best represent a student's abilities, progress, or most successful texts in a particular context. Portfolio evaluation reflects the practice of most writing courses, where students use readings and other sources of information as a basis for writing and where they revise and resubmit their assignments after receiving feedback from teachers or peers. The texts are typically selected by students, often in consultation with a teacher, and comprise four to six core items in categories that reflect the goals of the writing course. They can serve to either showcase a student's best work or display a collection of both drafts and final products to demonstrate process and improvement. Each piece of work initially contributes diagnostic information to teachers and student writers, and finished work is selected for inclusion in the portfolio to receive a final achievement grade. Figure 6.8 is an example of a rubric for a portfolio assessment in an academic writing class.

timed in-class argumentative essay
> Reflection questions for brief response: What is the structure of this essay? What do you particularly like about the essay? What are you most dissatisfied with?

research project (including drafts and materials leading to the final paper)
> What difficulties did you encounter writing this? What did you learn from writing it?

critical summary (of a reading)
> Why did you select this article to summarize? What is the structure of your summary? Why is it organized like this?

writer's choice (any text of your choice written by you at any time)
> What is this? When did you write it? Why did you choose it? What does it say about you?

n overall reflection of the portfolio (a letter to the teacher integrating the entries)
> What were the goals of this course? How does each entry help to achieve these goals?

Fig. 6.8. A portfolio assessment for a genre-based undergraduate academic writing class

Portfolios have the advantage of increasing the validity of assessments through multiple samples and ensuring that evaluation washes back into teaching. Hamp-Lyons and Condon (2000) point out that portfolios strongly support pedagogies that involve multi-drafting, revision, peer review, collaborative learning, and reflective writing. Reflection, in fact, is actually one of the main advantages of portfolios. As a result of assembling their texts over time, students are able to observe changes in their work, compare different genres and writing experiences, and reflect on their writing and the criteria employed for judging it. It is therefore an assessment that promotes greater responsibility for writing (Purves et al., 1995). Many portfolios, such as the one described in Figure 6.8, therefore include a reflective essay or letter that introduces the portfolio, justifies and links the entries, and perhaps relates them to the goals of the course.

In genre-based writing courses, portfolios help to link the products of different teaching-learning cycles or the different genres that have formed the focus of the course. They therefore not only represent multiple measures of a student's writing ability, providing more accurate assessments of competence across a range of genres, but also help students to understand more about the genres they have studied. Multi-genre portfolios, perhaps including both narrative and expository genres, can highlight how texts are organized differently to express particular purposes. Alternatively, a portfolio can illustrate how one genre often relates to or interacts with others as part of a routine sequence or "genre set," as discussed in Chapter 4, such as when students assemble all the genres for a formal job application. Because the criteria used for assessment have been made explicit, students can use these criteria to select pieces for the portfolio and to understand more clearly the connection between what they are taught and how they are assessed. For teachers, this also provides more information about students' progress to help them give greater support to writers.

Scoring a portfolio presents its own difficulties, however, and the heterogeneous nature of what is being assessed may make it harder to ensure reliability across raters and rating occasions than is the case with a single piece of writing. Standardizing a single score to fairly express a student's ability from a variety of genres, tasks, drafts, and perhaps different subject discipline material can be extremely difficult. However, the use of explicit genre descriptions and competency statements can help make the grading process much smoother and fairer.

Diagnostic Assessment and Feedback

It should be clear from the scoring rubrics, competency statements, and assessment guides given as examples in this chapter that achievement assessment can also serve *formative,* or diagnostic, purposes, allowing teachers to respond to student writing and to reinforce and extend their instructional programs. It can also be seen that the study of grammar is regarded as an integral part of writing and of learning to write. In order to use language effectively in social contexts, to engage with others, express purposes, and convey ideas, it is necessary not only for students to have something to say, to generate *content,* but also for them to have *ways of saying it.* They need to see how language choices relate to different situations, and this involves learning about language, both through teaching and through targeted feedback as an integrated part of the exploration of texts and contexts. Using language in this way, to talk about texts, allows teachers and learners to see, describe, and evaluate the kinds of meanings that students are trying to express in their writing and to help them do this more effectively.

Research on feedback, however, has been discouraging. It suggests that students often find teacher comments unclear, confusing, inconsistent, or vague (e.g., Hyland & Hyland, 2001; Zamel, 1985). In a survey of the L1 literature, Knoblauch and Brannon (1981, p. 165) conclude that "commenting on student essays might just be an exercise in futility. Either students do not read the comments or they read them and do not attempt to implement suggestions and correct errors."

The value of error correction as an element of teacher feedback is a particularly controversial issue. Responding to error is a key element of process approaches to teaching writing, and it is the point where teachers typically intervene to introduce the forms students need. Truscott's (1996) much quoted review of the literature on student response, however, concluded that error correction is ineffective in improving student writing. Students often revise their texts with no real understanding of why the changes are necessary, and in many cases, deletions are not rephrased, so that original ideas are lost rather than amplified or rewritten. It is possible, therefore, that feedback contributes little to students' longer-term writing development, and because of this, teachers are often encouraged to focus on issues of meaning and the process of writing, rather than on genre features of form and organization.

Despite these rather depressing views, teacher-written feedback has been found to be highly valued by second language writers (F. Hyland, 1998), and many learners particularly favor feedback on their grammar (Leki, 1990). Error-free work is often a major concern for L2 writers, possibly because of prior learning experiences and the fact that many of them will go on to be evaluated in academic and workplace settings where accuracy may be essential. ESL students, therefore, usually welcome and expect teacher comment on their errors; this is largely supported by the fact that they try to make use of the feedback they are given (F. Hyland, 1998). Moreover, the view that there is no direct connection between correction and learning is greatly overstated. Most feedback-linked revisions seem to result in both improvements to the current text and a reduction in errors in later assignments (Ferris, 2002). Master (1995), for instance, found that corrective grammar feedback was appreciated by students and was effective when combined with classroom discussions while Fathman and Whalley (1990) discovered that texts improved most when students received feedback on *both* content and form. It seems, therefore, that it is not feedback itself that is the problem, but how it is provided.

By integrating teaching and assessment, genre-based writing programs have the potential to overcome many of these problems. The provision of explicit genre descriptions, scaffolded writing practice, and a language for discussing texts means that feedback can be provided that closely relates suggestions for improvement to what students have learned. Teachers can therefore refer back to specific knowledge and strategies and can respond from a position of shared knowledge with students concerning what writing the genre requires, rather than simply offering decontextualized and ad hoc reactions to error.

Teachers should not respond just to grammar issues, however, but to whole texts and all aspects of student writing: to structure, organization, style, content, and presentation. But this does not mean it is necessary to cover every aspect on every draft. Those instructors using the teaching-learning cycle can focus their feedback on different aspects of the genre in successive iterations of the cycle, for instance, or hold group sessions to discuss common problems with specific students. The main benefit lies in the fact that because they are using the same terminology and targeting the same key features that were introduced to learners during the scaffolded stages of writing, they can offer feedback with greater confidence that students will recognize and make use of their suggestions. Moreover, teachers are also able to report in detail what students know and can do with language, and this can, in turn, wash back into the design of future courses or the next cycle.

In genre-based instruction, then, feedback is given to support students' writing development in systematic ways, reinforcing genre knowledge, community conventions, and suggestions for improvement. One example of how these expectations are communicated to ESL learners is suggested by the computer program BRIDGE, used with Civil Engineering students at the Papua New Guinea University of Technology (Marshall, 1991).

The program is designed to assist teachers in creating useful feedback for students on their reports, which describe the design and testing of model bridges. It is based on a formal schema for the genre of feedback, as follows:

1. Giving a qualitative evaluation
2. Stating what the student did well
3. Suggesting what needs improvement
4. Explaining the improvements required
5. Reminding the student why it is important for the report to be written in this way
6. Giving a quantitative evaluation

The program contains:

- A scoring scheme, comprising a list of the main features of the report genre that should be present
- A list of the qualities required for each feature, together with comments about each
- A set of grade equivalencies for deriving qualitative comments from numerical evaluations
- A textual script for producing the feedback

The content of the feedback is created by the program, which prompts the teacher to indicate which items or qualities are present in the student's report and then, if they are present, if they need improvement. From this input, the computer makes a quantitative evaluation and produces a report. A sample report is shown in Figure 6.9. While the program does not reduce the teacher's marking workload, it does generate far more feedback, an average of three or four pages for each report, than would normally be possible, and it gives students more targeted information on their writing.

Genre-based feedback, therefore, not only justifies a grade, if one is given, but helps students to see what lies beyond the grade and provides them with the means of improving on it. But genre assessments typically involve more than simply as-

Wallace Moromoro

Below are comments about the effectiveness of your BRIDGE REPORT. On your report, you will find red circles where mistakes in English occur. Please correct these to obtain extra points.

Title page   This is good—you included the title, who wrote it, and when it was completed. It would be better to also include:
    o   who it is for—this is a sort of distribution list

Contents page   I think this is very good—you included the list of sections and page numbers

Summary   Could be much improved. You included the important points and the conclusions and recommendation. But you should also include:
    o   the purposes—what exactly are you seeking to do?
Maybe you could also look again at the following:
    o   the important points—this should contain a brief description of what was done and found
    o   the conclusions and recommendation—what are the main ones that the decision maker needs to know quickly? They should be specific.
Don't forget, the summary allows readers to decide whether or not to read the whole report, focuses their attention on important points, and enables decision makers to obtain essential information quickly.

Introduction   I think this is quite good—you included the background to the project and the purposes. But you should also include:
    o   the plan of the report—create a "map" for the reader

Aims   I think this is not bad—they are satisfactorily expressed. But they should also be:
    o   listed and numbered—include the most important aims and number them for reference
Don't forget—it is important to show that you understand the purpose of the tests.

Materials   Very pleased to see you included the equipment used and the materials used.

Procedure   This is good—you included the bridge, design, reasons for the design, the construction, and the testing method.

Test results   Not bad—you included observations and comparisons. However, you should also include:
    o   calculations—e.g., show your calculations of the bridge rating
    o   interpretations—how do you account for the difference in performance of the bridges?
Please remember that this section describes what you observed and what your interpretations are, i.e., your evidence. It therefore gives credibility to your report.

Visual aids   I think this is good—they are well drawn, labeled, captioned, and numbered. They should also:
    o   be suitably placed in the text and referred to

Conclusions   Could be much improved—they are relative to the aims. However, they should also be:
    o   expressed as a checklist—dot points or numbers are best here
    o   comprehensive—you should cover all the aims stated
Remember this section summarizes the results and so focuses the mind of the reader.

Recommendation I like this—you included consideration of strength and consideration of cost.

Overall score: 12 out of 20

Fig. 6.9. Output of computerized feedback for Civil Engineering report (Marshall, 1991)

signing grades and offering feedback on form. Finding an appropriate structure and expression for what you have to say is only part of the story, for in the real world, there is the significant matter of engaging with a live audience. An essential aspect of ESP teaching is that students are asked not merely to master a group of relevant genres but to better understand the rich contexts of an academic or professional culture. Students need to process and understand disciplinary discourses on their own terms, by drawing from their other community memberships and from experts in the field, and by discussing the role of communities in shaping successful texts.

The role of gatekeepers and the influences of community hierarchies can be rich sources of material for discussion in these circumstances and encourage student reflection and self-evaluation. Figure 6.10 shows an amended activity from Swales and Feak (2000) that requires graduate students to devise the qualities they would look for as members of a conference program committee reviewing abstracts in their field. These qualities, produced by students themselves, result from learners reflecting on the values of their discipline and considering vital contextual information in writing. These points, therefore, provide criteria to help them write and evaluate genres that are important to them.

Diagnostic and formative assessment are no less important to instruction in systemic functional approaches. Feez (1998) provides a good example of the close integration of assessment and teaching in this model, offering a set of general criteria that allows teachers to assess students' abilities to work

Composition theory	Mechanical engineering	Environmental science
Topics of current community interest	Novelty, originality	Urgency of the problem
Clearly defined problem	Applicability	Good supporting data
Problem addressed in novel way	Completeness	Applicable to real world
Current or "buzzy" terminology	Hot topic	
References to scholarly literature		

Fig. 6.10. Contextual factors for abstract criteria (based on Swales & Feak, 2000, pp. 38–39)

with whole texts and that can be fine-tuned for particular genres (Fig. 6.11). Teachers can use this kind of checklist to respond to writers directly, through feedback that precisely targets problem areas for effective revisions and additional learning, and indirectly, through modifications to their teaching. Feez (1998, pp. 132–135) then shows how this checklist was used to analyze an ESL learner's text, a short description of the adult migrant writer's home country (Fig. 6.12). This provides explicit language criteria to assess the class members' scripts and to identify the remedial action required in the next teaching-learning cycle—a set of objectives to teach the class to write a short description (Fig. 6.13).

rpose and staging	Has the purpose been achieved, even partially?
	Is the staging contributing to or detracting from achievement of the purpose?
xt unity	Is the text made cohesive through the use of:
	- lexical sets, to do with both the field and the writer's attitude
	- conjunction
	- reference
	- distribution of information across paragraphs and clauses
ause grammar	Are noun groups, verb groups, and prepositional phrases put together to construct effective single-clause sentences? Consider:
	- use of declarative, interrogative, and imperative forms
	- use of doing, thinking and speaking, feeling and perceiving, being and having processes (verb groups) and accompanying participants (noun groups) and circumstances (prepositional phrases)
	- use of theme/first position in the clause to establish what the message is concerned with and placement of new information at the end of the clause
oups/words	Consider the learner's control of:
	- verb groups (verb forms, tense, voice, modals, number, agreement)
	- noun groups (plurals, articles, numeratives, describers, qualifiers)
	- prepositional phrases (use of prepositions with noun groups)
	- vocabulary sets related to field (specific/general, concrete/technical/abstract, nominalizations, describing words and phrases) and attitude (intensified words and phrases, expressions of modality, describing words and phrases)
aphology	Consider the learner's control of:
	- spelling
	- punctuation
	- layout

Fig. 6.11. An assessment checklist for beginning ESL writers (Feez, 1998, p. 131)

Student text:

General statement   *I wos born in Bosnia.*

Description   *My sity is Sarajevo. My Sity Lived 600,000 People. Sarajevo*
~~havenit~~ have many fobriks. I hove in ~~Bosnia~~ 4, cisters and 2
~~brab~~ 2 braders. Mo fomily. My ~~Sr~~. contry have ma live and
montes. Darajevo have Olipics centrum for vimda. Thse
mountains. Are vry wndfl lo snowgl deatiful especly one son. ~~I~~
~~Imane abhter an one son~~, I hve ane dohta o. one con,

Analysis:

Purpose and staging   - Purpose achieved, but staging could be improved by previewing subtopics in
general statement and keeping them in order in the description stage.

Text unity   - Needs more lexis for subtopics (*weather, cities, family*).
- Needs basic linking words and practice in using them (*also, so*).
- Needs more personal attitude words to give overall impression of author's
feelings about the country, city and family (*beautiful, huge, impressive*).
- Needs more pronouns for reference and practice in using them (*it, this, they*).

Clause grammar   - Needs practice with constructing effective single-clause sentences.
- Can construct declarative. Make subject/finite order explicit for interrogative.
- Information distributed erratically. Assist with techniques to order information
(*there are*, theme/given information at beginning and new information at the end)
- Uses mainly *being* and *having* verbs as appropriate to genre, but needs some
thinking/feeling/perceiving verbs.
- Only one circumstance used (*in Bosnia*). Assist to construct more appropriate
to genre (location in time and place, of manner, etc.).

Groups and words   - Needs more resources and practice with simple past and present verbs.
- Model and practice *it + present continuous* for weather descriptions.
- Develop use of noun groups so more adjectives can be used.
- Develop prepositional phrases to augment circumstances.
- Needs to build vocabulary sets related to field (factories, relevant
geographical words, family words) and attitudinal and descriptive words.

Graphology   - Needs spelling strategies and practice as part of vocabulary building.
- Punctuation appropriate.
- Immature layout. Model basic paragraphing to complement text structure.
- Immature script; needs handwriting practice. Discuss print vs. cursive.

Fig. 6.12. Sample analysis of learner descriptive text using genre criteria
(Feez, 1998, pp. 132–134)

Assessment Tasks

Finally, a few words about task design in L2 writing assessment. This is a large topic and is more fully covered elsewhere (e.g., Hyland, 2003; Weigle, 2002), but it is worth drawing at-

Goal

• To enable learners to write a short description of the place/country they come from

Objectives

• The learners will discuss:
- different uses of written descriptions, e.g., postcards to friends, class book to contribute to a teaching center open house
- the things they would like people in Australia to know about the place/country they come from

• The learners will:
- build vocabulary for describing places
- learn to spell the words they collect

• The learners will build knowledge of:
- the structure of a short description
- strategies for categorizing and organizing information
- the language features used for describing, i.e., noun groups, *being* and *having* verbs, personal pronouns, simple phrases with noun and verb groups and circumstances of place, using *and* to join simple clauses

• The learners will build handwriting and presentation skills.

• The learners will understand the writing process, i.e., preparing to write, drafting, conferencing, editing, proofreading, publishing.

• The learners will organize their writing materials and equipment effectively.

The teacher will:

• provide reference material for context building and text modeling, e.g., library visit, Internet, encyclopedias, books about the learner's country of origin, model texts

Fig. 6.13. Objectives for teaching the writing of a short description (Feez, 1998, p. 134)

tention to what a consideration of genre brings to this process. As we have seen, while genre-based assessments may serve different purposes, they are essentially concerned with measuring the extent to which students are able to construct particular genres effectively. By taking the importance of genre into account in task design, the designer ensures that the knowledge and skills to be tested are both clear and concrete, derived from a model of a particular kind of text and the particular linguistic and contextual knowledge that is required to produce it. Designing assessment writing tasks so that they are related to what has been taught, to students' future needs (as far as these can be determined), and to clear scoring criteria ensures that tasks will be relevant, achievable, fair, and (hopefully) interesting to student writers.

In practical terms, task design involves four basic elements: a rubric, a prompt, an expected response, and a post-task evaluation.

- **A rubric:** the instructions for carrying out the writing task. While the level of detail provided to students will vary, the information provided in genre assignments—both before the assessment, in prior learning, handouts, and practice activities, and in the rubric itself—is typically as explicit as possible. This information includes not only the genre to be used but also procedures for responding, the time allocated, the format expected, and the weight given to particular parts.
- **A prompt:** the stimulus the student must respond to. In genre assessments, prompts are generally quite detailed and situate the writer in a recognizable context. They will therefore include both contextual and input data (Douglas, 2000, p. 55), information that establishes the setting, participants, purpose, and so on and that provides the visual/aural material to be processed. In terms of response, students are usually required to interpret and respond to either a *situational frame* or a *text* (Kroll & Reid, 1994), as in the examples in Figure 6.14.
- **An expected response:** what the teacher intends students to do with the task. A consideration of genre in task design means that teachers have explicit criteria against which they can judge student performance on a task, and this helps them to be clear in their own minds regarding what they want from the assessment task and to communicate their requirements plainly to students. By providing rich input data and comprehensible prompts, teachers can elicit a certain response, generating discussion of a selected topic using appropriate language and generic structures. *Authenticity* is a key consideration of task design here as the prompt will seek to elicit the kind of writing students will be expected to do in the future. This means that the task (and genre) will vary with the students and the reasons they have for writing.

You are an official for the Ministry of Education. You have been asked to write an article for a
udent magazine in support of the view that university students should be required to pay for the
ll cost of their education. You expect your audience to disagree with you, so present the argument
a problem that your position will solve.

You have been a tenant in a small apartment for the last six months and have always paid your rent on
ne. There have been a number of problems with the apartment, but you have not complained. There is a
ak in the bedroom ceiling, the hot water system is faulty, and there is a bad smell from the drains.
ow you have just received a letter from your landlord saying that he wants to increase the rent.
rite a letter to persuade your landlord not to increase the rent.

You are the supervisor of a team of engineers responsible for on-call emergency repairs at a large
spital. Using the technicians' notes, telephone records, job entry sheets, and other data provided,
rite a one-page incident report for July 13.

With a partner, use the research data provided to produce a poster for a conference presentation.
onsider the title, organization, and layout of your poster, and decide on the information you will
lect and how you will present it. Remember to caption your diagrams and include the main
dings.

Fig. 6.14. Examples of framed and text-based prompts

- **A post-task evaluation:** an assessment of the effectiveness of the task. Task evaluation includes issues such as
  whether the task discriminated well among students,
  whether the products were easy to evaluate, and whether
  the students able to write to their potential (Reid & Kroll,
  1995). In a genre-based assessment, the teacher has to decide if the task is relevant to the course and to the students' real-world needs, if it provides clear specification
  of the required genre, if it suggests the appropriate tone
  and audience relationships, and if it avoids cultural bias
  and obscure knowledge.

To illustrate how tasks can relate to explicit assessment criteria in genre programs, Figure 6.15 presents two sample tasks
suggested for the report-writing competency criteria given in
Figure 6.4 and intended for adult immigrants seeking to engage in further study (NSW AMES, 1998).

Task 1. Graph: traveling to and from work

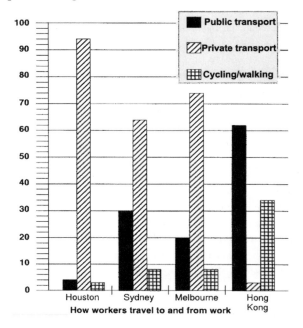

The graph shows the percentage of workers in Houston, Sydney, Melbourne, and Hong Kong who travel to and from work using public transport, private transport, or by walking or cycling. Write a report describing the data and the similarities and differences in the ways people get to and from work in the different cities. Suggest reasons for the similarities and differences. You may use your dictionary.

Length: approximately 200 words
Time Limit: one hour

Task 2.
Write a report on an Australian animal. You may want to write about some of the following features:

• appearance
• behaviors, including diet
• location and environment
• threats to animal's safety
• other factual information

You may use your dictionary.

Length: approximately 200 words
Time limit: one hour

Fig. 6.15. Sample assessment tasks for *Certificate in Spoken and Written English* (level III) *Can write a report* competency (NSW AMES, 1998)

Summary

Chapter 6 has addressed the issue of assessment and explored some principles and practices of genre-based writing assessment. A key feature of genre-based assessment is the use of clear and explicit criteria to evaluate student writing performance; this enables feedback and further instruction to target student needs precisely, establishing an integral relationship between teaching and assessment. The fact that the tasks students are asked to write reflect their learning experiences in the course and, as far as possible, their writing goals following it means that assessments may be seen as both relevant and authentic. Finally, since all written work is evaluated against explicit criteria that are linked to course content, students are in a better position to understand what counts as effective writing and to evaluate their own work, developing autonomy and independent learning skills. Key points of the chapter are:

1. Learners are assessed against explicit criteria based on the knowledge and skills (competencies) required to construct particular genres. These criteria should provide the basis for teaching, feedback, diagnostic intervention, and measuring achievement.
2. Tasks reflect the objectives of a course and relate to the writing skills and understandings that have been taught.
3. The use of explicit and agreed-upon scoring criteria— whether in the form of story plans, writing frames, competency statements, or analytic rubrics—helps to ensure that assessment tasks are reliable and valid, providing fair, consistent, transparent, and meaningful feedback and grading.
4. The integration of teaching and assessment means that feedback can be precisely targeted and made intelligible to students in terms of what they have learned about the genre.
5. Assessments should draw on clear and relevant contexts that are familiar to students and likely to relate to their real-world needs and experiences.

6. Assessment tasks need to specify clear instructions and requirements for completing the activity, as well as sufficient contextual and input material to make it meaningful and interesting.
7. Mixed-genre portfolios have advantages over single scripts since they provide students with an opportunity to demonstrate their abilities in different genres and their understanding of the writing process.

Once again, then, teaching writing using genre approaches emphasizes the importance of making known what is to be learned and assessed. Chapter 7 examines some of the ways that teachers and students can analyze written texts to discover their structure and features and to determine their relevance and suitability for particular groups of learners.

Tasks and Discussion Questions

1. Why are explicit criteria so important for teaching and assessment purposes? How do the examples of criteria given in this chapter relate to what you do in class? What would be your main concerns about adopting such criteria, and how could you address these?
2. Look again at the key principles of genre-based assessment listed in this chapter, and consider how you would apply these in a specific L2 writing course you have experience with. Can you envisage any problems in applying these principles? Which ones, and what problems? How would you deal with these difficulties?
3. Review one of the sets of assessment criteria given in this chapter, whether based on a story plan, move structure, text features, functional stages, or competencies. Consider its strengths and weaknesses for both diagnostic and achievement purposes. How might you use these criteria to assess the writing skills of a particular group of learners you are familiar with?

4. Do you think it is appropriate to include students' personal reflections on their learning and their understanding of writing practices as part of your assessment of their writing?

5. One of the main advantages claimed for genre-based writing assessment is that because the same genre criteria are used for both teaching and assessment, feedback can be precisely targeted and thus more useful and intelligible to learners. How far do you think this is true?

6. Write a rubric for a genre-based writing assessment task for either an imaginary group of students or a class you are familiar with. Consider how it relates to the four elements of task design, and explain why this is an appropriate task for the learners in terms of their needs and class objectives.

7. Devise a portfolio that would be an appropriate course assessment for a particular group of students you are familiar with. List the genres you would require students to include and the reflection questions they should respond to. Provide a written justification for your choices.

Chapter 7

Doing Genre Analysis

Previous chapters have focused on areas of theoretical and practical relevance to teachers interested in what genre approaches have to offer writing instruction: outlining what genre is, why it is useful, and how it has been applied in second language writing classrooms. We have not yet, however, looked in detail at how teachers, students, and researchers go about analyzing texts—that is, how we come to understand the ways genres are constructed and used. The identification and analysis of text features have not typically figured in second language writing instruction, and only recently have they started to appear in teacher-education courses. For these reasons, I have left them to the end of this book. Teachers may believe that they have enough to do already without adding text analysis as well, and they may even feel apprehensive at the prospect of it. But while analysis is often regarded as "research" and as removed from the everyday business of "teaching," it is, in fact, a very practical activity that is central to an awareness of how texts work and to bringing language into the teaching of writing.

This chapter, therefore, turns to look at texts more directly, to offer something of a practical guide for teachers on ways to research texts and contexts in order to help students gain greater control over their writing. First, I outline some basic features of genre analysis and then look briefly at how texts and their contexts can be analyzed and at some ways of using corpus tools in genre analysis.

What Is Genre Analysis?

Genre analysis is a branch of discourse analysis that explores specific uses of language. It is driven by a desire to understand the communicative character of discourse by looking at how individuals use language to engage in particular communicative situations. It then seeks to employ this knowledge to support language education.

Just as Chapter 2 showed that *genre* is understood and applied to teaching in different ways, there are also numerous ways to approach genre *analysis.* Some of these ways focus exclusively on text structure; some give greater attention to sociocultural factors; some closely examine the practices of writers; and others explore the expectations of readers (e.g., Hyland, 2002). Whatever the orientation, however, all genre analysts see language as a key feature of writing and as the way we create social contexts. Ultimately, all approaches share the same goal of adding to a model of language use that is rich in social, cultural, and institutional explanation; that links language to contexts; and that has practical relevance for teachers by offering useful ways of handling conventionalized aspects of texts.

Genre analysis is therefore a powerful tool to help teachers uncover connections between language and types of texts and between forms and functions, enabling us to offer students information and activities that raise their awareness of genres and perhaps make them better writers. But while we need to look at texts to understand how they work, genres are much more than texts. As Swales (1990) points out, focusing exclusively on the printed page does not tell us *why* genres have come to acquire certain features and not others. Genre analysts, therefore, look in various places to discover how private intentions have a public face, not only examining texts but also interviewing those who routinely use the genre and observing the ways texts are used. In sum, genre analysis seeks to:

- Identify how texts are structured in terms of functional stages or moves

- Identify the features that characterize texts and that help realize their communicative purposes
- Examine the understandings of those who write and read the genre
- Discover how the genre relates to users' activities
- Explain language choices in terms of social, cultural, and psychological contexts
- Provide insights for language teaching

Basic Principles for Conducting Genre Analysis

Bhatia (1993, pp. 22–34) suggests some basic steps for conducting genre analysis. While these steps are not designed specifically for teachers and may seem rather elaborate for classroom purposes, they nevertheless emphasize the importance of locating texts in contexts and of taking care to reflect on what is happening during analysis. Figure 7.1 shows an expanded version of Bhatia's steps.

1. Select a text that seems representative of the genre you intend to teach.

2. Place the text in a situational context—i.e., use your background knowledge and text clues to understand intuitively where the genre is used, who uses it, and why it is written the way it is.

3. Search the research literature or textbooks for ideas and insights into the working of the genre and the way it is conventionally structured and written.

4. Refine the situational analysis on the basis of this reading to more clearly identify users' goals, who the writers and readers are, the network of surrounding texts, and the context in which the genre is used.

5. Compare the text with other similar texts to ensure that it broadly represents the genre.

6. Study the institutional context in which the genre is used (through site visits, interviews, looking at rule books, manuals, etc.) to better understand the conventions that text users often follow.

7. Select one or more levels of analysis (looking at common vocabulary and grammar, types of cohesion, move structure, and so on), and analyze the key features.

8. Gather information from specialist informants, if possible, to confirm your findings and insights and to add psychological reality to the analysis.

Fig. 7.1. Steps in genre analysis (after Bhatia, 1993)

Different types of research methods lead to different types of understanding, but this outline provides a useful checklist to ensure that research doesn't lose sight of the essential link between texts and contexts. It encourages us to start with whole texts and to explore both the key features of the text and how these express particular functions. This helps us to identify what is distinctive about the text and, in EAP and ESP contexts, to reveal the preferences for certain kinds of expressions that writers in different disciplines or institutions might have.

Identifying and Analyzing Text Features

A good place to start when looking at a text is to follow Bhatia's Step 2 and ask a number of questions about the text, trying to place it as a particular genre and identifying its key contextual characteristics. This helps to uncover features outside the text that influenced the way it was written and some of the assumptions the writer was making about his or her readers. The questions in Figure 7.2, suggested by Paltridge (2001, p. 51), provide a useful guide in this initial examination of a text.

What is the text about?

What is the purpose of the text?

What is the setting of the text? (e.g., in a textbook, newspaper, etc.)

What is the tone of the text? (formal, informal, etc.)

Who is the author of the text?

What is his/her age?

    Sex?

    Ethnic background?

    Social status?

Who is the intended audience of the text?

What is the relationship between the author and the intended audience?

What rules or expectations limit how the text might be written?

What shared cultural knowledge is assumed by the text?

What shared understandings are implied?

What other texts does this text assume you have knowledge of?

Fig. 7.2. Some initial contextual questions when examining a text (Paltridge, 2001, p. 51)

While it may be difficult to get clear answers to some of these questions without more detailed information, this is a good orientation to studying a genre. Beyond this general contextual analysis, however, an ability to analyze the language of texts depends on a certain amount of linguistic knowledge and the ability to think carefully about the language and uses of texts. In practice, teachers in SFL and ESP situations may tend to go about this slightly differently, with those in the systemic linguistics camp perhaps giving more emphasis to the grammar of the texts and those working in ESP perhaps looking first at the situational uses of target texts before examining their key features. The following examples give some flavor of these approaches to analysis.

Genre Analysis in SFL

As we have seen in earlier chapters, grammar lies at the heart of an understanding of texts in systemic functional approaches to genre. Whether teachers are assisting learners to write formal descriptive reports, summaries of academic articles, or creative narratives, they will need to understand the language of these genres. This kind of analysis normally involves looking at some of the following text elements:

- **Staging:** The means by which a text fulfills the social purposes of the writer, identifying the different stages and the features that tend to cluster in each stage
- **Clause structure:** The use of sentences with more than one clause and what comes first in those clauses (their themes), thus indicating the starting point of the message
- **Types of verbs:** Verb choices, as these indicate the predominant kinds of processes or actions in the text or point to particular stages of the text; also important is

whether the writer uses modal verbs
indicating certainty or obligation

- **Vocabulary:** Whether technical, bureaucratic, or
  everyday language is used; whether it
  expresses emotion, attitude, or evaluation; and whether it is descriptive

- **Noun groups:** Whether the text includes extended
  what setting will it noun groups, often an indication of *who has? access?*
  be used in formal scientific or technical writing

- **Circumstances:** The kinds of circumstances that occur *dictate*
  peer review in the text—time, place, manner, etc. *language used*

- **Cohesion:** The use of reference, conjunction,
  from word to and chains of related lexical items to
  word to express connections between parts of
  sentence to sentence the text
  p to p

Breaking texts down to these component parts allows teachers to see texts as meaningful message structures that relate to
what the writer is trying to do in a given context. It helps
teachers to establish which features should be emphasized
when teaching a particular genre and assists students to more
effectively express their experiences and attitudes in ways
that meet reader expectations.

Hood, Solomon, and Burns (1996, pp. 66–67) present these
issues as a series of questions that the analyst can use as a
guide when approaching written texts. To provide an example of how these questions can be applied, I analyzed the text
presented in Figure 7.3, which appeared in my mailbox while
I was writing this section of the book. Figure 7.4 shows Hood
et al.'s questions in the left-hand column and comments on
the language of the sample text of Figure 7.3 on the right.

The analysis shows how the layout of the text, its formal
vocabulary choices, and its long nominal groups allow us to
place the text firmly in an institutional rhetorical context and
help reveal it as a formal, bureaucratic text establishing clear
roles and relationships between writer and reader. The
writer's adoption of a polite and informative tenor, expressed
through vocabulary choices, passives, modal verbs, and avoid-

---

Internal memorandum

From	Tony Tung (FMO)	To	Dr. Hyland, Ken (EN)
Our reference	FMO/23/3/5	Copies to	
Telephone	615-1234	Your reference	
Date	August 5 2003	Dated	

Office window(s) found opened

Please be advised that during the recent Typhoon Imbudo, some of the windows inside your office were found opened and our duty security staff had to enter your office and lock up the windows in order to prevent damage to the building services, fixtures, and the property in the room.

We do not recommend open windows. The reasons and concerns are:

1) The design of the centralized air-conditioning system on campus has provided sufficient air changes to offices, classrooms, and lecture theaters, etc. That is to say, fresh air intake into the building is sufficient. There is no need to open windows for more air. Furthermore, to ensure health and comfort, when outdoor air is drawn in, it is first filtered to have the pollutants removed and cooled to lower the humidity before being admitted to the indoor environment.

2) Leaving windows open will allow the ingress of moisture, dust/dirt, and other pollutants that would promote mold growth on air louvers, ceiling, walls, books, and documents.

3) Opening windows will allow the ingress of rainwater, which would cause flooding and hence damage to the services and property inside the room concerned.

4) To leave windows open in our buildings would constitute a violation of fire safety and the Building Authority's requirements because of its design.

5) Energy is also wasted when windows are opened.

In view of the potential problems created by leaving windows open, I am writing to seek your kind cooperation to refrain from opening windows in your office. Should you have any queries on the issue, please feel free to call me at 615-1234.

Tony Tung
Facilities Manager (Safety and Ambience)

Fig. 7.3. A sample text

---

ance of *you* pronouns, avoids attributing blame or even responsibility to the reader for a transgression. However, the text staging, which identifies the reason for the text as a "problem," goes on to explain why this is a problem and then "recommends" a solution. When considered with the repeated restatement of the violation, the numerical listing of rule-like information points, the "potential problems" expressed as sentence themes, and the use of formal vocabulary, this structure leaves the reader in no doubt of the intended message.

Through this process of analysis, we can see that this is a

Guidelines	Notes on text
Consider the purpose and context • What kind of text is it? • Who wrote it? • For whom? • What is it about?	This is a memo from a department responsible for building management to a staff member concerning a breach of regulations. The purpose is to inform/remind the recipient of these regulations and change the action.
Consider the overall organization of the text • Can you identify stages in the text (e.g., a beginning, middle, and end)? • Can you describe the function of each stage?	The text has roughly the following stages: 1. Heading: states topic of the text 2. The problem or reason for the text (*windows inside your office were found opened*) 3. Information for the reader concerning the behavior 4. Request for change in behavior to solve problem 5. Writer and title
Consider how cohesive the text is and how cohesion is achieved • Are conjunctions used? • Is cohesion achieved through reference backward and forward in the text or by use of pronouns? • Do vocabulary choices help tie the text together?	Cohesion mainly through repetition and numbered points Some use of conjunctions: *in order to, furthermore, also* Reference: few pronouns: *I, you, your office* Vocabulary chains: - *air-conditioning, air changes, fresh air, outdoor air*, etc. - *moisture, dust, dirt, pollutants, mold* - *rainwater, flooding, damage* - *room, ceiling, walls, books, documents*
Consider the significant grammatical features • Does the writer use mainly declaratives (statements), interrogatives (questions), or imperatives (commands)? • Does the writer use modal verbs (*could, may, must*)? • Are there patterns in the use of types of verbs (i.e., action, mental, verbal, being or having verbs)? • Are there patterns in choice of tenses? • What is the percentage of multiple-clause sentences? • Are there theme patterns, or what comes first in sentences or clauses? • Does the writer use long noun groups? • Does the writer use many prepositional phrases indicating the circumstances around events?	Mainly declaratives rather than imperatives despite the clear attempt to get the reader to do something. Politeness markers: *please, kind cooperation*, no direct accusation Considerable use of *would* plus *will* and *should* Mainly action verbs: *enter, lock, prevent, provide, open, wasted, seek*, etc; verbal: *writing, call*; and being: *is* Examples of past, present, and future tenses. Heavy use of passive voice to avoid attributing responsibility to reader Several long sentences with multiple clauses Themes mainly concern things or actions rather than people; the text is mainly about correct actions. Some: *sufficient air changes to offices, violation of fire safety and the Building Authority's requirements, the design of the central air-conditioning system on campus* Several to describe place: *inside your office, in the room into the building, in our buildings, on air louvers*, etc.
Consider the vocabulary choices in the text • Are technical words used or everyday terms? • Are there relatively few or many content words? • Are there a lot of descriptive words? • Do the vocabulary choices carry strong feeling, emotion, or judgment, or are they more neutral?	Mainly bureaucratic terms: *ingress, ensure, promote, constitute a violation*, etc., carrying formal or authoritative connotations A lot of content words Neutral tone carrying authority and the assumption that the reader will comply with more information
Consider the layout and the script • Is the layout an important clue to the meaning? • Are some parts of the text emphasized in the layout?	The formal memo layout carries authority. The emphasis given by a title, rather than a subject line in the header, sends a clear signal of rule infringement.

Fig. 7.4. An example analysis using Hood et al.'s (1996) guidelines for studying written texts

macro-proposal, instructing the addressee to modify his or her behavior in some way. The most salient features of the text are the polite, modalized, or hedged commands it contains and the bureaucratic language used to express these, avoiding blame and even accusation for personal wrongdoing. In order to see if these features apply more generally to this kind of text, it is necessary to look at a number of examples of the genre to see what is common and what varies. When a clear idea of genre features begins to emerge, then students can be asked to study these and focus on them in discussions, scaffolding tasks, and writing activities.

Genre Analysis in ESP

In ESP analyses, the idea of communicative purpose has always played a major part in identifying a genre. Usually the analyst conducts an assessment of student writing needs by consulting those with an understanding of the target situation, making judgments about the students' current writing abilities, and collecting texts and other information from the context itself. As I noted in Chapter 3, a useful starting point in identifying the texts potentially important to learners are the names participants give to the genres they regularly use. Following this, studies of examples of texts from these genres and interviews with those who use them can be conducted to discover the functions the texts serve in that context, the value they have for users, the ways they are related or chained together, and how they are typically structured. Among many published examples, such analyses have included direct mail sales letters (Bhatia, 1993), thesis proposals (Paltridge, 1997), research articles (Swales & Luebs, 2002), and business faxes (Akar & Louhiala-Salminen, 1999).

An analysis undertaken for a genre-based writing course is sketched below. This study was done to provide information that could be used in a short course on research writing for publication with a mixed-discipline group of L2 graduate students in Hong Kong. Time constraints and the disciplinary variability of the class meant that it was necessary to deal with a few general characteristics of research writing relevant to all the students, and the genre of journal abstracts was selected as one of these. Not only would all participants need to write an abstract almost immediately, but the focus provided a neat rhetorical block of manageable size for a short course.

First, several samples of the genre were collected from journals recommended by expert informants from the students' disciplines. Two of these are shown in Figure 7.5 (the numbers have been inserted to indicate the text moves mentioned in Figure 7.6.

These abstracts were then analyzed, drawing on the research literature for assistance. The analysis suggested that abstracts mirrored the structure of the research article itself, and this could be seen across different disciplines and in many of the examples we examined (Hyland, 2000). This structure is shown in Figure 7.6, with the numbers corresponding to those in the example texts.

From Business Studies

[1] This work builds on recent streams of research on both service quality and the relationships between consumption and gender. [2] It explores whether the sex of the service provider should be regarded as an element of the servicescape that influences perceptions of service quality in various contexts. [3] For each setting, two possibilities were explored. The first was that men might believe male servers provide higher quality and women believe female servers do, due to in-group bias or homophily based perceptions. The second was that consumers' "server stereotypes" concerning which sex does a better job of serving in a particular setting would interact with the sex of the service provider to influence perceived quality. [4] Across the three settings studied, server stereotypes were found to interact with sex of server and/or sex of consumer to affect ratings of some dimensions of service quality. [5] The reasons for and implications of the inconsistent effects of stereotypes are addressed.

From Biology

[1] Acetaldehyde is one of the intermediate products of ethanolic fermentation, which can be reduced to ethanol by alcohol dehydrogenase (ADH). Alternatively, acetaldehyde can be oxidized to acetate by aldehyde dehydrogenase (ALDH) and subsequently converted to acetyl-CoA by acetyl-CoA synthetase (ACS). [2] To study the expression of ALDHs in plants, [3] we isolated and characterized a cDNA coding for a putative mitochondrial ALDH (TobAldh2A) in Nicotiana tabacum. [4] TobALDH2A shows 54–60% identity at the amino acid level with other ALDHs and shows 76% identity with maize Rf2. TobAldh2A transcripts and protein were present at high levels in the male and female reproductive tissues. Expression in vegetative tissues was much lower, and no induction by anaerobic incubation was observed. [5] This suggests that TobALDH expression is not part of the anaerobic response but may have another function. The use of specific inhibitors of ALDH and the pyruvate dehydrogenase (PDH) complex indicates that ALDH activity is important for pollen tube growth and thus may have a function in biosynthesis or energy production.

Fig. 7.5. Sample journal article abstracts

Move	Function
1. Introduction	Establishes the context of the paper and motivates the research or discussion
2. Purpose	Indicates the purpose or hypothesis, outlines the intention behind the paper
3. Method	Provides information on design, procedures, assumptions, approach, data, etc.
4. Results	States the main findings, the argument, or what was accomplished
5. Conclusion	Interprets or extends the results, draws inferences, points to wider implications

Fig. 7.6. A classification of rhetorical moves in article abstracts (Hyland, 2000)

Following the move analysis, key features of the texts were examined. This involved looking at how the different moves were usually expressed and what features stood out as a result of their frequency or importance. Some of the features identified are listed here:

- *Tense.* Generally the background introduction and purpose tend to be expressed using the present tense (*builds on, explores, is, can be*), with writers switching to report their methods and results in the past (*were explored, were found, would interact, isolated, characterized, were present, was much lower*) and then returning to the present tense again in the conclusions (*this suggests, may have, indicates that, are addressed*). This is perhaps an attempt to produce an effect of immediacy and current relevance in those parts of the text of wider interest to readers (e.g., Swales & Feak, 1994, p. 213).
- *Voice.* While writer pronouns often occur, with *we* common in jointly authored texts, there is also considerable use of the passive voice (*were explored, were found, can be reduced*) and inanimate subjects (*this work builds on, it explores, TobALDH2A shows*) in this sample.
- *Themes.* Some of the themes highlight the discourse or judgments (*this work builds on recent streams of research, the reasons for and implications of the inconsistent effect of stereotypes*), but they are mainly what Gosden (1993) calls "Real-world Domain" themes in that they refer to entities, events, or processes that are part of

the research (*across the three settings studied, acetalde-hyde is one of the, expression in vegetative tissues was*). This emphasis on what is being studied and the processes used in the study serves to highlight the empirical aspects of the study rather than the writers' evaluation of them or a personal relationship with the reader.

- **Verb choices.** Presentation verbs often distinguish the purpose and result moves with items such as *discuss, describe, explore,* and *address* indicating intentions and *show, demonstrate, find,* and *establish* signaling results.

- **Hedges.** While writers are seeking to highlight what is new and interesting in their results, they nevertheless also pull back from overstating their findings. They tone findings down with hedges such as *found to interact with, some dimensions, suggests that, may have,* and so on. This may be intended to state the writers' confidence in the findings precisely, to avoid criticism, or to show respect for the alternative views of others.

- **Noun groups.** An extensive use of nominal groups allows the writers to package complex events or entities as single things so they can be thematized and discussed (e.g., *perceptions of service quality, the relationships between consumption and gender, in-group bias or homophily based perceptions, ethanolic fermentation, alcohol dehydrogenase,* and so on).

- **Promotional matter.** Introductory moves rarely provide simple background but seek to emphasize the importance, topicality, or relevance of the study to the discipline. By highlighting a link with previous theory or research, by stressing its practical value, or by promising a solution to a recognized problem, writers attempt to both give readers an idea of the article's content and strengthen the importance of their topic to persuade them to read further.

There is, of course, more that can be said about these texts, but this analysis was sufficient for this teaching and learning situation. Once these features had been brought to the attention of the learners, it was then possible for them to look at abstracts in their own fields, examining them for their move structures and how these were similar to and different from those in the sample we had analyzed in class. It was interesting to discover, for instance, that while all the abstracts brought into class contained a results move, stating the writer's central claims, the science abstracts often omitted an introduction and conclusion, so that a *Purpose—Method— Results* pattern was common. The social science abstracts, however, more often followed an *Introduction—Purpose— Results* format. Providing ways for learners to think about the distinctive features of these texts also served to help learners see differences in the practices of the disciplines and to ask questions about the underlying beliefs, conventions, and expectations of these disciplines.

Researching Genres as Practices

Clearly a student's ability to understand and write a particular genre will depend not only on classroom instruction but also on his or her knowledge and previous experience of the genre. It is both the texts and their use that are important to control of a genre. As Bazerman (1997, p. 19) eloquently reminds us:

> Genres are not just forms. Genres are forms of life, ways of being. They are frames for social action. They are environments for learning. They are locations within which meaning is constructed. Genres shape the thoughts we form and the communications by which we interact. Genres are the familiar places we go to create intelligible communicative action with each other and the guideposts we use to explore the unfamiliar.

While these frames for thinking and acting may be expressed and accomplished through language forms, these forms are themselves shaped and established by the very situations they help create.

To put this another way, most of the writing we do is produced in social contexts: in the workplace, in school, and at home. It therefore results, in part, from routine social activities or *practices*. The purpose and function of particular texts, the roles and relationships of their writers and readers, the context in which they are written and read, and the features they are composed of are all influenced by the community and the situation in which they occur. Because texts relate to such social and cultural practices, to getting things done in particular contexts, students who are unfamiliar with them will find the genres they encounter harder to process and to write. On the other hand, by understanding these practices and helping our L2 learners to understand them, we can make texts more accessible to them.

Perceptions and Questions in Researching Practices

A great deal of research has been conducted on writers and their behaviors, but because each situation is different, and because contextual factors play a large part in writing, there is still much to learn about how genres are written and responded to in different situations. Who is the target audience for a particular genre? What do writers need to know about their readers to write a genre successfully? How does this genre relate to other genres in the situation, and what genres does it respond to or assume?

Studying genre practices often begins with some vague idea of the context in which the genre is typically found and a curiosity about what can be learned by talking to those who use it regularly. For some purposes, it may be sufficient to gather enough information for a general idea of how a genre is employed. In fact, access to relevant sites can be difficult, and users may be reluctant to cooperate. However, only by developing a sense of the complexities of genre practices can teachers—and students—understand the social forces that impact on writing and how writers negotiate these.

- What writing strategies does a group of writers employ in accomplishing a writing task?
- Is writing done collaboratively or individually? Who writes, edits, or approves the text?
- Where is it written (home, work, school, etc.)?
- Who reads it, and what is their relationship and status relative to the writer?
- What format and mode is the genre produced in (e-mail, memo, word-processed, handwritten, etc.)?
- How is the genre related to other events and goals in the domain of activity?
- How is writing related to reading and speech in specific contexts?
- What are writers' attitudes to the genre and its role in their lives?
- How do writers feel about the institutional genres in which they participate?
- Which genres are privileged (and which ones less so) in different contexts?
- What other texts influence the genre? Is it a response or an initiation? Is a template used?
- What does this audience typically look for in a text in this genre, and how do they read it?
- What do writers need to know about the target audience to write successful texts?
- What do text users regard as the function and purpose of the genre?
- What do they see as its key functions? Do these features differ from one text to another?
- What do readers regard as an effective example of the genre? Can they provide text examples?

Fig. 7.7. Some useful questions for researching genre practices

Exploring practices thus offers another view of genre—an additional dimension to fill out and enrich a focus on texts themselves. It reveals that texts are varied; that they can be negotiated and resisted; that they can change; and that people have different ideas about their use. In other words, *it allows students to see texts as part of contexts.* It helps them to see how they are embedded in institutional life, communities, and cultures. To understand practices is to *demystify forms and patterns* that might otherwise be seen as arbitrary and conventional; it helps *explain* why writers do what they do, and such understanding can help learners avoid seeing genres as simply templates for writing. Asking the kinds of questions listed in Figure 7.7 can therefore offer a clearer picture of what a genre is and why it is as it is.

Methods for Researching Genre Practices

Information about genre practices is best approached using small-scale research and *qualitative* methods. While *qualitative research* means different things to different people, in

• *Study real-world settings.* Focus on particular people at a particular place and point in time rather than setting up experiments or decontextualized writing situations. In other words, research is contextualized, and the researcher avoids intruding on the subjects or manipulating the context.

• *Study the activities of groups.* Although researchers look at what individuals do, it is important to relate these behaviors and views to the understandings and actions of other members of the group.

• *Study the whole picture.* Focus on what the genre does and how it functions in its specific context, such as an office, department, institution, etc. This also means exploring the relative positions and roles of those who write and read the genre and the ways it relates to other genres and activities. Consider the ways the genre affects other people and texts and the consequences it has.

• *Study the genre users' own views* This is known as an *emic* perspective, taking seriously what participants believe they are doing and what they think about their roles, relationships, and practices.

• *Study the literature.* Use previous research as a source of insights and understandings.

Fig. 7.8. Guidelines for studying genre practices

practice it generally involves adopting the broad guidelines outlined in Figure 7.8.

The social practices that surround genres can be studied in a number of ways, and the research method adopted will largely depend on the questions asked and the approach the teacher feels most comfortable in using. Generally, though, the fullest picture of what is going on will require using several techniques in combination, usually observation, interviews, and text analysis. I have discussed methods for studying writing and genres elsewhere (Hyland, 2002; 2003), but exploring genre practices mainly involves observing genres in use and systematic procedures for collecting and analyzing genre users' perceptions of what they are doing. The main approaches are summarized below.

Questionnaires are useful for exploratory studies into what goes on in a writing context and for identifying issues that can be followed up later through more in-depth methods. They have been used to collect self-report data on writing and reading practices (what users think they do with a genre) and to discover the kinds of writing that a community requires from those writing particular genres, such as what subject teachers demand of students. Questionnaires have the advantages of being relatively quick and easy to administer, of allowing the views of many informants to be collected, and of providing results that can be easily compared and understood. Because the information is controlled by the researchers' questions, they also allow considerable precision and clarity, although it is remarkably easy to design ambiguous questions, and for this reason it is always a good idea to trial the questions first.

Interviews enable participants to discuss their understandings of writing and writing situations in their own words and in more detail than through questionnaires. Interviews can be conducted with individuals or with small groups (focus groups) and have been widely used in writing research, either as the main source of gathering data or in combination with other techniques to get a "thicker description" of a situation. They can range from simply working through a list of predetermined questions, much like a spoken questionnaire, to a relatively unstructured format where the interviewer is guided by the responses of the interviewee to allow unanticipated topics to emerge (Cohen, Manion, & Morrison, 2000, pp. 267–272).

Diary studies provide a first-person account of writing practices through regular, candid entries in a personal journal, which is then analyzed for recurring patterns or important events. Participants are usually asked to enter all their thoughts about using a genre and what they did when using it, such as how they collected data or the ways they considered their readers. This is done on a regular basis, and when a substantial amount of material has been produced, the diary is examined for patterns that are then interpreted and discussed with the writer. Diaries can therefore provide valuable insights into both social and psychological aspects of genre use that might be difficult to collect in other ways.

Observation is often used to supplement self-report methods such as questionnaires and interviews to gather direct evidence of what people do. Unlike everyday "noticing," observation for research purposes involves systematic and conscious recording, often based on prior decisions about what to observe. Noting everything is impossible, and so some observers decide to use pre-defined boxes that they check when an expected action occurs. Obviously, this kind of clear structure is easier to apply and yields more manageable data than on-the-spot descriptions, but pre-selection may ignore relevant events that the analyst did not anticipate. We are only likely to record what we think is important, which means all observation necessarily favors some behaviors and neglects others, so at first it may be a good idea to identify categories in advance. Observation can include a focus on:

- *Writers and what they do when they compose:* their discussions or collaboration with others, their use of reference sources or document templates, their collection of information, and so on
- *The genre itself:* what other texts contribute to it, the texts or activities it responds to and those it leads to, and its passage through an institution
- *Text receivers:* who sees the text, how they read it, the actions they take after reading it, and so on

It is worth making the point that studying genres as a set of practices embedded in the everyday lives of text users presents a way of understanding texts that is very different from that of most L2 writing classes. In educational settings, genres are seen as objects of study that are explicitly talked about and taught. In the settings where they are used, however, written genres are often incidental to other activities, whether persuading colleagues, claiming benefits, or selling widgets. Genres are used to get *other* things done, and this may be overlooked in writing instruction. For this reason, situated learning theorists such as Lave and Wenger (see Chapter 1) regard learning as an integral aspect of "activity in the world" so that writers can only gradually gain access to the ways things are done through participating in those things. But to ask L2 writers to learn genres in this way is perhaps asking a lot as they are simultaneously grappling with a second language and using that language in real contexts. Still, classroom teachers need not ignore the role and uses of genres in the real world. Johns (1997, p. 105), for instance, argues that "much student research on texts and processes can be completed in literacy classrooms, but students also need to go outside: to observe, to question, and to develop hypotheses."

By visiting sites where genres are used, by observing the ways they are used, and by interviewing users, students can apply the methods outlined earlier to discover for themselves how genres are subservient to the goals of everyday tasks and how they are defined by people in terms of those tasks. Just as learners should be encouraged to analyze texts, they can also gain an understanding of why, how, and by whom texts are produced and used through the study of genre practices.

Genre and Corpus Analysis

Genre analysts have been greatly assisted in their efforts to identify the principles and regularities of texts in the last 20 years by the use of corpora and computers. A *corpus* is a store of naturally occurring examples of language that has been collected for linguistic study. While it does not contain any new theories or information about language, it can offer fresh insights on familiar but perhaps unnoticed features of language use. This is because a corpus is a more reliable guide to what language is like than human intuition. While we all have experience of the genres we use regularly, much of this experience remains hidden so that, for example, even the best teachers are often unable to explain to their students why some phrasing or expression is preferred over another in a given context.

The idea behind a corpus is that it represents a speaker's experience of language in some domain. This makes the approach ideal for studying the features of written genres as it provides a way of describing them more accurately so that students can learn to write them more effectively. Using any one of a number of commercially available and relatively inexpensive text-analysis programs, teachers can examine fairly large amounts of texts to supplement their intuitions—not to confirm whether something is possible or not but to describe whether it is frequent or not. As Sinclair (1991, p. 17) points out, this moves the study of language away from ideas of what is correct toward a focus on what is typical or frequent.

Counting Word and Item Frequencies

One major use of a corpus is to identify the frequency of the words or grammatical patterns it contains. Figure 7.9, for instance, is a screenshot from a widely used program called

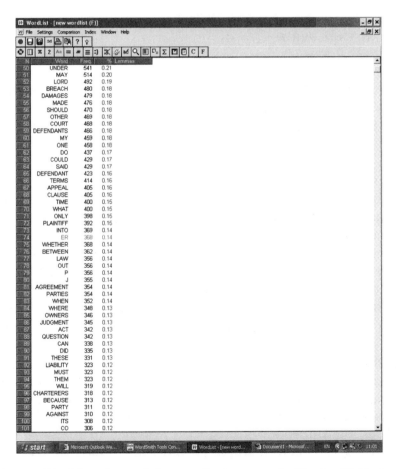

Fig. 7.9. Word list of court judgments by frequency in *Wordsmith Tools.* (*Wordsmith Tools* used Courtesy of Mike Scott, Liverpool University.)

Wordsmith Tools that shows a rank-ordered list of the most frequent words in a corpus of written courtroom judgments. The words appear in the first column and are followed by their frequency, and then the percentage that the word comprises of all words in the corpus is given. While grammar words are always the most frequent items in any text or corpus, a look further down the list reveals key items of vocabulary in a genre, enabling the teacher to identify and target key items in class.

Frequency counts are useful for describing the features of a genre and making comparisons between different genres. Questions such as these can be addressed through use of a corpus:

- What adjectives are most often used to describe places in recount genres?
- What tense is most commonly used in the methods section of physics lab reports?
- What is the usual way of opening or closing a business letter?
- What is the most common way of expressing possibility in an argument genre?

Corpus frequency studies have contributed to genre-based L2 writing instruction in numerous ways. They have, for instance, challenged traditional textbook prescriptions advising science students to avoid the active voice in their writing by revealing considerable use of this structure in academic research papers (Tarone, Dwyer, Gillette, & Icke, 1998). They have also shown the value of teaching specific genres by comparing the frequencies of different items across genres. Biber, Conrad, and Reppen (1994), for instance, found that ESL textbooks often overemphasize the use of relative clauses, agent marking with *by*-clauses, and continuous tense. Ljung (1990) discovered that the 56 leading EFL textbooks in Sweden contained an atypically high proportion of words denoting concrete objects and physical actions while the kinds of academic genres that students were expected to write had far higher frequencies of words denoting abstractions, mental processes, and social phenomena.

The advantages to writing teachers of feature counts in specialized corpora are also underlined by the fact that many words differ by discipline as well as genre (Hyland, 2000). A simple frequency count of two similarly sized corpora from introductory textbooks, for example, shows great variations in the most frequently occurring nouns, suggesting a number of items that might be worth teaching to students in these subjects (Fig. 7.10). These significantly more frequent words are known as *keywords.*

More sophisticated comparisons can be undertaken using software that counts not only words but also grammatical features. By a semi-automatic procedure known as *tagging,* codes can be added to each word indicating its part of speech; so, for instance, the word *work* is tagged as either a noun or verb each time it occurs, allowing much more detailed analyses of target genres. Biber's (1988) research, for instance, shows how written expository prose is characterized by bundles of grammatical features such as frequent nouns, long words, attributive adjectives, and prepositional phrases because they often function to present densely packed information, while second-person pronouns, direct questions, present-tense verbs, private verbs (*feel, think*), and *that*-deletions are less frequent because of their more interactive character. In genre-based

| Applied Linguistics | | | Biology | | |
Number	% of total	Word	Number	% of total	Word
423	0.8663	language	166	0.4304	species
149	0.3052	speech	150	0.3889	DNA
128	0.2622	example	143	0.3708	spores
127	0.2601	interaction	135	0.3500	organisms
106	0.2171	act	117	0.3033	bacteria
101	0.2069	communication	116	0.3008	fungi
97	0.1987	students	95	0.2463	figure
93	0.1905	text	89	0.2307	organism
93	0.1905	acquisition	75	0.1945	RNA
91	0.1864	acts	68	0.1763	spore
90	0.1843	face	62	0.1607	cells
89	0.1823	input	59	0.1530	section
86	0.1761	rules	58	0.1504	genus
85	0.1741	communicative	55	0.1426	cell
79	0.1618	knowledge	49	0.1270	disease

Fig. 7.10. Most frequent nouns in introductory textbooks in two disciplines

writing programs, the use of a tagged corpus can assist teachers in key teaching decisions, helping them to decide on the relative merits of recommending the past or present tense when teaching report genres, for example, or whether it is more useful to focus on VERB + *to* infinitive or VERB + *that* (e.g., *decided to* vs. *decided that*) when teaching narratives.

Comparative frequencies are also a useful way of determining the structures or items that are overused or underused in the writing of L2 students in given genres. Research by Granger (1998) and Hinkel (2002), for instance, shows that L2 academic essays contain a smaller range of vocabulary than L1 essays, with far higher rates of vague nouns, private verbs, *be*-copula constructions, and emphatics, all of which are more typical of informal speech than written discourse.

A good example of this kind of research is provided by Milton (1999), who used a learner corpus to explore his impression that his students were overusing certain fixed expressions in their essays. While such "lexical bundles" are of increasing interest to language teachers, novice writers who lack good models of target academic genres are often tempted to overuse them to avoid grammatical errors, leading them to a repetitive style of writing. By comparing a student essay corpus with a parallel corpus of L1 essays, Hong Kong school textbooks, and published research articles, Milton was able to confirm that the L2 students used the same phrases far more often than L1 writers. He was then able to draw up a list of alternative phrases from the L1 samples that he could include in his classes to help his students vary their writing of academic essays (Fig. 7.11).

Concordancing

In addition to frequency counts, a corpus is most usually explored using a concordance program, which brings together all instances of a search word or phrase in the corpus as a list of unconnected lines of text and so allows the user to see regularities in its use that might otherwise be missed. These lines, therefore, give instances of language *use* when read horizontally and evidence of *system* when read vertically. This

		Frequency of phrases per 50,000 words in each corpus			
	Lexical phrases with greatest difference	L2 student texts	L1 student texts	School textbooks	Published articles
used in tudent texts	*In the/this case*	0	9	11	16
	It has also been	0	8	0	5
	It can be seen that	0	8	0	4
	An example of this is	0	8	0	3
	This is not to say that	0	7	0	2
rused in L2 ent texts	*First of all*	170	1	13	5
	On the other hand	239	31	25	30
	(As) we/you know	118	2	22	3
	In my opinion	110	12	8	0
	All in all	59	2	1	0

Fig. 7.11. Lexical phrases in a Hong Kong learner corpus compared with other samples (Milton, 1999, p. 26)

can provide the following kinds of information for writing teachers:

- The preferred patterns of use of a word—e.g., whether first-person pronouns are associated with claims, criticisms, or research procedures in academic research papers
- The differences between words that students often confuse —e.g., *bored* vs. *boring, interested* vs. *interesting,* etc.
- The most appropriate words to use—e.g., whether to use the preposition *in, that,* or *to* with *interested* and *interesting*
- "Semantic prosody," or the connotative meanings a word acquires because of its regular association with other words—e.g., the word *commit* carries unfavorable implications because of its association with words such as *crime, murder, mistakes,* etc. (Partington, 1998, p. 67)
- How words change their meaning as a result of the surrounding text—e.g., the word *quite* boosts the meaning of non-gradable words such as *impossible, definitely,* and *agree* and hedges gradable words such as *interesting, beautiful,* and *cynical* (Hyland, 1996)

In genre studies, concordance results are useful for seeing how words are sometimes associated with different meanings and uses in different genres. Thus, the word *significant* is used in a technical sense of "not the result of chance" in academic research genres, collocating with words such as *statistical, change, variation,* etc. In newspaper articles, however, it carries the looser meaning of "important" and collocates with words like *event, decision,* and *misjudgment.* Similarly, the adjective *massive* is used in science writing in the sense of "large in mass" and modifies words like *star, planet,* and *black hole,* while in journalism it is used in the sense of "very big" and collocates with *gamble, profits,* and *blow* (Lee, 1999, cited in Hunston, 2002, p. 162).

In addition, because most concordance programs allow the user to automatically sort the concordance lines by alphabetical order on the first word to the left or to the right of the search word, frequent collocational patterns in a genre become much more apparent. Thus, in a genre study of acknowledgments in Ph.D. theses by Hong Kong students, for example, Hyland and Tse (2004) discovered a strong tendency to use the noun *thanks* in preference to other expressions of gratitude. By sorting concordance lines in order of the word to the left of this search word, we then discovered that this noun was modified by only three adjectives: *special, sincere,* and *deep,* with *special* making up over two-thirds of all cases. Figure 7.12 is a screen shot from the program *MonoConc Pro* showing part of the results of this sorting.

Concordance software is also useful to teachers in genre-based writing courses as it makes searches for word combinations possible, revealing frequencies and meanings of key phrases that vary by intervening words. Thus, entering the expression *it * that* will search for the word *it* followed by *that* in the near vicinity, producing examples such as these in a corpus of abstracts in academic research papers:

it is likely that	*it shows that*	*it is worth noting that*
it seems that	*it is claimed that*	*it is shown that*
it is clear that	*it is true that*	*it is more likely that*

When these examples are studied more carefully, they reveal that academic writers use this phrasing extremely frequently to express their evaluation of whether the following statement is likely to be true or not. In addition, the results show that

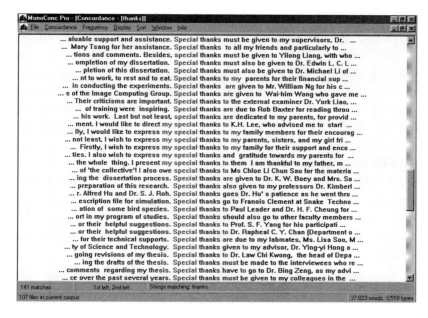

Fig. 7.12. A screenshot from *MonoConc Pro* showing a left sort on the word *thanks*. (*MonoConc Pro* used courtesy of Michael Barlow, Athelstan.)

expressions of certainty occur more often than those expressing doubt. This kind of information can help student writers not only to make use of this collocation in their own writing but to use it in expected and, hopefully, effective ways.

The analysis of potentially productive phrases using the * wildcard is particularly useful for helping student writers to see how high-frequency grammar words often occur in regular patterns. Thus, the words *the* and *of* are among the highest frequency words in any text, but the frame *the * of* is particularly common in research article writing. In this genre, it is used with nouns to express meanings such as existence (*the occurrence of, the absence of*), process (*the beginning of, the onset of*), quantity (*the amount of, the frequency of*), and so on (Luzon Marco, 2000). So, using the wildcard enables regularly occurring patterns to be identified through high-frequency grammar words, even though the lexical items within these patterns may be infrequent. Figure 7.13 is a screenshot from another language-analysis program, *WordPilot 2002*, showing concordance lines of this structure from a biology

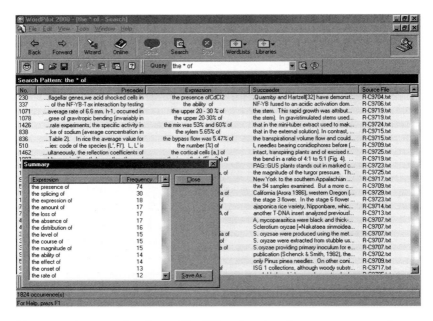

Fig. 7.13. A screenshot from *WordPilot* showing the most common forms of *the * of* in biology articles. (*WordPilot* used courtesy of John Milton, Compulang.)

corpus. A pop-up window gives a concordance summary of the most frequent forms.

Once again, armed with this kind of information about their target genres, L2 students are able to make choices that are better informed, guided by "expert" practice and the expectations that the genre tends to motivate among its routine readers. The high productivity of *the * of,* therefore, justifies its inclusion in courses assisting EAP students to write effective academic research papers in the sciences. Moreover, in biology, the collocations *the presence of* and *the splicing of* would seem to offer students valuable forms for expressing meanings relating to existence and to research processes in their writing.

Some Practical Notes

Not only is corpus analysis an increasingly important tool in genre-based writing instruction, but it is now fairly easy for teachers to collect or buy collections of texts, store these on a home PC, and analyze them using widely available and relatively inexpensive software.

Commercial corpora. Corpora of various kinds can be purchased easily, although not always cheaply. Most are of a general nature, however, and care needs to be taken in identifying the specific genres that material is taken from. Some language-analysis programs, such as *MonoConc, WordPilot,* and *Microconcord,* include text samples, but the main commercially available written corpora are:

- *British National Corpus:* (<http://info.ox.ac.uk/bnc/index .html>): 100 million words representing a wide cross-section of current spoken and written British English
- *BNC Sampler Corpus:* a reduced version of the above, containing one million words of various spoken and written genres
- *International Computer Archive of Modern English Collection* (<http://nora.hd.uib.no/corpora.html>): includes the *Brown Corpus* (one million words of written American English of 500 text samples in 15 text categories), the *Lancaster-Oslo/Bergen Corpus* (a parallel corpus of British written English), and the *Kolhapur Corpus* (an equivalent corpus of Indian English)
- *Newspaper corpora:* many national newspapers sell CD-ROMS of all the articles in the paper for a particular year, which are searchable by concordance packages

Learner corpora. While there are a number of learner corpora in existence, only the *International Corpus of Learner English (ICLE)* is commercially available on CD-ROM. This is a corpus of argumentative essays of between 500 and 1,000 words written by university students of English and representing Chinese, Czech, Dutch, Finnish, French, German, Japanese, Polish, Russian, Spanish, and Swedish language backgrounds. It is not, however, difficult for teachers to create a learner corpus of their own by asking students to submit their assignments electronically and gradually building up a larger and more representative collection of their work. It is then possible to analyze students' developing control of a genre and identify where they seem to be having difficulty.

The Internet. Often, researchers collect their own specialized corpora to better represent the genres they are teaching. Material can be collected and converted to electronic form using an optical scanner or directly from Internet sources. Web editions of newspapers, legal and government documents, business texts, and specialist magazines can be collected to produce large amounts of machine-readable texts in various genres, although copyright laws may prevent their long-term storage. The Internet also makes it possible to trial concordance techniques. So, teachers can get a good sense of what concordance programs can do by visiting these sites and trying out the software:

- *Corpus of Business Letters* (<http://www.cl.aoyama.ac.jp/~someya/>): a searchable ESP corpus of one million words
- *Cobuild Corpus Sampler* (<http://titania.cobuild.collins.co.uk/form.html>): 50 million words of British and American written and spoken material parts of speech, tagged to allow searches on words, phrases, or parts of speech
- *Virtual Language Centre Concordances* at <http://vlc.polyu.edu.hk/concordance/> includes the Brown and LOB corpora, computing and business texts, journalism, students' writing, and fiction.

Finally, the major text-analysis software tools can also be explored and ordered online, and some can be downloaded on a trial basis, at:

- *Concordance* (<http://www.rjcw.freeserve.co.uk/>)
- *MonoConc Pro* and *MonoConc 1.5* (<http://www.athel.com>)
- *Wordpilot 2002* (<http://www.compulang.com/>)
- *Wordsmith Tools* (<http://www.lexically.net/wordsmith/>)

Although there are currently few dedicated corpora for studying genres, teachers can nevertheless collect relevant texts and employ these concordance programs to both provide better descriptions of target genres and devise activities that assist their students to write them more effectively.

Summary

This chapter departed from theory and pedagogy to look more closely at genre analysis, describing and examining the ways applied linguists explore texts in relation to their communicative contexts. We have seen that while the term *genre* embraces a number of different approaches, they all seek to reveal how writers attempt to create texts that relate to readers, to other texts, and to the writer's purposes. An important theme of this chapter has been the view that genre analysis is not a purely theoretical, esoteric and impractical activity unrelated to real-world concerns but that, on the contrary, it has clear and practical relevance for teachers of L2 writing. The main points are:

1. Genre analysis begins with selecting a representative text and making intuitive judgments that allow this text to be seen as a particular genre.
2. SFL analysis requires an understanding of the ways a writer's grammatical choices work to express particular textual, ideational, and interpersonal meanings, with patterns of theme, modality, types of nouns and verbs, and cohesion helping to construct functional stages of the text.
3. ESP analyses begin with collecting examples of relevant genres in a particular context, often with the help of expert users, before identifying the move structure of a text and the main features of grammar and vocabulary it contains. ESP uses more varied models of language than SFL.
4. The study of text features needs to be combined with the study of the social and cultural practices that surround

them. This helps us to identify and understand the social forces that impinge on the ways genres are written and read, the purposes they serve, and the ways they change.

5. If students themselves analyze texts and contexts in the writing class, they see that genres are not just forms and come to understand how genres are part of cultural and institutional life.

6. The computer analysis of text corpora is an invaluable tool for genre analysis as it indicates the high-frequency words, phrases, and grammatical structures that characterize a given genre and reveals how these are typically used in patterns of collocation, or association, with other words or phrases.

7. Concordance lines show patterns and variation in how words relate to their surrounding co-text, providing insights into meanings and uses in particular genres. This regularity not only helps describe the typical features of text collections more accurately but is invaluable for teaching students to write the genres they need.

A Brief Conclusion

As teachers of second language writing, we may not usually see ourselves as applied linguists or discourse analysts. We have instead, perhaps, tended to draw more often on the insights of composition theory, cognitive psychology, or traditional grammars (e.g., Matsuda, 2003). Increasingly, however, we have grown ever more conscious that these dominant pedagogical orthodoxies are unable to address the *language* as well as the *writing* needs of our students. We have recognized that part of what it means to teach writing is to meet students' social, political, and cultural needs beyond the classroom and that writing instruction must help demystify prestigious forms of discourse, unlock students' creative and expressive abilities, and facilitate their access to greater life chances. To accomplish this, we require a systematic means of describing texts and of making our students' control over them more achievable. In short, a well-formulated theory of how language works in human interaction has become an urgent necessity in the field of second language writing teaching.

Genre theories are a major response to this need, providing teachers with a way of understanding how forces outside the individual help guide purposes, establish relationships, and ultimately shape writing. In this book, I have tried to suggest some of the ways that genre theory addresses these issues. In addition, by showing how genre theory situates writing in a social world and acknowledging the centrality of language in written communication, I hope to have illuminated something of the potential of genre-based pedagogies for teachers of second language writing.

Tasks and Discussion Questions

1. Look again at Hood et al.'s (1996) guidelines for studying written texts in Figure 7.4. Select a text, and use these guidelines to analyze it. What does your analysis tell you about this text?

2. Butt et al. (2000) and Knapp and Watkins (1994) suggest that a common structure for narratives is Orientation—Complication—Resolution—Coda (see also Fig. 6.3). Collect a number of short stories from magazines or elsewhere, and decide how well they fit this structure. What variations can you find?

3. How might you use one of the texts from Question 2, together with this model of structural stages, in your writing class? What stage are the students likely to find most difficult, and how would you help them with this?

4. Look at a formal letter you have received recently. How does it seek to engage you as a reader, and what kind of relationship does the writer seek to create with you? Does the writer employ an informal, personal

tone or a distant bureaucratic one? Examine the language features to see how the letter does this, particularly the choices of voice, tense, personal pronouns, and modal verbs. In what ways might this analysis be useful in teaching L2 writing students?

5. Choose a text from a genre that is suitable for a particular group of ESL writing students, and analyze it in terms of its stages or move structure and its key language features. From your findings, develop teaching activities to develop students' genre awareness and writing skills.

6. Consider the methods suggested for researching genre practices: questionnaires, interviews, diaries, and observations. Which method or methods do you think would be most effective in understanding how a genre is perceived and used in a particular site? Why? Which method or methods would you feel most able to use confidently?

7. Select a written genre that you would like to know more about, and identify a site where it is used. This could be an office, a factory, a school, a social club, the home, or elsewhere. Bearing in mind the guidelines in Figure 7.8, and using one or more of the methods suggested in this chapter, arrange to visit the site, and conduct a small-scale research project into the ways the genre is employed and understood in that site.

8. Go to the *Virtual Language Centre* website at <http:// vlc.polyu.edu.hk/concordance/>, and practice some of the techniques for analyzing corpora discussed in this chapter. Look for frequencies of what you consider to be common words, and examine concordance lines for collocation patterns and meanings. Can you find evidence for different meanings in words that occur with different prepositions (e.g., *possible for, possible that, possible to*)? What do neighboring words tell you about the meanings of relatively uncommon words such as *wake, sheer,* and *dire?*

9. Devise a task suitable for a group of business students using the *Corpus of Business Letters* at <http://www .cl.aoyama.ac.jp/~someya/>. Base the task on what you consider to be key features of this genre or on exploring the recommendations of an English for Business Writing textbook.

Bibliography

Akar, D., & Louhiala-Salminen, L. (1999). Towards a new genre: A comparative study of business faxes. In F. Bargiela-Chiappini & C. Nickerson (Eds.), *Writing business: Genres, media and discourses* (pp. 207–226). London: Longman.

Atkinson, D. (1996). The philosophical transactions of the Royal Society of London, 1675–1975: A sociohistorical discourse analysis. *Language in Society, 25,* 333–371.

Bakhtin, M. (1986). The problem of speech genres. In C. Emerson & M. Holquist (Eds.), *Speech genres and other late essays* (pp. 66–102). Austin: University of Texas.

Barton, D., & Hamilton, M. (1998). *Local literacies.* London: Routledge.

Bazerman, C. (1994). Systems of genres and the enactment of social intentions. In A. Freedman & P. Medway (Eds.), *Genre and the New Rhetoric* (pp. 79–101). London: Taylor and Francis.

Bazerman, C. (1997). The life of genre, the life in the classroom. In W. Bishop & H. Ostrom (Eds.), *Genre and writing: Issues, arguments, alternatives.* (pp. 19–26). Portsmouth, NH: Boynton/Cook.

Benesch, S. (2001). *Critical English for Academic Purposes.* Mahwah, NJ: Lawrence Erlbaum.

Bereiter, C., & Scardamalia, M. (1987). *The psychology of written composition.* Hillsdale, NJ: Lawrence Erlbaum.

Berkenkotter, C., & Huckin, T. (1995). *Genre knowledge in disciplinary communication.* Hillsdale, NJ: Lawrence Erlbaum.

Bernstein, B. (1990). *The structuring of pedagogic discourse: Vol. 4. Class, codes and control.* London: Routledge and Kegan Paul.

Bex, T. (1996). *Variety in written English.* London: Routledge.

Bhatia, V. K. (1993). *Analysing genre: Language use in professional settings.* London: Longman.

Bhatia, V. K. (1997). The power and politics of genre. *World Englishes, 17*(3), 359–371.

Bhatia, V. K. (1999). Integrating products, processes, and participants in professional writing. In C. N. Candlin & K. Hyland (Eds.), *Writing: Texts, processes and practices* (pp. 21–39). London: Longman.

Biber, D. (1988). *Variation across speech and writing.* Cambridge: Cambridge University Press.

Biber, D., Conrad, S., & Reppen, R. (1994). Corpus-based approaches to issues in applied linguistics. *Applied Linguistics, 15*(2), 169–189.

Bishop., W., & Ostrom, H. (Eds.). (1997). Genre and writing: Issues, arguments, alternatives. Portsmouth, NH: Boynton/Cook.

Board of Studies. (1998). *K–6 English syllabus: Modules.* Sydney: Board of Studies.

Bridgman, B., & Carlson, S. (1984). Survey of academic writing tasks. *Written Communication, 1,* 247–280.

Brown, J., & Duguid, P. (1989). Situated cognition and the culture of learning. *Educational Researcher, 18,* 34–42.

Bruner, J. S. (1990). *Acts of meaning.* Cambridge: Harvard University Press.

Burns, A., & Joyce, H. (1997). *Focus on speaking.* Sydney: NCELTR.

Burns, A., Joyce, H., & Gollin, S. (1996). *"I see what you mean": Using spoken discourse in the classroom.* Sydney: NCELTR.

Butt, D., Fahey, R., Feez, S., Spinks, S., & Yallop, C. (2000). *Using functional grammar: An explorer's guide* (2nd ed.). Sydney: NCELTR.

Candlin, C. (1993). Series editor's preface. In V. K. Bhatia, *Analysing genre: Language use in professional settings* (pp. ix–xi). London: Longman.

Casanave, C., & Hubbard, P. (1992). The writing assignments and writing problems of doctoral students: faculty perceptions, pedagogical issues and needed research. *English for Specific Purposes, 11*(1) 33–49.

Chang, Y.-Y., & Swales, J. (1999). Informal elements in English academic writing: threats or opportunities for advanced non-native speakers? In C. N. Candlin & K. Hyland (Eds.), *Writing: texts, processes and practices* (pp. 145–167). London: Longman.

Christie, F. (1987). Genres as choice. In I. Reid (Ed.), *The place of genre in learning: Current debates* (pp. 22–34). Deakin, Australia: Deakin University Press.

Christie, F. (1989). *Language education.* Oxford: Oxford University Press.

Christie, F. (1991). Literacy in Australia. *Annual Review of Applied Linguistics, 12,* 142–155.

Coe, R. M. (1994). "An arousing and fulfilment of desires": the rhetoric of genre in the process era—and beyond. In A. Freedman & P. Medway (Eds.), *Genre and the New Rhetoric* (pp. 181–190). London: Taylor and Francis.

Coe, R., Lingard, L., & Teslenko, T. (Eds.). (2002). The rhetoric and ideology of genre. Cresskill, NJ: Hampton Press.

Coffin, C., Curry, M., Goodman, S., Hewings, A., Lillis, T., & Swann, J. (2003). *Teaching academic writing: A toolkit for higher education.* London: Routledge.

Cohen, A. (1994). *Assessing language ability in the classroom* (2nd ed.). Boston: Heinle and Heinle.

Cohen, M., Manion, L., & Morrison, K. (2000). *Research methods in education* (5th ed.). London: Routledge.

Cook, G. (1989). *Discourse.* Oxford: Oxford University Press.

Cope, B., & Kalantzis, M. (Eds.). (1993). *The powers of literacy: A genre approach to teaching writing.* Bristol, PA: Falmer Press.

Crowston, K., & Williams, M. (1997). Reproduced and emergent genres of communication on the Internet. In *Proceedings of the 30th Hawaii international conference on system sciences* (Vol. VI, pp. 30–39). Maui, HI.

Delpit, L. (1988). The silenced dialogue: Power and pedagogy in educating other people's children. *Harvard Educational Review, 58,* 280–298.

Devitt, A. (1991). Intertextuality in tax accounting. In C. Bazerman & J. Paradis (Eds.), *Textual dynamics of the professions* (pp. 336–357). Madison: University of Wisconsin Press.

Devitt, A. (1997). *Genre as language standard.* In W. Bishop & H. Ostrom (Eds.), *Genre and Writing.* Portsmouth, NH: Boynton/Cook.

Dias, P., Freedman, A., Medway, P., & Pare, A. (1999). *Worlds apart: Acting and writing in academic and workplace contexts.* Mahwah, NJ: Lawrence Erlbaum.

Dias, P., & Pare, P. (Eds.). (2000). *Transitions: Writing in academic and workplace settings.* Cresskill, NJ: Hampton Press.

Dixon, J. (1987). The question of genres. In I. Reid (Ed.), *The place of genre in learning: Current debates* (pp. 9–21). Deakin, Australia: Deakin University Press.

Donato, R. (2000). Sociocutural contributions to understanding the second and foreign languge classroom. In J. Lantolf (Ed.), *Sociocultural theory and second language learning* (pp. 27–50). Oxford: Oxford University Press.

Douglas, D. (2000). *Assessing language for specific purposes.* Cambridge: Cambridge University Press.

Dudley-Evans, T., & St. John, M.-J. (1998). *Developments in English for Specific Purposes.* Cambridge: Cambridge University Press.

Fairclough, N. (1992). *Discourse and social change.* Cambridge: Polity Press.

Fairclough, N. (1995). *Critical discourse analysis.* Harlow, UK: Longman.

Fathman, A., & Whalley, E. (1990). Teacher response to student writing: Focus on form versus content. In B. Kroll (Ed.), *Second language writing: Research insights for the classroom* (pp. 178–190). Cambridge: Cambridge University Press.

Feez, S. (1998). *Text-based syllabus design.* Sydney: McQuarie University/AMES.

Feez, S. (2001). Heritage and innovation in second language education. In A. M. Johns (Ed.), *Genre in the classroom* (pp. 47–68). Mahwah, NJ: Lawrence Erlbaum.

Ferris, D. (1997). The influence of teacher commentary on student revision. *TESOL Quarterly, 31*(2), 315–339.

Ferris, D. (2002). *Treatment of error in second language student writing.* Ann Arbor: University of Michigan Press.

Flower, L., & Hayes, J. (1981). A cognitive process theory of writing. *College Composition and Communication, 32,* 365–387.

Flowerdew, J. (1993). Variation across speech and writing in biology: A quantitative study. *Perspectives: Working papers of the Department of English, City Polytechnic of Hong Kong, 5*(1), 75–88.

Freedman, A. (1994a). "Anyone for tennis?" In A. Freedman & P. Medway (Eds.), *Genre and the New Rhetoric* (pp. 43–66). London: Taylor and Francis.

Freedman, A. (1994b). "Do as I say?": The relationship between teaching and learning new genres. In A. Freedman & P. Medway (Eds.), *Genre and the New Rhetoric* (pp. 191–210). London: Taylor and Francis.

Freedman, A., & Adam, C. (2000). Write where you are: Situating learning to write in university and workplace settings. In P. Dias, & A. Pare (Eds.), *Transitions: Writing in academic and workplace settings* (pp. 31–60). Creskill, NJ: Hampton Press.

Freedman, A., & Medway, P. (Eds.). (1994). *Genre and the New Rhetoric.* London: Taylor and Francis.

Friedlander, A. (1990). Composing in English: Effects of a first language on writing in English as a second language. In B. Kroll (Ed.), *Second language writing: Research insights for the classroom* (pp. 109–125). Cambridge: Cambridge University Press.

Fucella, J., & Pizzolato, J. (1998). Creating web site designs based on user expectations. *ITG Newsletter 1*(1). http://internettg.org/newsletter/june98/web-design.html/.

Grabe, W. (2001). Reading and writing relations: L2 perspectives on research and practice. In B. Kroll (Ed.), *Exploring the dynamics of second language writing* (pp. 242–262). New York: Cambridge University Press.

Grabe, W. (2002). Narrative and expository macro-genres. In A. M. Johns (Ed.), *Genre in the classroom* (pp. 249–267). Mahwah, NJ: Lawrence Erlbaum.

Granger, S. (Ed.). (1998). *Learner English on computer.* London: Longman.

Halliday, M. A. K. (1989). *Spoken and written language.* Oxford: Oxford University Press.

Halliday, M. A. K. (1994). *An introduction to functional grammar* (2nd ed.). London: Edward Arnold.

Halliday, M. A. K. (1998). Things and relations: Regrammaticising experience as technical knowledge. In J. R. Martin & R. Veel (Eds.), *Reading Science* (pp. 185–235). London: Routledge.

Halliday, M. A. K., & Hasan, R. (1989). *Language, context and text: Aspects of language in a social semiotic perspective.* Oxford: Oxford University Press.

Hammond, J., & Macken-Horarik, M. (1999). Critical literacy: Challenges and questions for ESL classrooms. *TESOL Quarterly, 33*(3), 528–544.

Hamp-Lyons, L. (2003). Writing teachers as assessors of writing. In B. Kroll (Ed.), *Exploring the dynamics of second language writing* (pp. 162–241). Cambridge: Cambridge University Press.

Hamp-Lyons, L., & Condon, W. (2000). *Assessing the portfolio: Principles for practice, theory and research.* Cresskill, NJ: Hampton Press.

Hasan, R. (1996). Literacy, everyday talk and society. In R. Hasan & G. Williams (Eds.), *Literacy in society* (pp. 377–424). London: Longman.

Hinkel, E. (2002). *Second language writers' text.* Mahwah, NJ: Lawrence Erlbaum.

Hoey, M. (2001). *Textual interaction: An introduction to written text analysis.* London: Routledge.

Hood, S., Solomon, N., & Burns, A. (1996). *Focus on reading.* Sydney: NCELTR.

Hughes, A. (1989). *Testing for language teachers.* Cambridge: Cambridge University Press.

Hunston, S. (2002). *Corpora in applied linguistics.* Cambridge: Cambridge University Press.

Hunston, S., &. Thompson, G. (Eds.). (2000). *Evaluation in text: Authorial stance in the construction of discourse.* Oxford: Oxford University Press.

Hyland, F. (1998). The impact of teacher written feedback on individual writers. *Journal of Second Language Writing, 7*(3), 255–286.

Hyland, F., & Hyland, K. (2001). Sugaring the pill: Praise and criticism in written feedback. *Journal of Second Language Writing 10*(3), 185–212.

Hyland, K. (1990). A genre description of the argumentative essay. *RELC Journal, 21*(1), 66–78.

Hyland, K. (1994). Hedging in academic textbooks and EAP. *English for Specific Purposes 3*(3), 239–256.

Hyland, K. (1996). "I don't quite follow": Making sense of a modifier. *Language Awareness, 5*(2), 91–99.

Hyland, K. (1998). *Hedging in scientific research articles.* Amsterdam: John Benjamins.

Hyland, K. (2000). *Disciplinary discourses: Social interactions in academic writing.* London: Longman.

Hyland, K. (2001). Humble servants of the discipline? Self-mention in research articles. *English for Specific Purposes 20*(3), 207–226.

Hyland, K. (2002). *Teaching and researching writing.* London: Longman.

Hyland, K. (2003). *Second language writing.* New York: Cambridge University Press.

Hyland, K., & Milton, J. (1997). Qualification and certainty in L1 and L2 students' writing. *Journal of Second Language Writing, 6*(2), 183–206.

Hyland, K., & Tse, P. (2004). "I would like to thank my supervisor": Acknowledgements in graduate dissertations. *International Journal of Applied Linguistics, 14*(2).

Hymes, D. (1972). On communicative competence. In J. B. Pride & J. Holmes (Eds.), *Sociolinguistics* (pp. 269–293.). Harmondsworth, UK: Penguin.

Hyon, S. (1996). Genre in three traditions: Implications for ESL. *TESOL Quarterly, 30*(4), 693–722.

Johns, A. M. (1997). *Text, role and context: Developing academic literacies.* Cambridge: Cambridge University Press.

Johns, A. M. (Ed.). (2002). *Genre in the classroom: Multiple perspectives.* Mahwah, NJ: Lawrence Erlbaum.

Johnstone, B. (1996). *The linguistic individual.* New York: Oxford University Press.

Kay, H., & Dudley-Evans, T. (1998). Genre: What teachers think. *ELT Journal, 52*(4), 308–314.

Knapp, P., & Watkins, M. (1994). *Context—text—grammar: Teaching the genres and grammar of school writing in infants and primary classrooms.* Sydney: Text Productions.

Knoblauch, C., & Brannon, L. (1984). *Rhetorical traditions and the teaching of writing.* Upper Montclair, NJ: Boynton/Cook.

Kress, G. (1987). Genre in a social theory of language: A reply to John Dixon. In I. Reid (Ed.), *The place of genre in learning: Current debates* (pp. 33–45). Geelong, Australia: Deakin University Press.

Kress, G. (1989). *Linguistic processes in sociocultural practice.* Oxford: Oxford University Press.

Kroll, B., & Reid, J. (1994). Guidelines for designing writing prompts: Clarifications, caveats and cautions. *Journal of Second Language Writing, 3*(3), 231–255.

Lave, J., & Wenger, E. (1991). *Situated learning: Legitimate peripheral participation.* Cambridge: Cambridge University Press.

Leki, I. (1990). Coaching from the margins: Issues in written response. In B. Kroll (Ed.), *Second language writing: Research insights for the classroom* (pp. 57–68). Cambridge: Cambridge University Press.

Leki, I., & Carson, J. (1997). "Completely different worlds": EAP and the writing experiences of ESL students in university courses. *TESOL Quarterly, 31*(1), 39–69.

Lindsay, D. (1984). *A guide to scientific writing.* Melbourne: Longman.

Ljung, M. (1990). *A study of TEFL vocabulary.* Stockholm: Almqvist and Wiksell.

Lock, G., & Lockhart, C. (1998). Genres in an academic writing class. *Hong Kong Journal of Applied Linguistics, 3*(2), 47–64.

Luke, A. (1996). Genres of power? Literacy education and the production of capital. In R. Hasan & A. G. Williams (Eds.), *Literacy in society* (pp. 308–338). London: Longman.

Luzon Marco, M. (2000). Collocational frameworks in medical research papers: A genre-based study. *English for Specific Purposes, 19*(1), 63–86.

Macken, M., & Slade, D. (1993). Assessment: A foundation for effective learning in the school context. In B. Cope & M. Kalantzis (Eds.), *The powers of literacy: A genre approach to teaching writing* (pp. 203–230). London: Falmer.

Macken-Horarik, M. (1996). *Construing the invisible: Specialised literacy practices in junior secondary English.* Ph.D. diss., University of Sydney.

Marshall, S. (1991). A genre-based approach to the teaching of report writing. *English for Specific Purposes, 10*(1), 3–13.

Martin, J. R. (1989). *Factual writing: Exploring and challenging social reality.* Oxford: Oxford University Press.

Martin, J. R. (1992). *English text: System and structure.* Amsterdam: John Benjamins.

Martin, J. R. (2000a). Design and practice: Enacting functional linguistics. *Annual Review of Applied Linguistics, 20,* 116–126.

Martin, J. R. (2000b). Beyond exchange: Appraisal systems in English. In S. Hunston & G. G. Thompson (Eds.), *Evaluation in texts* (pp. 142–175). Oxford: Oxford University Press.

Master, P. (1995). Consciousness raising and article pedagogy. In D. Belcher & G. Braine (Eds.), *Academic writing in a second language* (pp. 183–205). Norwood, NJ: Ablex.

Matsuda, P. K. (2003). Second language writing in the twentieth century: A situated historical pespective. In B. Kroll (Ed.), *Exploring the dynamics of second language writing* (pp. 15–34). Cambridge: Cambridge University Press.

McKenna, B. (1997). How engineers write: An empirical study of engineering report writing. *Applied Linguistics, 18*(2), 189–211.

Meek, M. (1988). *How texts teach what readers learn.* Stroud, UK: Thimble Press.

Messick, S. (1996). Validity and washback in language testing. *Language Testing, 13,* 241–256.

Miller, C. (1994). Genre as social action. In A. Freedman & P. Medway (Eds.), *Genre and the New Rhetoric* (pp. 23–42). London: Taylor and Francis.

Milton, J. (1999). Lexical thickets and electronic gateways: Making text accessible by novice writers. In C. N. Candlin & K. Hyland (Eds.), *Writing: Texts, processes and practices* (pp. 221–243). London: Longman.

Mulholland, J. (1999). Email: Uses, issues and problems in an institutional setting. In F. Bargiela-Chiappini & C. Nickerson (Eds.), *Writing business: Genres, media and discourses* (pp. 57–84). London: Longman.

Murray, D. (1985). *A writer teaches writing* (2nd ed.). Boston: Houghton Mifflin.

Myers, G. (1990). *Writing biology: Texts in the social construction of scientific knowledge.* Madison: University of Wisconsin Press.

NSW AMES. (1998). *Certificate of spoken and written English. III.* Surrey Hills, Australia: NSW Adult Migrant English Service.

Nunan, D. (1988). *Syllabus design.* Oxford: Oxford University Press.

Ohta, A. (2000). Rethinking interaction in SLA: Developmentally appropriate assistance in the Zone of Proximal Development and the acquisition of L2 grammar. In J. Lantolf (Ed.), *Sociocultural theory and second language learning* (pp. 51–78). Oxford: Oxford University Press.

Paltridge, B. (1997). Thesis and dissertation writing: Preparing ESL students for research. *English for Specific Purposes, 16*(1), 61–70.

Paltridge, B. (2001). *Genre and the language learning classroom.* Ann Arbor: University of Michigan Press.

Pare, A. (2000). Writing as a way into social work: Genre sets, genre systems, and distributed cognition. In P. Dias & A. Pare (Eds.), *Transitions: Writing in academic and workplace settings* (pp. 145–166). Kresskill, NJ: Hampton Press.

Partington, A. (1998). *Patterns and meanings: Using corpora for English language research and teaching.* Amsterdam: Benjamins.

Pennycook, A. (1997). Vulgar pragmatism, critical pragmatism and EAP. *English for Specific Purposes, 16,* 253–269.

Prior, P. (1998). *Writing/disciplinarity: A sociohistoric account of literate activity in the academy.* Mahwah NJ: Lawrence Erlbaum.

Purves, A., Quanttrini, J., & Sullivan, C. (Eds.) (1995). *Creating the writing portfolio.* Lincolnwood, IL: NTC Publishing.

Raimes, A. (1992). *Exploring through writing: A process approach to ESL composition* (2nd ed.) New York: St. Martins Press.

Reid, J., & Kroll, B. (1995). Designing and assessing effective classroom writing assignments for NES and ESL students. *Journal of Second Language Writing, 4*(1), 17–41.

Richards, J. (2001). *Curriculum development in language teaching.* New York: Cambridge University Press.

Richards, J., & Rogers, T. (1986). *Approaches and methods in language teaching.* Cambridge: Cambridge University Press.

Rothery, J. (1996). Making changes: Developing an educational linguistics. In R. Hasan & G. Williams (Eds.), *Literacy in society* (pp. 86–123). London: Longman.

Shepherd, M., & Watters, C. (1999). The functionality attribute of cyber-genres. In *Proceedings of the 30th Hawaii international conference on system sciences* (Vol. IV, pp. 68–77).

Sinclair, J. (1991). *Corpus, concordance, collocation.* Oxford: Oxford University Press.

Spears, L. A. (1995). Nurses as technical writers: What they need to know. *Journal of Technical Writing and Communication, 25*(4), 401–414.

Swales, J. (1990). *Genre analysis: English in academic and research settings.* Cambridge: Cambridge University Press.

Swales, J. (1998). *Other floors, other voices: A textography of a small university building.* Mahwah, NJ: Lawrence Erlbaum.

Swales, J. (2000). Languages for specific purposes. *Annual Review of Applied Linguistics, 20,* 59–76.

Swales, J., & Feak, C. (1994). *Academic writing for graduate students: Essential tasks and skills.* Ann Arbor: University of Michigan Press.

Swales, J., & Feak, C. (2000). *English in today's research world: A writing guide.* Ann Arbor: University of Michigan Press.

Swales, J., & Luebs, M. (2002). Genre analysis and the advanced second language writer. In E. Barton & G. Stygal (Eds.), *Discourse studies in composition* (pp. 135–154). Cresskill, NJ: Hampton Press.

Tarone, E., Dwyer, S., Gillette, S., & Icke, V. (1998). On the use of the passive and active voice in astrophysics journal papers: With extensions to other languages and fields. *English for Specific Purposes, 17*(1): 113–122.

Taylor, L. (1994). *The Laurie Taylor guide to higher education.* Oxford: Butterworth-Heinemann.

Tribble, C. (1996). *Writing.* Oxford: Oxford University Press.

Truscott, J. (1996). The case against grammar correction in L2 writing classes. *Language Learning, 46,* 327–369.

Vygotsky, L. (1978). *Mind in society: The development of higher psychological processes* (M. Cole, V. John-Steiner, S. Scribner, & E. Souberman, Eds.). Cambridge: Harvard University Press.

Wallace, R. (1995). *English for Specific Purposes in ESL undergraduate composition classes.* Ph.D. diss., Illinois State University.

Weigle, S. C. (2002). *Assessing writing.* Cambridge: Cambridge University Press.

Wells, G. (1999). Language and education: Reconceptualising education as dialogue. In W. Grabe (Ed.), *Annual review of applied linguistics* (Vol. 19, pp. 135–155). New York: Cambridge University Press.

Widdowson, H. (1978). *Teaching language as communication.* Oxford: Oxford University Press.

Wray, D., & Lewis, M. (1997). *Extending literacy: Children reading and writing non-fiction.* London: Routledge.

Yakhontova, T. (2002). "Selling" or "telling"? The issue of cultural variation in research genres. In J. Flowerdew (Ed.), *Academic discourse* (pp. 216–232). London: Longman.

Zamel, V. (1985). Responding to student writing. *TESOL Quarterly, 19*(1), 79–101.

Subject Index

Academic writing, 43, 46, 61, 73, 96, 99, 106, 112, 141–157, 174–177, 180, 184, 198, 214–220
Assessment, 118, 132, 159–177, 186–190
   diagnostic, 160, 179
   genre-based, 160–168, 186, 189–192
   prompt, 126, 188
   reliability, 160–161, 179
   scoring, 178
   tasks, 186–190
   validity, 161

Certificate of Spoken and Written English, 101, 172–173, 190
Choices in writing, 97
Clause structure, 198
Coherence, 26, 51, 80, 114–115, 126, 176
Cohesion, 199, 201
Communicative language teaching, 8
Comparing texts, 137–138, 146
Competencies, 163, 173
Concordancing, 133, 216–222, 224
Consciousness raising, 140, 144
Content (of text), 72–75, 174
Context, 50, 77–83, 124, 206–210
   of learning, 93
   of use, 30, 77–83, 93, 206–210
Corpora, 212–214, 221–222
Corpus analysis, 212–220
Course design, 87–94, 109–117
Critical literacy, 41–43
Critical pedagogy, 15–18, 37

Diary studies, 210
Disciplinary differences, 64, 138, 151–155, 197, 203
Discourse analysis, 104, 174
Drafting, 102

Editing, 102, 135
Empowerment, 11
English for Specific Purposes, 18, 25, 43–50, 59, 109, 116, 122–124, 129, 140, 174, 184, 197, 198, 222–223
Error correction, 180
Explicit teaching, 8, 10–11, 163

Families of genres, 65–66, 110–111
Feedback, 104, 159, 179–190
Frequency counts, 213–217

Generic Structure Potential, 26
Genre
   argument, 28–29, 32–33, 34, 66–68, 102, 127
   argumentative essay, 91, 115, 161, 176, 177
   article abstracts, 203
   business e-mails, 106
   case study, 153
   description, 29, 33, 67, 175, 186
   discussion, 66–67, 140, 169
   engineering report, 46, 183
   explanation, 29
   exposition, 28–29, 34, 58
   investigative project report, 152, 159, 175
   legal documents, 48
   narrative, 44, 57–58, 75, 91, 115, 169, 170–171, 175, 178
   project proposal, 153
   recount, 44, 63, 117, 135, 139, 174, 214
   report, 29, 33, 50, 110
   research article, 46
   sales promotion letter, 105–106
   teacher feedback, 62
Genre analysis, 44, 151, 195–211
Genre knowledge, 54–83

Author Index